ZIKR

ZIKR

*In the Light and
Shade of Time*

An Autobiography

MUZAFFAR ALI

VINTAGE
An imprint of Penguin Random House

VINTAGE

USA | Canada | UK | Ireland | Australia
New Zealand | India | South Africa | China

Vintage is part of the Penguin Random House group of companies
whose addresses can be found at global.penguinrandomhouse.com

Published by Penguin Random House India Pvt. Ltd
4th Floor, Capital Tower 1, MG Road,
Gurugram 122 002, Haryana, India

Penguin
Random House
India

First published in Vintage by Penguin Random House India 2022

Copyright © Muzaffar Ali 2022
Photos by Gauri Gill, Mahendra Sinh, Karam Puri, Avinash Pasricha and Ben Ingham

ISBN 9780670096107

Typeset in Adobe Garamond Pro by MAP Systems, Bengaluru, India
Printed at Thomson Press India Ltd, New Delhi

www.penguin.co.in

I dedicate this book to all those who have taught me a single word,
including my grandson, Imaan

I dedicate this book to Meera, my wife, who has helped
bring my life together

All translations, from Urdu to English and from Persian to English, are by Muzaffar Ali, the latter done with the help of Dr Akhtar Mehdi, retired professor of Persian at the Jawaharlal Nehru University, New Delhi

Contents

Chapter 1

View from the Window

'*Bas-ki dushvaar hai har kaam ka aasaañ hona,*
Aadmī ko bhī mayassar nahīñ insaañ hona.'
('All things can't always become easy,
Thus it is difficult for a man to be human.')

—Mirza Ghalib

I write this from my home in Qaiserbagh, Lucknow, my father's home, sitting at the window he once sat at. His photographs look down at me as the days, from well before I was born, unfold before my eyes.

Why should one write an autobiography? I have often wondered about the need for one. Yet, recent times have made it important to realize the relevance of my time and my outlook. My engagement with my medium, my sensibilities, the changing milieu have slowly moved me to express myself and define my dreams.

My father lived his life as a humanist, a life true to his country and its ideals of harmony, opposing anything that divided man. The first Saturday of every month, come what may, one would hear around ten or twelve discordant voices singing, '*Aisa ho sansar hamara, aisa ho sansar, jagrut ho jan jan ke man mein manavta ka pyar* (Such should be the world we live in, such should be our world, where the highest concern in every

1

heart is the love for humankind) . . .' This was followed by tea and Good Bakery almond biscuits. This insignificant group comprised educated Lucknowites who conformed to his philosophy of oneness of the human race and rejected everything that divided mankind. Led by my father, they saw the world as one family. The group was called the Indian Humanist Union. They might have been a spent force, but the ideas they stood for could change the world. Such ideas never die. They go into hibernation, like many a tree or a bush in winter biding its time for the spring to come. These ideas are poetry in themselves, waiting for words to discover them, for music to embrace them.

Gone were the days of Krishna's dalliance with his *gopis*. Gone were the sounds of the gentle tinkling of bells threaded through with the melodious strains of the sarangi. Gone were the days when the birth of a new thumri (a genre of light classical vocal music of north India conducive to dance) was celebrated with endearing expressions in dance that blended feelings in a way that would melt the most hardened of souls. Abba Jaan, as we called my father, saw Lucknow slip into decay before his eyes. The city went from a peaceful and culturally rich setting to one whose fine arts and cultural values underwent an ugly degeneration.

The window of Abba Jaan's room in Kotwara House, Qaiserbagh, overlooking the Amir-ud-Daulah Public Library across the road, has borne witness to India in its varied shades. To him, the library stood as the sole hope for the survival of a civilized city, the quiet of its high ceilings a bulwark against the growing cacophony of the outside world.

The road that runs between the library and Kotwara House was built by the British in 1858 to ensure that the Qaiserbagh Palace Complex could never be fortified against them, as had happened in 1857, in the First War of Indian Independence. It stands testimony to those terrible times. Abba Jaan would gnash his teeth at what the British had done to Qaiserbagh and the glorious legacy of a gentle, romantic, united Awadh. It was only in 1859, after breaking down the north and south wings of Qaiserbagh Palace, that the British ire had subsided—or maybe they lacked the budget to raze to the ground that formidable palace that had stood its ground against the colonial might for eleven months, fearlessly issuing *farman* (edict) after farman against the British. Perhaps they realized that to rule Awadh after 1857, they had no choice but to appease the all-powerful taluqdars. And in 1861, Qaiserbagh was divided among them through an ordinance.

But who cares? Nor would I, had I not been born in Qaiserbagh and seen it through the piercing eyes of my father. The man who kept looking out of that window, at the changes with each passing year, was Raja Syed Sajid Husain of Kotwara. His English Savile Row suits and striped silk shirts—part of my nostalgia for elegant dressing—were replaced by coarse, handwoven, handspun khadi after 1947, and a vow to never wear anything else till the day textile mills in India were nationalized. He could envision a world beyond his time, and his sharp gaze assured him of the power of rational knowledge going public. His faith in the institutions that were coming up in independent India was unshakeable, and, slowly, all his valuable books flew out of his home and into different sections of the Amir-ud-Daulah Public Library. He was planting the seeds for the future. He was not sure who would value all this after him. I felt a bit insulted at this, thinking Abba Jaan did not trust me enough to hold dear what he treasured. But deep down, I knew I could not fully vouch for myself to be so responsible. I had destroyed a valuable first flight cover stamp and envelope from his very rare stamp collection. He had lost confidence in me. And I had to regain his trust. I had to learn the value of things not for myself but for others. I had to develop a sense of history, a sense of record that we as Indians were losing over time. Abba Jaan made me value life differently.

Raja Sajid Husain's life-size painting hangs on the wall of the imposing entrance to the library, watching over all the quiet readers who step into this expanse of books to pursue their quest for knowledge. I do not know what that window will continue to show and whether the city will ever honour a space where so much, including so many different scenes of national importance, has happened. Will we always be oblivious to the culture of sensitivity and refinement for which Lucknow has been known the world over?

As I sit by the window overlooking the library, I think of all that would have gone through Abba Jaan's mind. Knowing him, it must have been the shape of things to come, through the perspective the times that had rolled by had given him. He had known of the loot, destruction and degradation of Qaiserbagh at the hands of those who were heedless to its significance. He and his Corona typewriter were inseparable. It was placed in a drop-down wooden box in a niche by the window, and on it he would struggle to find solutions to the problems he perceived. As a child I was mesmerized by the rhythmic pounding of the keys, never really understanding his angst. It was only when I chanced upon his booklet *Solution of Our Problem*, published by his friend Madan Lal Bhargava, during one of my visits back from college that I realized the intensity of what he felt. A compilation of letters to the editors of the *Pioneer* and *National Herald*, the booklet outlined solutions to varied problems plaguing our society—such as the cancer of communalism, the use of Roman for the propagation of the Hindustani language, the construction of footpaths, audio–visual education as the only way to catch up with the rest of the world, and many more.

I consider myself fortunate to have been born out of that pain, a pain that is as intangible as it is invisible.

* * *

By the time I was six, much water had flowed down the Gomti. Abba Jaan was a changed man. The abolition of zamindari in 1950 had served a severe blow to the taluqdars of Awadh, of which he was one.

The taluqdars formed a powerful group of aristocrats established in three different periods: 1207 to 1707, the Sultanate–Mughal period; 1722 to 1857, the Nawabi period; and 1857 to 1947, the British period. The Kotwara state emerged as a feudal order that was re-established in 1007 by Raja Swaroop Singh of the Chaura dynasty of Gujarat, who had fled at the impending threat of attack by Mahmud of Ghazni. He knew that he could never unite the Chauras under one banner to face the powerful onslaught of the sultan, whenever it came.

One legend adds a mythological twist to the story of Raja Swaroop Singh's establishment of Kotwara as his new territory. The Chaura Rajputs claim direct descent from Lord Rama. It is said that Raja Sopi, as Swaroop Singh was known, traversed northwards to the kingdom of his forefathers. Having come from a war-torn country, he rode first to Ayodhya, to pay homage to a place which was sacred to him. The name Ayodhya signified that no human blood would be shed on its soil, no war would be fought on its ground. Here, the Chaura king laid down his weapons and prayed for guidance. Clouds gathered and lightning flashed. He moved in their direction. Tirelessly he rode, night and day, till he reached the fertile Terai region of the Himalayan foothills. The dense trees told him that he had reached his journey's end. The human world had surrendered to the world of the beasts. He rested under the generous shade of a semal tree. The cool breeze from the surrounding forest had lulled him to sleep when a voice thundered from the darkness of the forest. 'Sacrifice the brown bison you see amid that herd. Where the head falls is the ancient seat of your forefather, Raja Muratdhwaj. Re-establish yourself there.' The resounding voice was that of Lord Vishnu. Upon awakening, Raja Sopi slew the bison and made the spot his seat forever.

Who was Raja Muratdhwaj? Was anyone on the throne with Lord Vishnu's blessings obliged to know this? My father, though a rational thinker, believed that mythologies and their characters carried a larger truth for a generation to understand. He sat by the window and did his thesis on the Chauras of Gujarat, and in the process discovered the import and significance of these mythologies. It was his duty to understand his legacy and create a sense of responsibility to take it further, beyond the limited realm of religion. As I grew to understand the benevolence of Raja Muratdwhaj, I wanted to learn more about him and how he was remembered through folklore and legend.

In 1488, Raja Sopi's descendant, Raja Mull, converted to Islam during the reign of Sultan Bahlol Lodi. Raja Mull was a true Rajput and loved hunting. The huge tracts of forests made Kotwara a hunter's paradise. Thousands of acres of thick jungles surrounded the mud fort he had built for himself, which he called Anhalwara after the capital of the Chaura Empire, Anhalwara Patan, in Gujarat. The forest, as well as his own lively nature and adventurous spirit, endeared Raja Mull to the Lodi sultans. He was among the earliest Rajas to be given the status of a taluqdar by them. The sultans would spend weeks in the forests, hunting and feasting. The Brahmin *rajgurus* (state priests) of Kotwara did not like this. They complained to the ranis that Raja Mull had lost his dharma by feasting with the Muslim sultans. One day, the raja returned to the palace to find all the ranis upset with him. He was not allowed entry into the *zenana* (women's quarters). Even his favourite queen, who used to be the most welcoming and seductive when he returned safely from his expeditions, now refused his darshan. He went through a miserable time trying to fathom the cause of this alienation. Of course, no one had the courage to tell the raja the truth. Finally, when he did come to know, he roared in disgust, asserting that if they felt he had really lost his dharma by just being a good friend of the sultan, then let it be truly lost. So saying, he embraced Islam.[*]

Mughal Emperor Aurangzeb appropriated Kotwara during his reign. It was only in 1779 that state rule was restored to Raja Sopi's scion, Raja Tarbiat Buksh Khan. In 1857, the eighty-fourth Kotwara descendant, Raja Madar Buksh Khan, died without a male heir. His widow, Rani Chand Bibi, married her eldest daughter to Syed Nazar Husain, the grandson of Syed Alimuddin, whose wife was the daughter of King Ibrahim Shah Sharqi of Jaunpur.

It was left to Nazar Husain's son, Raja Syed Raza Husain, my father's grandfather, to bring up Abba Jaan after he was orphaned at the age of twelve. Raza Husain had built his fortune not only through his lands but by building bazaars and markets for business. He planted thousands of hectares of forests, created a trust for the management of his Imambara, for Muharram and the mosques, and appointed a pandit, Gaurishankar Vajpai, as its head trustee.

* * *

Abba Jaan often narrated stories to us at mealtimes. Many left me spellbound, even after having heard them over a hundred times. The story of the fiery steed my father loved as a child was one. The horse's black-and-white markings, Abba Jaan told me, were such that when he sped, he looked like lightning striking the ground. He was called Barq, lightning. My father would feed him carrots and talk to him about his dreams. One day, Raza Husain hitched Barq to his two-seater phaeton to take young Sajid for a drive through the forests of Razanagar Grant. True to his name, Barq took off through the forest like lightning. The wind blew hard across their faces, tearing through Raza Husain's parted Rajput beard. Grandfather and grandson could feel the adrenaline rush as they raced through the trees, their shadows growing sharper and longer. Abba Jaan could only see the horse's mane and his grandfather's flying beard. The horse went faster and faster.

They heard the invisible train too late. They saw the smoking engine hurtling towards them at top speed on the recently laid railway tracks. Stopping Barq at this point would have been their end. Raza Husain raised

---

[*] Raja Sajid Husain, *Chauras of Gujarat*, PhD dissertation, University of Lucknow.

his whip high as a signal to Barq to take a leap across the tracks. The horse leapt across with the phaeton, missing the train by a hair's breadth! They breathed a deep sigh as they turned around to see the endless train charge past as their phaeton carried on through the forest. It was a moment that would remain etched in Abba Jaan's mind for all time to come, in memory of his dynamic grandfather.

My great-grandfather hated cars and loved horses and carriages, and allowed no car into the Kotwara region. He had written a book on horses and their ailments, and trained them to perform great feats, which the village folk loved. A believer in the sanctity of the horse in Islam, he would speak to them every day in accordance with the Hadith of Prophet Muhammad. When he spoke to the horses, they reacted and behaved as he desired. One of the horses in his stable was Zuljinah, named after the sacred horse of the grandson of the Prophet, Imam Husain. No one was allowed to ride Zuljinah who was taken out in public only during the Muharram procession. People believed that touching him would cure them of disease. Such stories about horses prevailed till the advent of the automobile erased the last of such legends.*

Raza Husain passed away in 1924. Within a few days his eldest son and heir, Mustafa Husain, was murdered. This served as a great blow to his widow, Rani Sartaj Mahal, a Rajput princess who chose to live a down-to-earth life, looking after her meagre needs herself. She would even churn her own ghee, much to the amusement of Abba Jaan and his sisters. Who could imagine that beyond the veil of her frugal life in her haveli was hidden a large cache of gold guineas? As children we had often gone on treasure hunts to find this wealth but were chased away by bats who we believed were guarding it. It was said that when the estate went into the Court of Wards several bullock carts' worth of gold was transported to the government treasury.

Next in the line of succession was my father. He was only fourteen at the time, and the Kotwara state was transferred to the Court of Wards, a legal body created in India by the British East India Company on a model similar to the Court of Wards and Liveries that had existed in England from 1540 to 1660. Its purpose was to protect heirs and their estates when the heir was deemed to be a minor and, therefore, incapable of acting

---

* Ibid.

independently. Estates would be managed on behalf of the heir, who would also be educated and nurtured through the offices of the Court to ensure that he gained the necessary skills to manage his inheritance independently upon coming of age.

Everything changed. Abba Jaan was removed from his idyllic life in Kotwara and sent to La Martiniere College in Lucknow as a boarder to reside with the vice principal, Lt Col W.E. Andrews. As he pulled into Lucknow, he saw an open Rover. It was love at first sight. He was given a new Rover Tourer, the colour of which I wish I had asked, like many other things he talked about and I have not seen. Surely this convertible must have reminded him of driving through the Kotwara forest, as in the two-seater phaeton pulled by Barq.

One day, when Abba Jaan was driving from Dilkusha Palace to La Martiniere, he stopped his Rover at a railway barrier. As the train sped across, a gun fired, missing him, but hitting the speeding train. The sound of metal being hit resonated in the air. Pandemonium ensued as the railway guards popped out to find the source of the sound. A man with a rifle was seen running away as the train crossed the bridge. It was with a sense of déjà vu that my father was reminded of the moment when Barq had saved their lives in the forest. He had just taken over his grandfather's seat. Was the life of a raja full of such perils?

My father, still being a minor under protection, was always shadowed by the district authorities of Lakhimpur Kheri. The Court of Wards took stock of the situation and decided that Oxford would be a safer place for Abba Jaan to continue with his education. Of course, my father had no choice in the matter, and so off he went to Kotwara, to bid farewell to his grandmother, the dowager rani of Kotwara. It was at her haveli that one of Abba Jaan's assailants confessed. He was the son of a faithful employee of the Kotwara state and was under tremendous obligation to the dowager rani's late husband. He placed before them the Rs 1000, given to him for this task by the dowager rani's youngest son. A similar amount had been promised upon completion of the mission. He broke down, pleading forgiveness. The man was led out of the *garhi* (palace grounds) and given three times the amount. This was a secret he was to die with. She had lost one son; she didn't want to lose another!

The British deputy magistrate, B.E. Drephas, who saw great poise and promise in Abba Jaan, put my father on a ship to England.

Orphaned once again, Abba Jaan had to shoulder the responsibility of looking after his little sister, Kaniz Sakina, ten years younger than him. The Court of Wards advised that she be sent to Caineville House School in Mussoorie, a boarding school run by an Irish lady, Francis Adams. Girls from distinguished families in such situations often found their way there. Abba Jaan went to see her before leaving for Oxford. He took her shopping at the Mall in Dehradun, and Bitto, as he would call Kaniz, bought four of everything—one for herself and three for those less fortunate than her at school. Even though Bitto and Sajid were orphans, she never considered herself unfortunate.

Brother and sister got themselves photographed by an English photographer, Vernon & Sons. Photography was a necessary ritual that played a regular role in the life of the good-looking siblings. Several decades later, on a visit to Dehradun, I walked into Vernon & Sons, which had obviously changed hands, and its old-world character had vanished. Only the weather-beaten art deco wooden signboard remained. Looking around, a grand 5x5 frame caught my attention. It was a magnificent portrait of my phuphijaan, Kaniz Sakina! The studio owner quoted a price of Rs 10,000, which I could not afford. Our old driver Abdul Samad, whom we all called Munna, had accompanied me. He now worked with the Geological Survey of India. Munna whisked me out saying he would come back later and negotiate. He finally brought the price down to half, but I never made it back to buy the photograph. Munna is now no more, and neither is there any trace left of the Vernon & Sons shop. Yet I feel certain that the portrait will pop up somewhere, one day.

Caineville House transformed Phuphi Jaan from a scared little girl who feared the dark to an independent woman poised to face the world. She grew up to become fearless and self-reliant. The bond between the two siblings stayed strong, despite her subsequent migration to Pakistan with her husband upon its formation.

Chapter 2

A Button for Freedom

'Ham parvarish-e-lauh-o-qalam karte raheṅge,
Jo dil pe guzartī hai raqam karte raheṅge.'
(I will continue to nurture the pen and the tablet,
What my heart goes through, I will keep expressing.)
—Faiz Ahmad Faiz

I was always interested in stories of Abba Jaan's life from when he was around my age. I could put myself in his position and be the person that he was. Between his photographs, evocative storytelling and old cars parked in the Kotwara garages was a world of wonder. The 1928 Isotta Fraschini, with coach work by Cesare Sala, which one day I swore to bring back to life, stood testimony to this link. I remember distinctly the dial set below the dashboard with a connecting push button in the passenger seat. Pushing that button was like a miracle for me. It would guide the driver on where to go and what to do.

The Isotta was the first car Abba Jaan bought in England. The dowager rani of Kotwara had paid for her grandson's indulgence. It was not a car; it was a person. It was made for my father, and one can't imagine one without the other. He returned from Britain with spectacular photographs of his cars and vivid memories that went with them. I discovered the essence of automobile design through the Isotta.

England was like paradise for the Indian aristocracy. A source of great knowledge and style, both of which came at huge costs! They also came at huge risk of awakening the aristocracy to the systemic exploitative machinery that was set into motion by the colonial rulers in the name of progress, pushing the haves into the lap of mindless luxury and the have-nots into an abyss of darkness and ignorance.

Abba Jaan could see the good, the bad and the ugly in each situation in an instant and did not waste a moment to say it. This made him swerve left of centre all the time while appreciating the positive values of the taluqdars. He was extremely down-to-earth yet attached to status symbols. While these symbols, too, expressed his revolt against conventions that defined people, he was prone to self-indulgence. He loved cars, and big ones at that.

Abba Jaan's shoe polish incident comes to mind here. Once, walking down Piccadilly, my father stopped to get his shoes polished. He looked around in wonder admiring the shining automobiles driving up and down elegantly as the brush moved rhythmically—left-right, left-right—on his black shoe, now taking on a new shine. The polish boy nudged him to change his foot, which he did distractedly, and quipped in a shrill tone, 'How do you like our rule down there in India?' My father, taken aback by the cheeky polish boy's question, retorted, 'Mind your business, whatever you're called . . .' and tossed him more coins than he deserved and walked away. The boy tucked them into his pocket with a sly chuckle. 'Me name is Colin. Always at your service, sir.'

Selling luxury cars like the Rolls-Royce or the Bentley, especially to the Indian aristocracy, was a lucrative business for Great Britain, and Abba Jaan was sure he would not fall into this trap. He had all the star-like qualities, and Rudolf Valentino was the rage of the time. Valentino already owned an Isotta Fraschini town car when he ordered another Isotta to be bodied by Fleetwood. Unfortunately, Valentino passed away at the young age of thirty-one due to ill health and never saw the car. Abba Jaan met a dealer who sold him the idea of a new and rare style, not the British way but the Italian way—a style that Valentino had fallen for. It was something that Abba Jaan could see himself driving from Lucknow to Kotwara through the verdant greens of the Terai forests. A straight 8-litre engine burning its way to the heart carrying a 3-tonne and 21-feet-long machine with it. Maybe his grandfather would have made an exception for this. Cars were made of dreams, and he knew that. A dream that I inherited from him.

Heads would turn as the Isotta roared its way around Mayfair. Abba Jaan was reminded of Colin, the polish boy. He deliberately drove past his polish stand, waving nonchalantly: 'Ciao.'

Years on, as Abba Jaan excitedly recalled his experience, I imagined myself at the driving wheel, with its intricate meters ticking away. Zipping around London to the distinctly Italian roar of its straight 8-litre engine—it was like a moment of epiphany. The fire of design, which was to be my lifelong pursuit of joy.

Abba Jaan finally drove into Oxford only to be told that college rules did not allow a first-year student to keep a car! Flabbergasted at the ridiculousness of this rule, he drove out, went straight to an outfitter, donned a kilt and vowed never to drive through the Oxford gate again.

Several decades later I took the journey from London to Edinburgh, where I felt I had lived before through Abba Jaan. The photographs stood reference to a blind nostalgia, with his evocative recollections filling in the blanks. What was his empathy with Scotsmen, which kept reappearing in the loving recollections of his chauffeur, James? I made this real and meaningful for myself with my newfound love for Highland folklore and music originally inspired by Abba Jaan.

'O ye'll take the high road and I'll take the low road, and I'll be in Scotland afore ye . . . But me and my true love will never meet again, on the Bonnie Bonnie banks o' Loch Lomond . . .'

Abba Jaan had a passion for getting photographed, for a sense of record. He met Swan Watson, a famous photographer who specialized in studio portraiture. When Abba Jaan went to see him, Swan was fascinated by this great machine he had driven in and agreed to shoot them outdoors by the lochs. Abba Jaan and the Isotta stood like a statement frozen in time. Swan also photographed them later with James at the Edinburgh University. He was so taken with Abba Jaan that he also photographed him with his Sunbeam. These photographs are as valuable to me today as the cars themselves. He would say, 'My photographs won't die like me. They'll keep you alive too.'

These photographs brought to life the Isotta and the memories of Abba Jaan driving through dales and lochs, mountains and curves, as the monstrous green machine, with beige canvas suitcases packed with clothes and books, turned around and made its way to Edinburgh University in Bonnie Scotland as bagpipes welcomed him. He must have pressed the FAST button in the interior cabin, separated from James by a glass partition. FREEDOM!

This was no ordinary machine. It represented an era when cars were designed by artists and made by craftsmen. He used it rarely and judiciously, so he bought a Sunbeam coupé and a Citroen for daily use. James continued to look after all his cars. One Christmas, James invited my father to his village near Edinburgh, Linlithgow, the birthplace of Mary Queen of Scots, for lunch. James was proud to belong to that place. It was a white Christmas, and everyone was appropriately dressed with something in red. As my father came out the children shrieked, 'Look! Look! In the snow even the darkies are turning white!'

I drove back taking a detour through Linlithgow with Abba Jaan's recollection of James humming the song of 'Loch Lomond', a tale of freedom and defeat, in resonance with the aftermath of 1857 in Awadh. The song was born out of the famous battle of Culloden Moor, where 7000 highlanders were defeated on 17 April 1746. 'Loch Lomond' tells the story of two Scottish soldiers who were imprisoned. One of them was to be executed, while the other was to be set free. According to Celtic legend, if someone dies in a foreign land his spirit will travel to his homeland by 'the low road'—the route for the souls of the dead. It was a tragic tale that must have touched Abba Jaan so far away from Kotwara, with no one in the world to care for him. The Highlands had become his second home, and James, his butler and his cook, were his extended family.

Edinburgh was all about a new world that was so tangible and real for him, which I just had to see and feel for myself. A new sense of liberty. A new identity with a historical past. A new recognition with the future and symbols that connected them. The semal tree and the appearance of Lord Vishnu to Raja Sopi in a dream in the dark wooded forests of the Terai. This finally became the Kotwara insignia, which Abba Jaan took upon himself to get designed in Edinburgh. I added the horses to highlight the idea of self-reliance.

Abba Jaan remembered every little detail of his time spent in Edinburgh. From his phone number to the number of his house and the street it was on, to the names of all those who visited him. He was especially friendly with Nawab Hamidullah Khan of Bhopal, for whom he hosted a banquet upon his visit. I wish I had written down the names of those who had posed for the group photograph! 'I wish I had' is a phrase that gets the better of me as I document this past.

Back in India, the socio-political system was grappling with a growing fire for freedom. The taluqdars of Awadh, who had sided with Begum Hazrat Mahal during the 1857 War of Indian Independence, were slowly and gradually being divided along communal lines. The Hindus sided with the Hindu Mahasabha and the Muslims with the Muslim League. There were a few who were with the Congress. It suited the British to have it this way with the rise of the call for freedom. They had quickly realized that the Hindu and the Muslim taluqdars should be individually pampered, yet a divide was created, which would only grow deeper with time.

The taluqdars of the British period were given honours and titles depending on how useful they were to the colonial powers and their contribution to the war funds. The British administration kept close tabs on each of them through the deputy collector of the district. The behaviour of each mattered a lot. This was the slice of history that I tried to capture in my feature film *Jaanisaar*, released in 2015.

When my father returned from Scotland, he went to pay his respects to the taluqdars and elders who had been close to his grandfather. While it suited the British to keep the taluqdars polarized, deep within, the taluqdars of Awadh were secular to the core. Abba Jaan introduced me to the rich milieu and culture of the taluqdars. He told me so many stories and anecdotes that they became larger than life for me. It happened to be the month of Muharram when Abba Jaan visited Maharaj Krishan Dutt Singh of Oel. He found the Maharaja sleeping on the floor on a thin, coarse mat. Surprised, my father asked why he had left the comfort of his opulent silken bed and was lying on the floor. Annoyed, the Maharaja replied, 'Don't you know? It is Muharram!' To which my father replied, 'So what does that have to do with you?' At this the Maharaja flared up, 'You are a fool, Sajid! A ruler has no religion but the religion of his subjects.'

Abba Jaan was very different from the usual taluqdars of his time. He could never position himself as a 'Muslim' aristocrat siding with Muslims. His education in Edinburgh had made him very open-minded. He found a lot in common with Scotsmen, as far as the British dominance of the Indian nation went. He had joined the Communist Party of Scotland and, despite his luxurious lifestyle, was in deep sympathy with the downtrodden. He travelled across most of the world and was particularly impressed with the China of that time. He always used to quote an incident when he went to a Chinese home and saw that in the household each member was from a different religion, which they kept to themselves. This made a deep and lasting impact on his mind. As it did on me. Abba Jaan had no parents and therefore no conditioning of any sort. When I see films made on the rajas of that time I realize how off-the-mark and clichéd they really are.

My father had much in common with Mustafa Kemal Atatürk and became an ardent admirer of his. He, too, believed in Romanizing all Indian languages, much like Atatürk did with Turkish. Even though he belonged to the ruling class, Abba Jaan himself was always opposed to the monarchy. In his heart of hearts, I know he secretly agreed with Turkey breaking out of the shackles of imperialism to become a republic!

The Ottoman Empire had reached its zenith between 1520 and 1566, during the time of Sultan Suleiman the Magnificent. It had expanded to cover vast territories of the world to include Turkey, Greece, Bulgaria, Egypt, Hungary, Macedonia, Romania, Jordan, Palestine, Lebanon, Syria, some regions of Arabia and large parts of the North African coastal strip. Suleiman was considered by many Sunni Muslims to be both a religious leader and a political ruler. But by early 1600s the Ottoman Empire had begun to lose its economic and military dominance to Europe, which had gained enormous strength with the Renaissance movement and the Industrial Revolution. Over the next hundred years, the Ottoman Turks lost battle after battle, with the Balkan Wars of 1912–1913 sounding the death knell for their empire.

The Ottomans suffered a humiliating defeat in the First World War, and with the subsequent Treaty of Versailles, signed in 1919, their territories were reduced to a minimum. Finally, it was the successful Turkish War of Independence, led by Atatürk against the occupying Allies in 1922, that led to the emergence of the Republic of Turkey and the abolition of the Ottoman monarchy.

Undivided India was torn politically between its vast Muslim population and its struggle for independence. The British played a major role in shaping minds and loyalties. Fifteen million Indians fought a war that was not theirs. The Indian troops became the backbone of the British Army. Muslims were both at the core of the Indian Army and, subsequently, of India's Freedom struggle. One million Indian soldiers died. The leadership working on fanning anti-British sentiment used this emotionally.

Sensing unrest within the empire, Ottoman sultan Abdul Hamid II (1842–1918) had launched a pan-Islamist movement with a two-fold agenda—to protect the empire from Western attack and division, and to crush the democratic opposition at home. His emissary, Jamaluddin Afghani, evoked religious passion and empathy among Indian Muslims, with several religious leaders working to spread awareness and develop Muslim engagement on behalf of the Ottoman Caliphate.[*]

The Khilafat Movement (1919–24) was a pan-Islamist political opposition campaign launched by Muslims in India. It was led by Maulana Shaukat Ali, Maulana Mohammad Ali Jauhar, Hakim Ajmal Khan and Abul Kalam Azad, and it was aimed at restoring the caliph of the Ottoman Caliphate as an effective political authority.

An alliance was formed between the Khilafat leaders and the Indian National Congress in 1920, wherein the leaders promised to work and fight together for the causes of Khilafat and Swaraj.

But chinks began to appear in the armour soon. The Muslims were divided between working for the Congress, the Khilafat cause and the Muslim League, and the Khilafat leadership was fragmented along different political lines.

The Ottoman Empire officially ended on 1 November 1922. With this, the Khilafat movement collapsed completely. The last sultan, Mehmed VI, fled the country, and the caliphate was abolished.

But Abba Jaan fell prey to the Ali Brothers' campaign of reinstating the Royal Ottoman family in India by finding suitable husbands for the princesses. In 1931, Maulana Muhammad Ali arranged the marriage of Princess Durru Shehvar, daughter of Sultan Abdul Mejid II, and his brother's daughter, Princess Niloufer, to the two sons of Nizam Mir Osman Ali Khan of Hyderabad.

In 1936, Maulana Shaukat Ali arranged the marriage of another Ottoman Princess, Selma Hanimsultan, the granddaughter of Sultan Murad V, to my father. Abba Jaan and Selma's marriage was solemnized at

---

[*] Shamshad Ali, *Indian Muslims and the Ottoman Empire, 1876–1924*, PhD dissertation, Aligarh Muslim University, 1990.

Patiala House in Delhi. It was a simple ceremony attended by the maharaja of Oel, Josh Malihabadi, Bahzad Lakhnawi, Vasl Bilgrami and Dr Abdul Wajid Khan, to whom my father's sister would soon get married.

The marriage with Selma did not last long, and she migrated to Paris, where she gave birth to a daughter, Kanize, and died. World War II broke out, cutting off all communication with the civil society in India. Selma had made sure Kanize would not be easily traceable. Abba Jaan tried hard but failed. Kanize was adopted by a Swiss couple, Monsieur De Naville and his wife, who put her in a Christian convent. It was only in 1962 that she found her way to her father in India.

Abba Jaan resolved that he would only marry again if he found a traditional person of his own ilk in Lucknow. He came to know of my mother through his own mother's cousin, the thakurain of Qadipur, who had a strong influence on him. Late in 1942, my father married Kaniz Hyder, daughter of Nawab Mohammad Hasan Khan of Muradabad, who was living in exile in Bilhera House with his sister, the rani of Bilhera.

I have not seen anyone change as much as my father from the time of Independence. He fought for freedom, but it came with an unprecedented, unforeseen cost. For my father's only sister married Dr Abdul Wajid Khan from Rampur, who opted for Pakistan—a severe blow. Abba Jaan himself never went to Pakistan. He used to say, '*Kawwa meri haddi na le jaye us paar* (A raven may not take a single bone from my body across to Pakistan).' He knew over a decade before that the Muslim League would result in an ugly India, fractured along communal lines as per the design of our colonial masters. He fought his first provincial election in British India in 1936–37, at the young age of twenty-seven, from Shahabad, the seat that includes the Kotwara region, and defeated his opponents for eighteen years, finally retiring early from politics as chairman of the Uttar Pradesh Legislative Assembly, when he lost the elections in 1952. He was an elected member of the legislative assembly, as an independent candidate, and this opened a new vision for the people of the district, minimizing, for them, the impact of migration in 1947 and also leading to the rehabilitation of the Sikh population in large numbers in the Terai region.

Abba Jaan had formed his own party and called it the Hal Jutta Party, a party of farmers. He even penned an anthem for the party, '*Hal jutta bhai hal jutta, jai jai bhaiya hal jutta* (Toiler of the soil, hail thee, O toiler of the soil).' Vijay Lakshmi Pandit was also a member of the legislative assembly at the same time as him and would often drop by for lunch at Kotwara House in Qaiserbagh to meet Abba Jaan's sister, with whom she was very friendly. On every visit she would ask him to recite his party anthem, which he did with full gusto and great belief.

Except for what I have heard in stories, I have faint memories of that time. Once, my father was seeking help from a close family relative during the election, who was also a taluqdar and an ardent Muslim Leaguer. The uncle readily agreed and asked my father to come to the mosque on a particular Friday after the Friday prayers. On the appointed day, my father arrived in his traditional best at the village mosque. There was a larger-than-usual turnout as his campaign managers had announced that Raja Sahab will come and join the namaz. The uncle announced at the beginning of the prayers that he would be making a special announcement after the namaz and the *khutba* (an address given at the end of the namaz). The namaz came to an end, and an authoritative voice boomed from the pulpit. His hold on his people was evident in his tone and tenor. 'All you present here have to promise that you will do as I say.' Having got an unconditional affirmation, he went on to add, 'If you wish to stay in this world and get your jobs done, vote for the Congress. If you want a place for yourself in heaven, vote for the Muslim League. And if you wish to go to hell, vote for my nephew, Sajid Husain. Now, all of you will promise me that you will vote for Raja Kotwara and go straight to hell!' My father was taken aback and cursed himself for seeking his Muslim Leaguer uncle's help. It took a considerable amount of firefighting to mend the damage. But it made him a wiser man, more prepared for the dangers ahead.

The post-1952 period saw the greatest change in Awadh since 1857. The remaining sheen quickly wore off, and the taluqdars of Awadh suffered a severe setback they still have not recovered from, except those who took to politics. My father had lost the election of 1952, and his self-respect kept him from going to Pandit Nehru, though the latter held him in high esteem as a man of human values and ideas. In 1948, Sardar Patel gave a speech in Lucknow at the Amin-ud-Daulah Park, warning Muslims that if they did not mend their ways such 'hot winds' would blow that it would be impossible for them to remain in India. When Pandit Nehru came to know of this, he called for Maulana Abul Kalam Azad to proceed immediately to Lucknow, where he was to chair a meeting of the Muslim intelligentsia to assure them that this was not what the Congress meant. He underlined that the person at whose home this meeting should be held should be a hardcore nationalist who was not a Congressman. The choice fell on my father, and Kotwara House in the historical Qaiserbagh was chosen as the venue. The date was 12 December 1948. It was Abba Jaan's pride that kept him away from active politics after 1952, but he continued to be an ardent admirer of Nehru, who, he believed, was the need of the hour to build a strong secular nation with visionary institutions to take India into the new world of independent nations.

Abba Jaan may have differed from Nehru on various matters, but he believed in his secular ideals which made India stand out in sharp contrast to Pakistan. He would write frequently to Nehru, who was a sounding board for his own ideas, and would elicit regular responses. The larger issues that concerned him were audio–visual education, hydel power by harnessing and connecting the waters of our rivers, and family planning. He sent a detailed plan to Nehru, to which he received a reply saying that we did not have the wherewithal to make all this happen. Abba Jaan's letter about building footpaths was made into a government order. He would often go to Delhi to meet Nehru. Once, in 1962, I accompanied him with my stepsister, Kanize. The conversation ended on her extraordinary life story and that of her mother. Indira Gandhi was there too, and I found both father and daughter most gracious and refined. Twenty years later, she would appoint me on a committee for software development for Doordarshan in India. And another twenty years later I was appointed as a member of the Prasar Bharati board.

I had seen my father dream and seen his dreams shatter. After 1952, Abba Jaan locked himself in his room with the window, from where he saw the city go by for almost two years, and emerged as a lawyer. His new motto was, 'A penny saved is a penny earned!' He fought every legal case to the best of his capabilities. His close group of friends comprised lawyers, and he was in constant consultation with them on one thing or the other. By now, all his Western suits, fancy cufflinks and pocket squares, scarves, fine leather wallets, belts and shoes had been replaced by one khadi sherwani and two khadi kurta pajama sets, his favourite being a khaki kurta and lungi, which he wore at home. My mother detested this outfit.

A generous soul, my mother allowed a fruit-seller, Sitara, to sleep under the fan in our large drawing room in the heat of the summer afternoon. Sitara was an obese woman with a man's short haircut and a loud voice, hoarse from shouting to sell her wares. My brothers and I found her both amusing and scary. Abba Jaan had gone to Lakhimpur, our district headquarters, for some work. His favourite khaki kurta and lungi had been washed and hung out to dry in the courtyard. It caught Sitara's fancy, and she asked my mother if she could have it. Only too delighted to get rid of the pair, my mother quickly handed them over to Sitara, who immediately changed and lay down in total bliss for her afternoon siesta on the cool mosaic floor. While she slept with her fruit basket next to her, the Issota entered the porch. There was much commotion when Abba Jaan walked up the stairway and entered the hall to find his kurta and lungi cladding this person. He felt humiliated realizing what was thought of an attire that he deeply respected. The moment created a minor earthquake, which, thankfully, over the years became a joke, a secret shared by my mother and me.

* * *

My early life in Lucknow is a collage of images and memories, often with little context, of people who still called my father Sajid, and my mother Bittan. Some pieces of this collage are moments, some incidents and some stories told by others. Some are poems, some songs. And some are just sounds of being addressed or summoned. 'Bare Miañ' as I was known, my younger brother Manjhu Miañ, and the youngest Guddu Miañ . . .

Besides my parents, there were many people who came into and went out of my life. We were never left alone at any point of time. There were only certain friends and certain homes I could visit or who were encouraged to visit me. And so, I spent many hours in the zenana as a child, listening to stories. I have faint memories of a dignified old lady— Aatuji, we called her—who told the best stories. Ladli Begum, another character, used to delight in telling us crazy tales, especially of opium addicts. One such story was about a pair of friends who were given the task of delivering two prized horses to a buyer. On the way, they stopped to rest under the generous shade of an imli tree and opened their opium boxes. Having had their fill, they were lulled to sleep by the cool breeze. They woke up a few hours later and reluctantly resumed their journey, all the while telling each other that they seemed to have forgotten something but couldn't exactly remember what. Upon reaching their destination, they realized they had forgotten the horses! These stories, apart from being humorous, served as a hidden warning to us children against the use of these easily available drugs.

I would often hear the same story from different women. They opened a very endearing side of themselves to me—no defences, no pretences. They went out of their way to please and reach out. They all bloomed under the gracious presence of my mother. In a way, my mother was the sum total of their happiness. There was no one untouched by her generosity.

I remember my mother as the most elegant lady, slender and tall with a powerful personality. My maternal grandfather, Nawab Mohammad Hasan Khan of Muradabad, had fled the ire of the British with just the shirt on his back. He settled with his family in Lucknow with his widowed, issueless sister, the Rani of Bilhera, who looked after them all. My nani (maternal grandmother), Chhoti Bi, was from Sheikhupur in Badaun, a descendant of Sheikh Salim Chishti, who was given the *jagir* (estate) of Sheikhupur by Mughal Emperor Akbar. She always wore a *ghuttana* (tight pajamas) with a long kurta, and a white *chadar* (sheet-like veil) over her *rupatta* (veil).

Chhoti Bi was a world in herself, a dervish of sorts. She was truly placeless, truly traceless. No one knew where she would stay the night to come. My mother was brought up by her father's sister. She was a deep reflection of her aunt and her magnanimity. Her aunt kept an open kitchen where anybody and everybody could come and eat and take refuge. She was the extension of her brother, Nawab Mohammad Hasan Khan, who would give away a new quilt every night. Her death served a severe blow to all who had come to love her, and her Brahmin driver committed suicide by banging his head on the bonnet of her car.

Unfortunately, her next of kin among the Bilhera taluqdars were not the same. In fact, everybody considered my mother, who had moved to 10 Qaiserbagh as rani of Kotwara, as the only one fit to carry forward her aunt's legacy.

Bilhera House was full of people of different sorts. Nooran and Batasan, both of whom were about my mother's age, came with her dowry from Bilhera House to Kotwara House. They hated each other and vied for my mother's attention, constantly putting the other down in front of her. Nooran and her several children became part of our family. Kallu, her second son, became integral to my nani's life and was called 'Chhoti Bi ka signboard', as he accompanied her everywhere, appearing just before she did.

My nana had another wife, Badi Bi. He had two children each from both his marriages. While they were all Sunnis, his sister, the rani of Bilhera, was Shia. Under her influence, Chhoti Bi's children, my mother and her brother became Shia.

My memories of my nana are mixed with much of what I have heard of him. What impacted me most was that when he asked for water, all the girls in the zenana ran to him offering a *katora* (bowl). I was told over and over again by my nana about the plight of Nawab Majiduddin Khan, my great-grandfather who was burnt alive by the British in a lime kiln and his body dragged around Moradabad, tied to the feet of his own elephant. The nawab, a great freedom fighter in 1857, was deceitfully arrested with the help of a British lackey, the then nawab of Rampur. What I do remember of my nana is the bell-like noise he made with a spoon and a plate, trying to distract me as a toddler. He passed away when I was hardly four years old. A tinted photograph of him in a *jamevar* sherwani still hangs in the drawing room of Kotwara House, next to the Swan Watson photographs of Abba Jaan.

The world of Kotwara House was my world. Batasan had a son, Munna, who was taught to drive by the state driver, Aghhan, a wiry, half-bent person who would drive like a maniac, taking his anger out on the car, the road and the people on it. *Purdahs* (curtains), would be drawn on the Ford's windows, and the car would tear through the crowded streets of Aminabad, coming to a screeching halt outside Madan Fabric Shop. My mother would lift the purdah slightly, and more than half the shop would be emptied into the car for her to choose from. She also had a few favourite haunts in Hazratgunj—Modern Silk House and Modern Novelties. These also had branches in Naini Tal, which we frequented. I would lose myself in Modern Novelties, a wonderland of books and toys.

During Muharram, several ladies came home to do *matam* (grieve). They were mostly Abyssinians who had come back with my mother's aunt from Karbala. Of these, Sibti Bahen was the most amusing and went with us to Naini Tal whenever our visit to that place coincided with Muharram. Sibti going to Kotwara Lodge was a spectacle. She was enormous and had to climb up the hill on all fours. But she didn't care, and always arrived huffing and puffing. Her animated narration of stories, about the people she'd met, the shopkeepers we knew, was hilarious. Aatuji had warned us that if travellers listened to the stories in the daytime, they would lose their way. I have a sneaky suspicion that she made this up to stop me clamouring for more, for I had an insatiable appetite for stories.

But when none of these storytellers were present, Abba Jaan filled the gap. He had to prove better than the rest. Which he did! My favourite was 'Tilism-e-Hoshruba', the most amusing, never-ending story of the magician Afrasiyab, the intelligent trickster Amru Ayyar and the warrior Amir Hamza. Filled with magic, intellect, trickery and chivalry, three genres of narratives are intertwined in one tale. Surely what I heard from my father was his own interpretation of how he saw these characters as prototypes of a contemporary world he had grown up in. Abba Jaan's stories were always told to us in installments, between his other tasks. He was good at building suspense, stopping at moments that kept us guessing impatiently till the next evening. He would have made a good writer had he taken up the profession.

Stories and more stories made up the lessons of life, and Abba Jaan was specially gifted in the art of telling them. His stories spanned the gullies of Lucknow as well as his journeys around the world. He was in awe of the human race and found it amusing, endearing and, at the same time, disgusting. He was also impatient with fools and intolerant of dishonesty.

During an appetizing meal of quorma, kabab and chapattis, dished out by Nooran, Abba Jaan narrated an incident when he was travelling by train to Kotwara. In his compartment was a 'Brown Sahib' in a suit, pith helmet and tie. Throughout the journey the Brown Sahib kept cursing everything Indian. Flies, dust, heat, people, smells, adding the prefix 'damn' to everything. My father kept to himself, reading his book. He got down at Oel to stretch his legs. The train whistled and, as it began to pull out of the station, my father jumped back in. And lo and behold, what did he see! The Brown Sahib with his tiffin box open, eating kabab and chapattis . . . He was taken aback to see Abba Jaan return. In a tone full of apology and embarrassment, he said, 'You know, I rather like these damn Indian shuppatties and kobabs.'

'Brown Sahab' seemed like a term coined especially for Awadh. Among the educated elite, the culture of the English reigned, and it was said that Deputy Habibullah was its greatest victim, having fallen prey to the disease when he went to drop his children to college in England. He was of a dark complexion and wore white suits and pith helmets in summer. One day, an Urdu poet went to visit him, and as is often the case with poets, a singular trait sparked off a couplet: '*Wah kya dhaj hai mere bhole ki, hat solay ki, shakl kolay ki* (What a sight is my innocent buffoon, a pith helmet on a face as black as coal) . . .' Today, a comment like this would be deemed racist, but casual British and Indian upper-caste racism then made this thought and expression permissible. There is another instance when, looking from his rooftop, Deputy Habibullah, taluqdar of Saidanpur, saw people moving about in new clothes. He asked a member of his staff, in his carefully cultivated English accent, '*Aj sab naya naya kapra kyon pahna hai* (Why is everyone dressed in fancy new clothes today)?' To which the staff replied, '*Huzoor, aaj hamlogoñ ki Eid hai* (Sir, today is the day of Eid for us).'

Deputy Habibullah immediately admonished the fellow, '*Hamko pahhle bolta to ham roza rakhta* (You should have told me! I would have kept a fast).

Often, taluqdars lived in a world of their own, populated by their own people, with their own rules and timings. They were, most of the time, out of place in situations of their own making. Abba Jaan would gnash his teeth at their idiosyncrasies and at the same time find their predicament amusing. He would regale us with true-life incidents woven into stories. Another mealtime, another story. We were having birhaiñ roti with qeema for lunch, a typical Lakhnawi monsoon delicacy. Each time there had to be one new person on the table for my father to open his story box! I had enjoyed hearing the same stories from him over and over again. I wanted my new friends to hear them too. This particular story was set in the period of the non-cooperation movement. The Qaiserbagh Baradari, which was the headquarters of the British India Association, with the taludqars of Awadh as its members, was just a few windows away from our dining room in Kotwara House. A meeting of the taluqdars was being held at the Baradari under the chairmanship of none other than the viceroy of India, to persuade them to stay in favour of the queen. One of the attendees, a rather effeminate raja from a very large state, was heavily under the influence of his mindless and illiterate attendant, Abdullah, who had dressed him for this very important gathering in a *lehnga, choli* and a heavily embroidered and bejewelled *chogha* in a bid to outdo the other taluqdars, as was the general idea on such occasions.

Then it came to the choice of a watch. Abdullah told his master, '*Aap itte bare raja, kahañ itni chhoti si ghari lagayyo* (How can such a big raja wear such a tiny watch)?' So saying, he dismissed the emerald-studded Cartier the raja had chosen, and instead hung a timepiece strung on a silken tassel around the raja's neck. Pleased as punch, the raja arrived at the Baradari. Everyone bowed as low as they could in greeting. He was given a seat in the front row.

The meeting began with the usual decorum and protocol. The raja soon got bored with the proceedings, lost interest and dozed off. Somewhere in the middle of the viceroy's speech, an alarm went off, throwing the meeting in a disarray. Everyone thought the 'swarajis' had struck. Slowly the audience's attention narrowed towards the source of the sound. It was the raja's timepiece! He woke up and pointed nonchalantly, proudly at his clock, '*Ka chakar-makar chakar-makar dekhat ho? Yau mor baajat hai* (Why are you looking here and there in a dumbfounded manner? It is the bell of my timepiece that you hear).' This was the same raja who would sleep on the ground during Muharram in reverence towards the faith of his people.

Kotwara House was the world of my father, his ideas, his visitors and his way of life. It was located in the heart of the city, and everyone from every background would drop by to see him. The house was full of humanist slogans pasted on the walls, including, 'Humanity will only progress when the last brick of the last church will fall on the head of the last priest.'

One frequent visitor was a person who would also visit the famous barrister Yusuf of Lucknow daily. While sitting with Abba Jaan he would curse the barrister every day for new reasons. Abba Jaan asked him why he visited the barrister so often if he hated him so much. '*Wah bhai wah. Aap nahiñ samajh paye* (You have not understood). I go there just to develop my sense of hatred towards that man!'

Today, when I think back, I realize I have such a huge cache of characters ready to find their space on the film screen.

We spend our lives enmeshed in a web of stories, whether as tellers of tales or listeners. If you are a mindless listener, storytellers can grossly mislead you, if they are telling a story to gain power over you or even just for simple profit. Listening to these small, harmless stories told by my father around the dinner table made me acutely sensitive to this truth.

The simple, gullible people who were swayed by such minds were, in my father's view, fools or dishonest as humans. He vehemently opposed anything that divided humanity and looked for binding factors in each faith. Maybe that is how I grew up to become a storyteller through my works—be it film-making or painting.

Abba Jaan was engaged with anything and everything that happened to the human race. He had a tremendous sense of record and kept newspaper cuttings from 1915, when he was only five years of age, spanning the two world wars, scientific developments and wonders of nature. He even invented a water cooler sitting at home in Qaiserbagh! His scientific approach drove me to take up science at the Aligarh Muslim University. I chose geology, to discover the secrets of nature below the earth, with the world's endless need for fossil fuel; botany, to learn the secrets of nature that grew out of the earth; and chemistry, which contained the secrets of elements, their salts and their compounds that made everything happen. While there seemed to be eternal truth in all this, it had no alignment with my own 'chemistry'—something I was yet to discover. I would see the world through the eyes of a poet, be it an optimistic way of looking at the world or otherwise. Be it a revolution or a romance. Or spiritual surrender! Yet I was destined to be an artist who would find deep resonance in science.

* * *

Kotwara was a place of simple innocence. Of people who could not even lie properly. My heart reached out to them. My mother was deeply drawn to the scheduled-caste women who would flock in hundreds around her for hours and days on end. We spent all our winters there. Muharram was another time when the entire palace was teeming with colourful women. I had my own favourites among them. We played and ran about, and in time to come they became a part of my art. There was a lady in Kotwara whom we called Dadi (paternal grandmother), married to an insufferable patriarch, Masitullah Khan. Dadi came to live with us while we were there one winter. She would narrate incidents involving my grandparents and great-grandparents late into the night, leaving us feeling both proud and wonderstruck.

It was here that I found, jacked up on bricks, a dream on wheels. In every taluqdar's home there was an abandoned dream on bricks, but never anything like this. This dream had been brought back from Edinburgh, reminiscent of my father's romantic days and his grandmother's indulgence. A 1929 Tipo 8A Isotta Fraschini. The name was enough to conjure dreams. It was rare, and only a few were ever crafted. It was a piece of art. The garage smelt of old wood, leather and ancient congealed oil. It would make a fabulous perfume if one had the nose and the means.

My carpenter Gajodhar would say, '*Kotwaro ka cut niralo hai* (There is something unique in the Kotwara style).' Several years later, all these people acted in the films I made there. Every inch of the visible design was born out of their nimble and artistic hands. Kotwara was to become my art in time to come. All the books, photographs, albums and postcards that my father brought from Edinburgh were kept in a library in Mustafa Manzil, facing the rising sun. Today, this is my inspirational space which I have not properly shared with people. Most of the time that we were in Kotwara, we lived in Mustafa Manzil. I continue to do so today, and it is strictly a no-shoe zone covered by Kotwara durries.

Chapter 3

A New Dawn

'Ab is ke baad subah hai aur subah-e-nau "Majaz",
Ham par hai khatm shaam-e-gharibaan-e-Lakhnau.'
('Beyond this darkness is the morn, a new morn at that,
With me Majaz comes an end to eves of angst and sorrow.')
—Asrar-ul-Haq Majaz

We began visiting Naini Tal in 1948. I was about four years old. I have vivid memories of staying at the Metropole Hotel, which belonged to Raja Amir Ahmad Khan of Mahmudabad, and was run very efficiently by a Parsi, Shaporji. We took a whole wing facing the tennis courts. The staff was well appointed, just as the British had left them. The head waiter was a Pandit from Almora, who knew all about the mysteries of mountain mythology, and I feel fortunate that I had the opportunity to spend a few summers with him. He was most dramatic and amusing. He taught us how to eat mangoes—they had to be followed by a cup of cold milk. He would then stroke his moustache and burp long and loud. The large ballroom had diamond-shaped bevelled windows interspersed with life-size mirrors—a magical place in the day.

One day, there was an unusually heavy downpour and lightning flashed through the windows, striking the huge mirrors and giving the eerie illusion of their being shattered. It was in this sinister atmosphere that he chose to tell the story of Naini Tal, of Shiva who carried the body of his beloved Sati in anguish all over the universe. Vishnu had cut her body into fifty-two parts with his Sudharshan Chakra. Where her *nain* (eyes), fell grew the expansive lake that continues to be known as Naini Tal.

Having proved the origin of the lake to a trembling child, the Metropole Pandit heaved a sigh of deep spiritual satisfaction. The lake would always remain an awe-inspiring mystery for all time to come. Every time I visited Naini Tal, I would seek out a Brahmin to take me through the wonders of these mountains.

The British had brought their own sense of romance to the hills. Naini Tal, like all hill stations, was a mini Britain of sorts. The Kumaon hills came under British rule after the Anglo–Nepalese War (1814–16), but Naini Tal was founded only in 1841, with the construction of Pilgrim Lodge by P. Barron, a sugar trader from Shahjahanpur. The Anglican Church, St John in the Wilderness, one of the oldest and finest churches in Naini Tal, was built in 1846, after which the town grew rapidly, with the construction of Belvedere, Alma Lodge and Ashdale Cottage. It became the health resort of choice for British soldiers and colonial officials, and their families trying to escape the intense heat of the plains. It later went on to become the summer residence of the governor of the United Provinces. Several schools came up for the floating British population. The taluqdars of Awadh built their summer homes here, designed by British architects. They turned the landslip into a great advantage and the 'Flats' discovered a culture of its own. It became a place for games and sports, a place for meetings where liveried bands would play British tunes.

I was enamoured by the hills. We started frequenting Naini Tal after Partition, when things took an ugly turn in Mussoorie. It had a fragrance I would like to bottle. There was nature and culture. Soon we started taking a home on rent and my mother always shared it with Dr Abdul Hameed, the most sought-after physician in Lucknow. He had many daughters, a few younger than me, a few older, and Zehra was my age. He had one son, Khalid, who is now Lord Khalid Hameed of Hampstead. Abba Jaan realized that our heart was in the hills. He was one of the founder members of the Naini Tal Boathouse Club, a jewel among colonial clubs, where Indians had not been allowed in pre-Independence days. In 1952 my father bought a house for my mother. It was a dream house, with a gorgeous view of the lake. We started settling there with every room done up to our taste. My room was filled with toys and a library of comic books.

Going to Naini Tal was a big event. I would prepare in great detail, and packing my books and clothes was a major exercise. I enjoyed going to the Flats, the Boathouse Club and walking up and down the Mall. Riding horses became a passion for me, and there were many beautiful horses with equally charismatic owners. Hashmat the horseman and his blackish-brown horse, Badal; the Punjabi horse Tiku, owned by the grand-looking Gulzar Khan, who always donned a *safa* (turban), a waistcoat and a baggy *shalwar* (loose pajamas gathered at the ankle). These horses racing through mountain paths and tracks around the lakeside got my adrenaline going. I admired these horsemen and how they served their riders clinging on to their horses' tails, going up steep climbs to China Peak, Land's End, Snow View and Tiffin Top. I don't think I have seen such dedicated service in the tourism world.

Naini Tal was another world. I recall there was one Syed Sahab who came with us and told me stories which I was a decade too young to hear. A couple of summers later I overheard him being admonished by my father, after which I never saw him again.

As I grew up, my circle widened and, like many teenagers, I grew interested in bodybuilding. I made friends in the bodybuilding fraternity, of which Darshan and Pyare Lal Sah were closest to me. Bodybuilding became a passion, and there was a room reserved permanently for a bodybuilder who would accompany us to Naini Tal. Often, he would double up as my maths tutor, a subject for which, unfortunately, I have never had any aptitude. I distinctly remember one of my maths tutors in Lucknow—Pandit Gokaranath, a bulkier, older version of Pandit Nehru. He would ride to Qaiserbagh from Gola Ganj on his cycle with rubber garters that kept his dhoti safe from getting entangled in the chain. Sometimes, I went to him. One day, a white Alsatian bitch landed up at his home, jumping roof to roof chasing monkeys. She was beautiful and most loving. Much to my father's surprise, my interest in meeting the maths tutor increased, and my classes at his home became more frequent. Since no one claimed the white Alsatian, Pandit Gokaranath asked me if I would be interested in taking her home. I jumped at the proposition. She was really very nice and stayed with me for several years till I gave her to my best friend, Taqi Hasan, when I went to study in Aligarh. Though my interest in maths had certainly increased, it didn't reflect in the marksheet!

I found myself, like many of my friends in Lucknow, living in a bubble. In dreams that were unreal and had no bearing on the future. Larger things were happening around us, over which we had no power. In 1952 zamindari was abolished, and my father lost the assembly election.

Everything changed. All the comfort we got from the presence of people like Aatuji or Ladli Begum or even Batasan, suddenly vanished. The most terrible things began to happen. One summer, my younger brother, Manjhu Mian, suddenly stopped talking and eating. He was taken to the best hospitals and given the best of treatments, but his situation worsened. It made our going to Naini Tal sad since we had nothing to look forward to. It was the end of a spell of romance about a place. My mother never got over it.

* * *

Colvin College in Lucknow had been specially created to educate the taluqdars' children. But some families preferred to send their sons to La Martiniere—mine did too; after all, it was my father's old school. I made several friends there, many of whom are still very close to me. Jamal Rasul Khan, Jimmy as he is known, is the son of Maharajah Aijaz Rasul Khan of Jahangirabad. I remember Jimmy had a black Studebaker Champion and a 36 Wolseley sedan. I spent quality time with him at his palace, which was elegantly conceived by a famous Armenian designer, Charles Lazarus, who was based in Calcutta. For me, a home was somewhere I could play, run and hide, jump and scream. This was one. Jahangirabad Palace was one of the finest homes I have ever played in. We mostly played Robin Hood. Jimmy was Robin and I was Will Scarlet—I always had to find a scarlet something or the other to hang on to. Naini Tal was the summer capital of Uttar Pradesh, and almost everyone you knew in Lucknow you were bound to meet in Naini Tal and certainly the taluqdar community, of which Jimmy and his brother were the most popular. We made up an intimate group with our mothers joining us at Hallet Castle, the Jahangirabad home in Naini Tal. Robin Hood continued till we reached Naini Tal. Jimmy's palace there had a lily pond, into which someone or the other, usually a junior, would be thrown.

Another friend was Sulaiman, son of the raja of Mahmudabad. He was a sombre young man who took life too seriously. His *ataliq* (personal tutor), who stayed with him the whole day, was one of the greatest conversationalists

I have ever come across. He narrated incidents with such a sense of wonder that I was always drawn to him in our free periods. Dressed always in a beige sherwani, he waited daily by Sulaiman's grey Ford Mercury, next to which was spread a large Persian carpet by two retainers who would retreat discreetly after placing an old-world *lota* and katora for water neatly on it. Parallel to his car stood my Ford Super Deluxe, also grey. Often, we were tempted to take off in our cars and stand outside Loreto Convent to gaze at the girls. This was our Lucknow, old and new, pious and mischievous, all converging in an odd way. Amir Naqi Khan of Basaha was also a very close friend, as was Taqi Hasan of Salempur. Amir Naqi, though very reserved and quiet, was full of knowledge of the arts and secrets of life, of coming of age and finding the opposite sex attractive, but within the decorum of a culture where much went unsaid. Our bond remains as strong.

Taqi, a passionate and able cricketer, was game for anything. He was a constant companion on my location surveys for films, would be part of the production process till 'pack-up' and help collect every prop that went into a frame. We shared a lot of intimate moments and secrets. His mother was my mother's best friend in the Qaiserbagh taluqdari fraternity before their marriage. Films, I have come to realize, are not made alone. You need a friend with whom you can let your hair down. Someone with whom you can laugh your tensions off. A friend who is not answerable to you, but one to whom you are. Taqi was that friend for me. He would keep me in check, making sure I made no mistakes in day-to-day production decisions. A simple question put everything in place, '*Amma kya kar rahe ho yaar* (What are you doing, my friend)?' During the shooting of *Umrao Jaan* in Lucknow, he gave me the most intricately etched agate pendant with ninety-nine names of Allah, to protect me, which I wear with reverence even now. Anything that belonged to him was mine. This was Taqi Hasan for me, morning, noon and night! A great asset is his son, Rushdi Hasan, a sensitive and highly responsible boy who has been bitten by the film bug.

This was the Lucknow of the mid-1950s and early 1960s, a Lucknow that was changing. India had been partitioned, and though not many Muslims moved out of compulsion from Lucknow, people from Sindh and Punjab found Lucknow an easy place to settle in. There were plenty of opportunities for business that hadn't been taken by the locals. The taluqdars shunned business, and there was a shift of economic balance in favour of the new settlers. I made new friends among them. They brought with them a culture different from ours—more flamboyant and aggressive. My new circle of friends included many who were not the gentle '*Ama mian chhodiye bhi* (My dear fellow, let it pass)' taluqdar sort, but the loud and '*Oye chal yaar* (Come on, buddy)' type. Ravindra Mohan became close to me. He was a year older than me, about seventeen years of age, and would drive into La Martiniere in a swanky Studebaker Hawk, with himself behind the wheel. He kept a knife tucked in his belt, as he said, for self-defence. He also boasted about his imaginary love affair with a Rajput taluqdar's daughter. He gave me an opening into a new world of showing off and telling lies, stories different from the ones I had grown up with. In comparison to the Mohans, my old aristocratic friends seemed pale. His unrequited love led him to shoot himself. I was shattered.

Another new friend, S.P. Singh, was an overgrown sardar who had outlandish ideas about enjoying life. He, too, carried a knife. One day, SP suggested we go for a drive. I agreed, and we bunked class and took off, leaving Munna behind. Munna had taken over when Aghhan, the state driver, died. As soon as we returned, Munna nervously checked the car's meter reading. We had driven around so much! What answer would he give Raja Sahab? But SP had an answer. He always had an answer: '*Utni back gear mein chala de yaar. Meter vapas vahin aa jaye ga* (Drive in reverse gear. The meter gauge will also get reversed).' By the time I got back to class, the principal had already reported my absence to Abba Jaan. SP advised that, as an excuse for bunking, I should try to run up a fever by walking around in the sun with two onions under my armpits. I did that and told Munna to inform Abba Jaan that since I had fever, Munna had asked me to rest in the car. When we got home, Munna went and reported the entire truth to my father, including the onions and faking fever bit. I kicked Munna in anger, and he went tumbling down the stairs. Revolver in hand, Abba Jaan chased me all over Qaiserbagh. When I look at that revolver, which is in my possession now, I thank my stars that he didn't pull the trigger!

* * *

Lucknow was full of people I cherished. Among them was Mamu Jaan, my mother's brother, Dr Mohammad Ahsan Farooqi, and his four children, all older than me but very interesting and inspiring. Mamu Jaan was humility and intellect personified. He was an Urdu novelist and a professor of

English at Lucknow University. A tall man with sharp features, he always had a paan (betel leaf) in his mouth. He lived in his own world, a pillow on his lap cushioning his book and a *paandaan* (betel-nut box) besides him. His white chikan kurta was perennially full of paan stains. '*Arre bhai, upar se sherwani aa jayegi* (My dear, the sherwani will cover all the stains)!'

He would enter the English department with his sherwani flying in the breeze, speaking aloud to himself,

> Hither, hither, dear
> By the breath of life,
> Hither, hither, dear!—
> Be the summer's wife!
> But those of you
> who have not been in love
> may leave the hall right now
> As we are going to talk about
> no one else but . . .
> Keats.

He made the last few lines sound as if the poem was by Keats himself. 'Hither, hither, dear . . .' was something he repeated frequently.

He had a great sense of humour and often indulged in baby talk. He gave quaint names to people and repeated them to make them sound funnier. Ucchako . . . Guchako . . . and so on. Maybe I inherited that trait from him. I would often twist names and words to make them sound funny for my children. I would call my sweet little daughter 'tawn ze bawn sawait'. It just meant too sweet but sounded funny when you said it. Mian Jaani Mian, as Mamu Jaan was called, was a fakir amid princes. He inspired my mother to study and made her do her BA much after we were born. I recall her inscribing 'Kaniz Hyder BA' proudly on her books.

Mamu Jaan's children were very amusing too, and Huzur Jaani, the eldest, taught me how to draw faces. Safia, his younger sister, had the most beautiful face I had seen, and my mother adored her beyond limits. Atia, the little one, was a total tomboy, and Chhote Huzoor, the youngest, was most interesting in his ideas but verging on insanity, to which he succumbed when they migrated to Karachi. Their going away to Pakistan was a blow to all of us, but most so to my mother. In a desperate bid, she even offered to get me married to the much-older Safia if they stayed back. But Mumani, Bajjo Jaani, as my Mamu Jaan called her lovingly, was sure that Pakistan was the only answer to her dreams. Mamu Jaan himself had no dreams, and he followed her blindly. Mamu Jaan's world was his books, his Parker pens and Bajjo Jaani. He was in love and living Keats all the time . . .

> *Jidhar jidhar Bajjo Jaani,*
> *udhar udhar Miañ Jaani . . .*
> Hither, hither, dear
> By the breath of life,
> Hither, hither, dear!—
> Be the summer's wife!
> Hither, hither, hither
> Love its boon has sent—
> If I die and wither
> I shall die content!

Bajjo Jaani had no idea that she was going to change his world, and with it, my mother's world forever. My mother went into a sadness from which there was no respite. As it turned out, Pakistan was not made for Mamu Jaan and family. They could never find their Lucknow there. There was no friendly classroom wall in Lucknow where his words would bounce off with the comfort of belonging.

> Though one moment's pleasure
> In one moment flies—
> Though the passion's treasure
> In one moment dies . . .

In Pakistan, he was often asked why he eulogized India, a country where cows were worshipped. He would retort that in Pakistan, donkeys are worshipped. The ever-buoyant Mian Jaani had nothing left to joke about. In his last days, he read Rumi aloud in the loneliness of the Sindh desert. It was uncanny that somewhere deep down I would follow in his footsteps. From his dissertation on Umrao Jaan to the way of Rumi, Mamu Jaan, the author of *Sham-e-Awadh*, faded into the sunset. A sunset from which rose a new sun—a new dawn.

Chapter 4

The Imli Tree

'Sarv-o-saman bhi mauj-e-naseem-e-sahar bhi hai,
Aye gul tere chaman meiñ koi chashm-e-tar bhi hai.'
(Birds and the stately cypress dance
in the morning breeze.
O flower, is there someone in your garden
whose eyes moisten at what they see?)
—Moin Ahsan Jazbi

I think of the lyrical sensitivity of Moin Ahsan Jazbi captured in this opening couplet as I walk through spaces and gardens of the city blessed by the name Aligarh. The morning breeze blows gently through old trees that have witnessed time. I stand under the generous shade of magnificent imli (tamarind) tree under which Naeem ran his cycle rental shop. It didn't charge him rent, and no one asked him how he found a place there. He was as relevant and gracious as the tree. With his trusting smile he would launch you into the world of your dreams on forty-eight shining spokes in the wheel. The tree might have even blessed you with a ready-to-eat tamarind fruit from its luxuriant branches. It was the same tree that befriended me in La Martinere in Lucknow, embracing the lake outside the Constantia building, where I had come to understand its language over ten summers.

I ask of the present generation of students, the flowers of today, to testify the truth of what Jazbi felt. The emotion of the beauty of nature. This is a timeless question felt by someone or the other. As timeless as the imli tree that grew from a seed fallen on the sacred earth of Aligarh a few hundred years ago.

The year was 1962. I was at the cusp of eighteen. The imli, fifty-eight years younger. I was young and windblown, lost to the world. The imli stood firm, waiting for the likes of me. I was to embark on a simple train journey that would change the course of my life. Little short of an overnight run from Lucknow, too short for reservations, I would go from a city of beauty to a city of dreams.

I could have gone anywhere after my Senior Cambridge from La Martiniere College, but I followed my father's advice, who was keen that I make something out of my life without any trappings of luxury. Living in Lucknow like the son of a raja, like many people of my ilk and generation, made no sense to him. Like any taluqdar of that time, his better days were behind him. My journey from now on had to be devoid of any feudal fragrance, and so, I stepped into anonymity.

I do not understand what it was that made him think of Aligarh for me at that time. Why did he send me to a Muslim university, with which he had no association of any sort? Was it because Sir Syed Ahmad Khan, its founder, had an LLD from Edinburgh University like him? Or was it the character of the effeminate Maulana Hasrat Mohani that fascinated him? Abba Jaan spoke of the maulana with great passion as someone who had arrived in Aligarh with his *paandaan*, and so was immediately given the title of 'Bi Chammo Jaan'. The maulana dreamt of *sampurn swaraj*, total democracy, and coined the slogan 'Inquilab Zindabad' (long live the revolution) in the early 1920s. He was expelled from AMU, then known as the Muhammadan Anglo–Oriental College, on three occasions for his criticism of the British government.

It almost felt as if I was being sent to Aligarh as the maulana's ward. Hasrat Mohani saw no contradiction between being a Communist and a Muslim. No conflict between being a maulana and a lover of Shri Krishna. In a growingly divisive country, such characters fascinated my father. If Aligarh could create an open-minded Hasrat, it could make something out of his son! It was also likely that my mother had something to do with the decision. She knew Mumtaz Haider, a regular visitor in the summers to

Naini Tal, where she stayed with my mother's close friend, the maharani of Jahangirabad, at Hallet Castle. Mumtaz Apa's father was the founder of the Women's College in Aligarh University, which impressed her no end.

I travelled to Aligarh unreserved, third class. My father had reminded me that even the maulana, who was a member of the Indian Constituent Assembly, always travelled third class. When asked why, the maulana had quipped, 'Because there is no fourth class.' He shared a tonga to Parliament. In Hasrat Mohani, Abba Jaan found the solution to all troubles. Thank God my father did not ask me to share a rickshaw from the station!

In the wee hours of the morning, the train moved into my new world—Aligarh. It was with an unclear future that I entered the city, sitting on a black trunk that read 'M.A. Zaidi'. Abba Jaan had said half-jokingly, 'In case there is a communal flare-up, you are Maurice Albert Zaidi!' I wondered where I could find the maulana to give him Abba Jaan's *adaab* (salutations) and tell him I had been sent to him so that he could make a man out of me. Maybe it would make my being a fresher easier. But I was eleven years too late.

I sat perched precariously on my Zaidi trunk as my rickshaw went hurtling down the Katpulla. I heard my father's voice, 'Don't pigeonhole a good idea.' Abba Jaan's random dos and don'ts. Did I come with the answer in my trunk or to find answers in the world of Aligarh Muslim University? Where I came from no one knew and was to know. I was to remain a silent observer all along, always a liberating idea. Abba Jaan himself had gone into anonymity. He wanted to be no one. Each idea he authored came from a different descent. He wrote from his typewriter to the editor of *Pioneer* under different names. Sajid became 'Dijas'. Then became 'Kotwara'. At other times he became an 'Educated Villager', and sometimes he was just 'Sajid Husain'. He would travel third-class sleeper, reserved, of course, under the name of S.H. Chaura, in his khadi safari suit, changed into his khadi lungi at night, folded his trousers and kept them neatly under his air pillow so that they remain ironed. He had attained his swaraj.

I went to Aligarh with no dreams. It was a city which slowly unveiled itself, the ugly, the bad and the good. In that very order. First, the summer heat in a three-seater room at Mac Donald Hostel. *Makhi, machhar, matri* (fly, mosquitoes, large biscuit) were what Aligarh was endearingly known for, and these became my constant companions till I left. Then, the ragging in Aligarh was referred to as 'introduction'. You were asked questions that you'd never been asked, and therefore you were not prepared for them. The questions seemed straightforward but were embarrassing to answer and thus hilarious.

And there was my mother, battling cancer in Lucknow. It was an earth-shattering beginning to an educational journey.

But I slowly realized that there was more to the city than what met the eye. Aligarh was the people I met, the meaning they gave to life and the association they created for spaces. And the poets of Aligarh taught me this art of associations. The people I met here must have indeed shaped others' lives as they did mine. They moved me to feel and think.

* * *

Aligarh opened a vista of a post-1857 era buildings, neo-oriental in appearance. The city itself had a similarity with many such cities across India, most of them built by ruling chiefs. All in all, you could feel the presence of a stable Victorian Britain in the Aligarh of those days.

The university itself was a sprawling complex of Colonial Moorish buildings in red bricks, with broad white plaster borders defining their shapes. It was connected by parks and boulevards lined with majestic trees of all sorts, which became the landmarks of my everyday bicycle journey through the campus. The university had come up with the contributions of some generous patrons and rulers, notable among them being the maharaja of Patiala and the nizam of Hyderabad. Designed with a modern Islamic vision, it had a unique feel, with elegant and spacious mosques and grand gathering spaces. Inspired by Oxford, the founder, Sir Syed Ahmad Khan, built hostels, cricket pavilions, a riding club, expansive hockey and football fields, and indoor gymnasiums and swimming pools that echoed the same architectural grammar as the historical homes of those who were the builders of this institution, like the grand Aftab Manzil and the residence of the nawab of Chattari.

Unfortunately, its new architecture post-Independence, in trying to create a modern Islamic idiom, was neither here nor there. As eminent painter Satish Gujral would often repeat to me, '*Hindustan ki filmein aur architecture dono himaqat ka namuna hain* (Indian films and architecture are both examples of our own stupidity).' Ugliness had begun to seep in through petty, untrained minds given the job to build according to the urgent needs of growth. The first breath of fresh air was the General Education Centre, which used a new vocabulary of material and form, very much inspired by the stone architecture of Delhi, like the India International Centre coexisting with the Lodi tombs in its gardens.

Conceived by the visionary Dr Moonis Raza, who later founded the Jawahar Lal Nehru University in Delhi, the General Education Centre was designed by the great architect Joseph Allan Stein. It was completed the year I landed in Aligarh.

My family had many friends and relatives in the city. Marris Road was the lifeline of Aligarh, and anyone who was anyone resided here. Dr Zahoor Qasim, the famous marine biologist who led India's first expedition to Antartica, lived here. His father's brother from Rakswara was married to Abba Jaan's elder sister. He was over six feet tall and could have walked into any Hollywood studio. He was an athlete and a star the likes of which Aligarh had never seen, driving around in a red-and-white Standard Herald, one of the sportier cars of the time. I felt proud staying with him for a few weeks till I got my hostel accommodation sorted. At times, he would drop me to class. But, I soon realized, it was not a good idea to stand out in the Aligarh milieu. Another home I stayed in for a short period was that of a cousin, Dr Mustajabuddin, who was related to my mother from her Moradabad lineage. He enjoyed playing bridge. Maybe if I had known how to play the game, I would have come to know the who's who of Aligarh, who played regularly at the Staff Club.

Then there was Mahmuda Khala, the principal of the Girls' School, whose home, Hamid Manzil, was located dead centre of Marris Road, near the Women's College. She was related to me through my nani, from her Sheikhupur lineage. Mahmuda Khala's sister was Begum Abida Ahmad, wife of India's former President, Fakhruddin Ali Ahmad. Some very attractive young ladies from the Girls' School would visit Mahmuda Khala, but unfortunately, I had to leave the room when they came.

But the beauty of the mornings in Aligarh had nothing to do with Mahmuda Khala's lovely students! The breeze reminded me of how beautiful Faiz had made the early mornings feel:

Naseem teri shabistañ se ho ke aayi hai
Meri sahar meiñ mahak hai tere badan ki si . . .

(The breeze has come from your garden
My morning has your body's fragrance . . .)

I was still oblivious to what the *sahars* (early mornings) and the *naseems* (early morning breeze) of Aligarh held in their *daaman* (folds of the skirt) for me. Later I was to plan to make a film on the trauma of pre-Partition Aligarh, which, like many of my films, would not see the light of day. It was for this film that was never made that I had Shahryar pen a poem as a dream of someone not knowing their future:

Manzar tarah tarah ke daaman meiñ bhar raheiñ haiñ
Ham ek naye safar ka saamaan kar raheiñ hai.
(Visions of all sorts I gather in my fold
As I prepare to embark on a journey new.)

I held close to myself the *Dast-e-Saba* (the hand of breeze) all along my stay in a city which was going to teach me how to dream and what to dream.

As I sat under the imli tree, I felt the intermingling of arts and life creep into me.

My imagination flowered slowly between science and art. My father was keen that I take up science to be relevant to the world, and without any resistance I had taken up geology, botany and chemistry. My only contribution to this choice was including geology. It fascinated me. The secrets contained in large landscapes and mountain ranges, the search for rock samples as we set out with khaki haversacks, hammer and chisel in hand. The echo of the hammer and chisel mixed with the chirping of birds and the sounds of the blowing wind through the lonely mountains. Poets in Aligarh were dreamers. For them all deserts were the desert of Najd (central Arabian desert, the setting of the immortal love legend of Laila and Majnu) and any passionate quest was Majnu's search for his beloved Laila. It was all about bewilderment and wonder. We began to see our geological exploration in this crazy romantic light. Slowly, I discovered that there was a bit of a scientist in every poet of Aligarh, and a poet in every scientist.

I had taken Shia theology as an optional subject, and it was when I was asking around about where its classes were held that someone pointed to Asghar Wajahat, who was also taking the same class. I gave him a lift to the theology department on my bicycle. It was the start of a strong friendship. A maulana took the theology class. We called him 'Ghodi' (mare) because, chewing his paan, he looked like a horse and would always talk with his mouth full. Often, he would forget his paandaan at home. Everyone would jump to volunteer to bring it for him. One by one, the whole class would disappear in search of the paandaan and then in search of the one who went to get the paandaan. Asghar and I became inseparable. We had lots in common, and he had also taken up geology.

The geology class was very hard work. But most disturbing was the expression on Asghar's face as we descended the winding road to the base of the mountains—from the steep climbs of Almora hills to the rich Dharwar, Vindhyan in the Sone River valley and the sandstone alluvium of Bihar. All the way Asghar looked as if he would throw up. Still, I enjoyed it. The soundscape thrummed with the poetry that we would recite to each other:

> *Raahe vafa meiñ jab koi*
> *Sang-e-garañ mila Kamaal*
> *Dekha sanam bana liya*
> *Socha Khuda bana liya . . .*
> (In the path of faith
> I confronted an unsurmountable rock,
> saw, and made it a beloved
> contemplated, and made it God . . .)

—Javed Kamaal

Besides Shia theology and geology, we had another thing in common—Faiz Ahmad Faiz. Every day we would discover a new poem by Faiz, a new dawn on my creative thought.

There are a few poets in each era who give a new meaning to language, a new sense to history and a new life to metaphors. Faiz was one. He gave the twentieth century a global way of seeing humanity. He was born in undivided India, witnessed the largest human holocaust at the time of Partition, but still saw in the two nations a strong common culture and language divided on communal grounds. He was brought up on a leftist, anti-imperialist ideology, which gave a new meaning to his romantic idealism. A context totally ahead of its time, totally universal. Such people do not pass away but continue to be celebrated year after year. They grow through others, as they inspire them to see the beauty and relevance of art in their times. Faiz has helped humanity transcend man-made barriers and imparted a larger purpose to art. Today, when the sense of human history is being submerged in an ocean of information, Faiz emerges as an intangible ship captain. Faiz has been and always will be a *faiz* (ever-giving) giver to people like us, whose work has been inspired by his mind.

If we look at the poems of Faiz in totality, we realize that as far as his beliefs were concerned, they were similar to those that all progressive writers consider to be their tenets. Yet in Faiz's poetry, these values are presented in the most unique and musical manner possible. His imagery contains within it the very essence of our countries' existence, and is imbued with truth and the democratic aims which shine forth from our best minds. His poetry embodies the basic requirements of a civilized existence, in which both the body and mind are nurtured in equal proportions.

Little did I imagine that Faiz would continue to appear at different times in my life. I saw him in flesh and blood for the first time in Bombay, at a *mehfil* (congregation) in 1971. I sat quietly and listened to him spellbound. Words that I had heard before, words that I knew by heart and words that I had never heard. Ideas that reminded me of my father's concerns.

These words echoed in my head till I met Faiz again years later and got the opportunity of sharing my first feature film, *Gaman*, with him. The experience elated me. He gave me the carte-blanche permission to use any of his lyrics in any of my works. This I did most judiciously, wanting to make him feel proud of me. Faiz held my hand in all my endeavours that dreamt of change, of a humane world—whether *Anjuman*, *Aagaman* or the hour-long *Sheeshoṅ ka Masiha*, on the Bhopal gas tragedy. The poet featured in my music album *Paigham-e-Mohabbat* and was also part of my fourteen-episode series *Zubaan-e-Ishq*.

Our burning desire for poetry brought Asghar and me closer. We would regularly meet poets and enjoy their poetry. In Aligarh, every poet had a group of admirers who would gather around them. Another incentive, of course, was the tea and cigarettes that were passed around in abundance to keep the audience captive. Tea could take us anywhere, even to the most boring people, in whom we would try and discover something amusing to pass the time. There is a poet in everyone—some you flock to listen to and others you run a mile from.

In my second year I moved to a single-seater room in Kashmir House. It was the last room, number 91, in the block. An imli tree cast a generous shade, playing a rabab (a stringed instrument from Kashmir) as its leaves danced on the white walls of the building. Without wanting to, I was suddenly among the elite. Kashmir House had only meritorious students, foreigners and boys from Kashmir. I was none of these. It is likely that our provost, Naseem Quraishi, came to know that I was the nephew of Dr Farooqi's, whom he held in the highest esteem. Or that I was the son of Raja Sajid Husain, in whose house Jigar Moradabadi, a famous romantic modern Urdu poet of his time, twenty years senior to Abba Jaan, played chess regularly with other poets, in the dark, cool rooms on the ground floor. The house, 10 Qaiserbagh, was a refuge for poets and a venue for a constant exchange of poetry that ended up with my father reciting his. This was just before the abolition of zamindari in 1952.

Nothing was said. And no one asked why. But it was very clear that Quraishi Sahab had a great weakness for Urdu literature and poetry.

Kashmir House also had Mumtaz Ali Khan, a highly meritorious student of engineering, from Lucknow but hailing from Rampur. He was my neighbour and probably secretly considered me, an ordinary BSc student, unworthy of occupying a room in this very special hostel. He was too perfect and busy in his own world to be a close friend then, but now in Lucknow we see each other often twice a day. Another neighbour, also admitted from the meritorious category, would wake up at odd hours of the night and knock at my door each time with a new ghazal. Finally I learnt to say, 'Achha ek cigarette nikalo, na tum bor ho na ham (Okay, take out a cigarette, so that neither of us has to suffer).'

* * *

As I settled down in university, poetry surrounded me constantly. The poets seemed far more interesting than my dry geology teachers. I even found some poetry that made me identify with my predicament in the subject of geology and became the motto of my geology batch:

> Ab iraada hai ki patthar ke sanam poojooń ga
> Taaki ghabrauń to takra bhi sakuń mar bhi sakuń . . .
> (I have resolved I will worship idols of stone,
> When in despair, I can bang my head against them and die . . .)

Soon I saw myself emerging as a different person. A romantic revolutionary dreamer. Geology was my dream, my city was my reality, and poetry was a virtual bridge which we crossed many times a day. *Shahr aur sahra* (city and desert)—the urban and the geological wilderness become my obsession of sorts.

Zahida Zaidi was our window to art. Zahida Apa, as she was known, was one of the four highly artistic, progressive and literate Zaidi sisters, much ahead of their time. She was a reader in the Department of English at the university. All the talent of Aligarh rallied behind her Art Club, and Naseeruddin Shah was one of this lot. Theatre and painting came together. This was an Anglicized group and made Aligarh a little more acceptable to a Westernized world. Zahida Apa inspired me to think from a feminine viewpoint, which was going to become my forte in films. There were many who came from very conservative backgrounds and could not understand the psyche of an independent, free-thinking woman like her. Through Zahida Apa I met Syeda Sayyadain in Delhi, whose father, Khwaja Ghulam-us-Sayyadain, was the second education secretary of India, under Maulana Azad as the education minister. Syeda introduced me to an American girl, Marsha Chapman, who gave me her tape recorder when she left. I used this throughout my stay in Aligarh to record the contemporary poets.

Urdu poetry and literature were a world unto itself. I was attracted to both, one from within and the other from the fringes. For the Urdu lot I was a bit alien. I slowly made my inroads through people like Dr Rahi Masoom Raza and his then beloved Nayyar Apa, who used to live in the grand Aftab Manzil. They got married a few years later. She was then still married to my phuphijaan's cousin, Col Sahibzada Yunus from Rampur. Their son, Nadeem Khan, was the cameraman for my film *Gaman*. Aligarh was a small cauldron of artists, and one had to dive into it. It was not just talent but an ecosystem where art could be perceived and become an inspiration for life. Rahi Sahab was the brother of Dr Moonis Raza, the then coordinator of GEC.

Looking back, I realized that Aligarh had the pace, leisure and culture to make people become what they wanted to be, most often at the cost of their parents, by taking decades to graduate or complete their research! They existed in a dreamworld and could read meaning into their dreams with the aid of the poetic world around. One such senior was Ashfaq Paape, who remained in one class for ten years. He would preside over all the introduction sessions that the juniors would undergo. He would choose songs and make them stand in front of the revolving pedestal fan and orchestrate the freshers to oscillate their heads in sync with the fan as they sang that song. Much later, I discovered he was of Rahi Sahab's vintage.

I remember two significant visitors to Aligarh who made a deep impact on me. One was M.F. Husain, an artist who was making the Kennedy Hall mural for the General Education Centre; and the other was Ebrahim Alkazi, a theatre director. I came to know both well as I moved from shahr to shahr. Husain was a storyteller on canvas, and I liked the intimate way in which he would share his thoughts. I last met him a few months before he passed away in London. Dropping me off in his Rolls-Royce, he told me that I was wasting my time making films and that I should paint like him instead. When I told him that it took me a long time to make a painting, he said, 'Meri tarah jaldi wali painting kiya keejiye (Like me, do quick paintings).' And then he recited a couplet, probably his own:

Na aane ki khushi na jaane ka gham,
Kamaye duniya khayeiñ hum.
(Neither happy about the incoming,
Nor sad about the outgoing,
Let world do the earning, let me do the enjoying.)

I am still grappling with this statement. It was only Husain who could live this in reality! That day at the Dorchester Hotel, I recorded a long interview with him on storytelling, which, unfortunately, got erased due to my own stupidity.

My passion for painting went back to Aligarh, where I was emerging as a dreamer. Art was something that could contain my dreams and yet, inspire me to dream more. I also became engrossed in Zahida Apa's Art Club. There was a group of us who were particularly passionate about art, of which one was Farhan Mujeeb and the other Inayat Zaidi. Both were budding artists. Farhan was an amiable, colourful character who was studying physics at that time and who eventually achieved great heights in his career as a painter. Each of us inspired and surprised each other by our works. I had my first painting exhibition in 1964 at the General

Education Centre at Kennedy Hall, with Rahi Sahab inaugurating the show. He wrote an inspiring couplet in the visitor's book,

Ek ham haiñ ke liya apni hi surat ko bigaad,
Ik vo haiñ ki jinheiñ tasveer bana aati hai.
(There is me who has destroyed his looks,
And there is he who creates pictures . . .)

Rahi Sahab was indeed a mentor and an inspiration. For a bit, I thought Rahi Sahab was doing my *khichai* in writing this couplet on my exhibition. Khichai was a must for a student to fit into the social fabric of the university and could last from six months to a year. When I joined as a fresher, I had been made to sing. I had learnt to be as humble and self-effacing as possible, lest I become a target for a heavy-duty khichai. But slowly, this self-effacing behaviour began to draw more attention and after the list of new recruits was over, I became the centre of attraction, '*Ab sawaal paida hota hai bhai Muzaffar ka* (Now the question arises of brother Muzaffar).'

Seniors of Aligarh knew how to track you down to shed your ego. They were creative enough to do exactly what needed be done with you to present you intelligently in the most stupid way possible, which stuck to you all your life. You became what the seniors wanted you to become for all time to come, even before your juniors. It was not such a cruel process because a junior had to be taken under a senior's wing and become his odd-jobs guy till he passed out. And the grace of the senior was to pamper him enough to make him his unpaid, respectful servant. This continues as a tradition even today. People specialized in this process, and once you get used to it you never wanted to leave Aligarh.

This year was my turn. I returned to Aligarh after my holidays. Every semester unfolded new happenings, new events. There was always a lot more to learn beyond the syllabus. I made friends with a senior, Amir Hasan Khan, who was an engineering student and stayed in another hostel next to Kashmir House. He had a mischievous streak writ large on his face, which changed interestingly with each *chamcha* attached to him. He called them *charkha* in his terminology. To have a group of charkhas in tow was also a prerequisite for an Aligarh senior, as the charkha would become a devotee of the senior for life.

The art of nursing a charkha was a culture in itself and part of the Aligarian sense of humour. A seasoned Aligarian without his charkha was a lost case. Asghar and I had some common charkhas. A new student, Shakil, had taken admission in Asghar's hostel and was finding it difficult to secure a reliable *dhobi* (washerman). One day we got another junior from my hostel to go as a dhobi and collect all his dirty clothes. Shakil was most delighted to see the dhobi and pleaded with him that what he was wearing was his last clean set of clothing and so needed his laundry back the next day. All his clothes arrived as a big bundle in Asghar's room. We conveniently forgot about it and would enjoy hearing him ask in sheer desperation, all who would pass by, if they had seen the dhobi. We then slipped a note under his door that the dhobi wanted sweets to return his clothes. The sweets reached the appointed place, and his dirty clothes landed at his door in the middle of the night. Dessert was called 'variety', and we had secured our 'variety' for the week. That we had made a charkha out of Shakil remained a secret for a year. Later, it was the same Shakil who became my neighbour at Kashmir House, and I had to suffer him all along in Aligarh and listen to his terrible poems.

In this cruelty there was gentility. Everyone eventually wanted to leave behind a good image. It was here that the Urdu language found its multiple shades, now slowly getting lost to the world. It made one learn to live with people and made the Aligarh *tarana* by Majaz, a passionate poet who dreamt of freedom and a generous world of love and to be loved. The air of Aligarh was the air of our nation.

Jo abr yahañ se utthega, wo sarey jahañ par barsega
Har ju-e-rawañ par barsega, har koh-e-garaañ par barsega
Har sarv-o-saman par barsega, har dasht-o-daman par barsega
Khud apne chaman par barsega, ghairoñ ke chaman par barsega
Har shahr-e-tarab par garjega, har qasr-e-tarab par kadkega
Ye abr hamesha barsa hai, ye abr hamesha barsega . . .
(The clouds that rise from here,
Will always rain,
On the world around they'll rain . . .
They'll rain to wash the mighty mountain range
They'll rain
To join each flowing stream . . .
They'll rain to make the cypress sway

They'll rain to make the jasmine bloom
They'll rain to make the desert green;
On its own garden they will rain
On others' gardens they will rain
They'll thunder on each city of joy . . .
And their lightning dazzle
Each palace of delight.
The clouds from here
Have always rained.
The clouds from here
Will always rain . . .)
                    —Excerpted from the Aligarh tarana by Asrar-ul-Haq Majaz

It was the air which gave one the resilience to face the world. To don a black sherwani and stand out. Over time the sherwani changed shades and became a national attire. The sherwani was a way of being known and reaching out. Droves of dashing young workers in black sherwanis would float around the annual *numaish* (exhibition) following groups of attractive girls from the Women's College. Ashfaq Paape would lead his group eating barolas (a savoury of potatoes). So addicted he was to the barola that he acquired the name 'Barola' as suffix to Ashfaq. To date, he is known to the Aligarians as Ashfaq Barola. Pape was left behind. Mazhar Jamil, also from my hostel but studying engineering, joined our group to visit the exhibition. I called out to him as he was getting lost amid the girls, '*Arre Mazhar Bhai—yahañ* (O Brother Mazhar, here).' He turned around to look at me when he heard a beautiful girl, '*Mazhar Bhai, sherwani mein jachte hain* (Brother Mazhar looks cool in a sherewani).' He walked towards me saying, '*Saale ik vada karo. Aaj se mujhe "Bhai" kahna band* (Just promise me one thing. You won't ever call me brother again).' But from that day onwards Mazhar Bhai never took off that sherwani.

He was passionate about poetry. Poetry was the passport to getting attention from the young ladies at Women's College. He remembered and recited Urdu poetry with such intellectual elan that he could be mistaken as the poet himself. He spent most of his time with poetry books and was the captain of the Sulaiman Hall 'Bait Baazi' team! He had the girls swooning over his memory and the aptness with which he found the perfect couplet for every occasion. But the 'Bhai' got imprinted to his name like the sherwani which never came off. Slowly it began to turn grey.

He would only wash his pajama knee downwards, as he claimed that was what was visible.

One day the hostel was being whitewashed, and the painter had put his ladder to rest on his door. Mazhar Bhai was deeply engrossed in his books. The painter's bucket kept hitting his door as the ladder rocked. A few times Mazhar Bhai gave an extended groan of '*Kaaun* (Who is that)?' The knocking persisted. Mazhar Bhai got up saying to himself, '*Saale chayan se padhne bhi nahin dete* (These bastards don't even let me read me in peace).' Saying this he pulled the door open. The painter fell off the ladder with his pail of white paint, turning the famous sherwani white forever!

The poetry action shifted to the Library Canteen, an old building near the Maulana Azad Library. The space was too grand for the likes of us, and we felt humbled by its vastness. It was run by a tall, good-looking poet, Javed Kamaal from Rampur. In his heyday he was believed to have been a gun-toting, knife-carrying don of sorts. This image helped him commercially as it invited no creditors, a problem that many restaurants in and around Shamshad Market faced. I remember Rahmat Cafe, where a couplet became popular for debtors, '*Rahmat ko baton mein, bahla ke pi gaya* (We distracted Rahmat and drank away).' Being in debt was a way of life. There was a friend who used to always borrow money in English. He said it sounded more credible and dignified. The Library Canteen with the don at the cash counter was a formidable sight. Many great things happened there. It had an aura of romance, especially when postgraduate girls would walk in, dressed most fashionably. Conversation would come to a grinding halt at all tables, and Javed Kamaal too would lose count of the change, his hands aimlessly feeling their way around the cash drawer. We often dreamt of walking into this congregation with a good-looking girl, and baffling Javed Bhai and all the students drinking their national drink—tea.

It was our friend Madhosh Bilgrami, son of Nawab Hoshyaar Jung Bahadur from Hyderabad, who gave us a glimpse of this dream. He was enamoured of his young and beautiful English teacher, and he expressed his desire to walk into the Library Canteen with her! He had to find a good enough reason as the matter was entirely one-sided. He was just a wishful 'worker', as we called those who were lost in a one-sided love affair! The look of a typical 'worker' was forlorn and vulnerable, and he was an easy prey for those specialized in making them into charkhas. A 'worker' is essentially a tireless *ashiq* who rides his charger, his bicycle, in a subtle way, following a beautiful face from her class to her hostel and then again from her hostel to her class, to the canteen and back to the hostel. The art of being a 'worker' entailed not to be seen but to look busy with some errand, other than the designated assignment of following the beloved. 'Work' fanned poetry and 'working' itself sometimes led to success, but more often to frustration. 'Work is worship' was their lifelong motto. However, some fortunately did get wedded to their 'work'.

Madhosh's birthday party was slated for that very evening. The English teacher was given the time of 5 p.m. There were still two hours to go. The next question that came up was: What should Madhosh wear? A sherwani for sure, but a sherwani with a difference. It struck Madhosh that he had a peacock-blue brocade sherwani that belonged to his father. We jumped at the idea of him in peacock blue and sketched an exotic image in words—of Madhosh emerging out of the trees, glowing in the dappled evening light like a dancing peacock on his hired bicycle.

The problem was that the sherwani was badly crushed and needed to be ironed. The plan was fraught with excitement, especially with the shortage of time. Off went Madhosh in his pajama, on his bicycle, to Dudhpur to his dhobi. We were told to go to the Library Canteen and take a table where the English teacher would have a good view of his arrival in the peacock-blue sherwani gleaming in the setting sun. Timing was most important. Maybe there was a dormant film-maker in me planning these exciting details! Cut to Madhosh arriving at the dhobi's who, as luck would have it, had gone for a wedding. After Madhosh had waited for an hour, the dhobi arrived in a happy mood. The *dukhtar-e-angoor* (wine) had caught his fancy at the party. In that mood the best of the poets could not have convinced him to light up the heavy iron to straighten out the crushed sherwani. Fortunately, Madhosh's offer of a cigarette worked. They both lit up and the iron-heating process began with the dhobi asking, '*Mian, kiski shaadi hai* (Sir, are you attending a wedding)?' Madhosh was too feudal to encourage such *fuzool* (futile) conversation with a dhobi, but the thought of displeasing him and jeopardizing the timing of meeting his flame enabled him to make some condescending noises to sooth the dhobi. But the dhobi took his time, cigarette dangling from his lips. Madhosh could not help but exclaim in his gruff and slanted Hyderabadi accent, '*Mian, sherwani jala mat dena. Kheemti hai* (Don't singe it, my friend).' To which the dhobi retorted, '*Miyan, na ye pahli cigarette hai . . . na pahli sherwani hai* (Sir, neither is this my first cigarette nor is this my first sherwani),' seemingly threatening to stop midway. The heavy accents of two cultures clashed like the clanging of sharp swords.

We were waiting impatiently, wondering what had happened to Madhosh. Zahida Apa, too, had been invited to give credibility to the party. The English teacher arrived dressed in a peacock-blue sari, very much like what Madhosh was to appear in! We received her warmly, seating her on the chair with a view of the grand arrival. Tea and other snacks, as planned, were ordered with a lurking fear of insufficient funds.

The bicycle took off with Madhosh riding as fast as the old thing would move. It was a good thirty minutes' ride, and he was running out of time. Suddenly he heard a sharp whistle. A puncture!

The tea was over, as were the snacks. We were too tense to bask in the glory of the English teacher's company as planned. She left in the fading evening light, and we watched her go, a poetic image taking shape in our minds at the cost of Madhosh's loss, seeing her go from his point of view . . . '*Dekha kiye ham unko jahañ tak nazar gayi* (I kept looking on till the end of what I could see).'

We kept sitting, with the bill in hand, waiting for Madhosh to arrive . . .

He appeared much later, panting . . . It had become too dark for the blue of the sherwani to glow. His love had left . . . The bill had to be cleared. Javed Bhai looked up. '*Kya hua, bhai* (What happened, brother)?' His eyes said it all. The sherwani looked good but was a few sizes too big.

These incidents were called 'activities', designed by one mind but growing out of proportion as others joined in with their ideas. An 'activity' was something that was creative and new. It was a memorable, funny and subtle way of enjoying your time with people.

Rahi Sahab had joined our table and sat with the beautiful English teacher while waiting for the birthday boy. He guffawed and said, '*Tumhari dawat hamlogoñ ki taraf se* (This party is on me).' Such were the ways of a senior who would grace a table, even for a short while, at any restaurant. He always paid. The arrival of Madhosh panting on his hired bicycle— you can well imagine the rest.

There were some people I introduced to Aligarh. People Aligarh had never seen or will never see. One such person was Waliullah Beg. 'Waliullah' means a saint, a representative of God. But don't go by the name.

He was far from that meaning. 'Wolly', as he was called, was nearest to his personality. He was the son of Justice Nasrullah Beg, a judge of the high court and an icon of Lucknow society. Wolly had only one sister, the beautician Shahnaz Husain. Wolly took his own beauty seriously. He carried a Pond's pink rouge wrapped in a small newspaper packet. He spent all his time in Kotwara House and would be regaled by Abba Jaan's stories at lunch, which, I have a suspicion, he did not fully understand as he laughed at all the wrong moments. After lunch he would pass out on my bed with his shoes on. Done with his nap in five minutes, he would jump up, take out the rouge packet and rub it on his fair, rough face. Caressing his own cheeks, he would say, 'See, fresh like a baby's bot.'

Wolly was very skinny, and wore tight black pants, pointed shoes and bright-coloured shirts made from thick curtain fabric hiding a bedsheet padding on his shoulders. I discovered this closely guarded secret when it fell down once while we were *gunjing* (strolling in Hazratganj), following a beautiful girl. His personality suddenly changed when this happened. He had a Bullet motorcycle, which added to his aura. Wolly would fail in school every year in a new subject, and had been changing schools and subjects ever since I knew him. One day he sold his bike to pay for his strange new passion for shoes. When we reached his father's house, Justice Beg asked, '*Wolly, tumhari Bullet kahan hai* (Wolly, where is your Bullet)?' Without batting an eyelid, Wolly, in his Anglicized Lakhnawi Urdu, said, '*Wo, Dad, Kanpur se aate time jal gaya* (Dad, it caught fire near Kanpur).' The judge asked, '*Kuch to bacha hoga* (Something must be left of it)?' To which Wolly replied, '*Wo sob bachha log khelne ki liye le gaye* (Dad, the children took the parts to play with).' Justice Beg took me aside and said, 'Baba wants me to swallow this. Can you imagine children carrying hot parts of a burnt bike to play! Please take him with you to Aligarh. I'll do the needful.'

One day there was a loud sound outside my room and a familiar voice screamed out, '*Arre vo Raja Kotwara ka ladka kahan hai* (Where is Raja Kotwara's son)?' I came out to see Wolly with all his luggage on a rickshaw. 'O God!' I said to myself. What would one do with him! He was quite organized and set himself up on the same floor, at the same hostel just a few rooms away. It came to be known that a character like Wolly had never come to Aligarh before, and never would come again. He would drink 'Cokar Colar' (as he called Coca-Cola) in one gulp, standing in his trademark bright tapestry shirt in Shamshad Market. Aligarh watched aghast. Wolly was beyond all the conventional definitions Aligarh was known for. 'Worker', charkha or even the victim of an 'activity'. He had to be a new definition in himself. So we decided to spin scary stories around him, stories that made him sound supernatural, sending students into hiding whenever he approached.

One day I told Shakil that Wolly, Asghar and I had gone to town to see a film. On the way back on a rickshaw around midnight, Wolly felt sorry for the rickshaw puller huffing and puffing while dragging our load uphill on the Railway Bridge, and out of compassion got down and started walking. As we finished the climb we turned around to look for Wolly, but he had disappeared into thin air. The rickshaw puller got scared and sped through the deserted streets to our hostel. When we reached our room, we found Wolly already there! Shakil was so scared that he never came to my room, which was next to Wolly's, ever again. This story went around, and Wolly started enjoying this scary aura that was being built around him. It made him do more strange things. His passion for buying shoes had grown beyond all limits. He owned scores of pairs and would line them up on the floor along all the four walls of his room. Soon they started spilling out into the corridor, but Wolly was not worried about their being stolen, sure that the students would be too scared to touch them. I warned him, 'No more shoes, Wolly, or I'll tell your dad!' One day he called me to show me yet another new pair of white shoes he had bought. 'It is like having five pairs in one,' he said, pointing to the small holes in the shoes and the five bright-coloured socks, which would pop out of the perforations to match with his shirts.

In Wolly, Aligarh had not only found a charkha but a windmill. Not just a windmill but a Don Quixote and a Sancho Panza.

Rahi Sahab was a colossus of poetry. A very good-looking man, he wore his sherwani with gracious aplomb, its open hem flying in the wind as he confidently hopped along with a disability which did not allow him to put his left foot fully on the ground. He was called Lord Byron of Aligarh, and certainly he was no less. Not once was he ever booed in a *mushaira* (poetry soiree). Not once did anyone have the courage to make a negative comment on his poetry. This aura drew us constantly to him, to listen to him recite. His *tarranum* (singing of poetry) was like the breeze of paradise.

Jin se ham chhūt gaye ab vo jahañ kaise haiñ?
Shaakh-e-gul kaisi hai khushbu ke makaañ kaise haiñ?
(Those from whom I have been separated, how are their worlds?
How is the flowering bough, how are their fragrant homes?)

The Women's College hall would resound with applause. Then silence would descend as the audience got ready to hear his next couplet. Rahi would lift his soulful voice,

Ai saba tu to udhar hi se guzarti hogī . . .
(O morning breeze, you must be passing that way . . .)

Again the hall would be filled with the din of appreciation.

Us galī meiñ mere pairoñ ke nishaañ kaise haiñ?
(How are my footprints in those lanes?)

As the applause rang again louder than before, a shrill voice exclaimed naughtily '*Dedh*', meaning 'one and a half', as his one foot never fully touched the ground. It was Mazhar Bhai!
    Rahi's sharp mind retorted like a sword that made the commenter shrink into himself,

Pattharoñ vaale vo insaan vo behis dar-o-baam,
Vo makiñ kaise haiñ sheeshe ke makaañ kaise haiñ?
(Stonehearted people, insensitive doors and arches,
How are those people, how are their houses of glass?)

There was pin-drop silence. '*Bazi maar li* (Won the game),' Mazhar said sheepishly to us. Rahi stood tall amid the poets who had recited before him. His disability was dwarfed by his talent.
    By the seventies Rahi was a giant in Bollywood, and after his dialogues for the epic *Mahabharat* by B.R. Chopra, he was a force to reckon with. One day Asghar and I went to meet him in Bombay. He was lounging in a silken lungi with his Bollywood cronies. The moment we walked in he welcomed us warmly and told his cronies to leave, as his Aligarh intellectuals had come and he had to catch up with the world there. '*Haañ bhai . . . batao . . . jinse ham chhoot gaye ab vo jahañ kaise haiñ* (O my friend, now tell me,

how are those from whom I have been parted)?' The Bollywood cronies left and tea was ordered for us. We pleaded that he recite some more couplets from the ghazal that had left Aligarh weeping.

> *Yaad jin ki hamein jiine bhi na degī 'Rahī'*
> *Dushman-e-jaań vo masīha-nafasań kaise hain?*
> (Those whose memories will not let me live, Rahi,
> Those enemies of my life, those who bring me back to life, how are they?)

As our conversation moved on, the doorbell rang. A very big producer was announced, and we were immediately asked to leave, just like the Bollywood cronies before us. We had not even had our tea! This was the way of this world.

It was true that Bombay was not for people who had lived life with the timeless ease of Aligarh. This was not the same Rahi we had met in Aligarh. That Rahi we will keep meeting in poetry, the Rahi of his own memories . . . Rahi without Aligarh was not the same, nor was Aligarh without Rahi . . .

> *Ajnabi shahr ke ajnabi raaste, meri tanhai par muskrate rahe,*
> *Main bahut der tak youñhi chalta raha, tum bahut der tak yaad aate rahe.*
> (Alien alleys in an alien city, smiled at my loneliness all the way
> I kept walking, for a long way, your memories came a long way.)

A few years later, when Rahi saw *Gaman*, he wrote a touching piece on it for a publication called *Shama*. It brought tears to my eyes as he concluded saying, 'Seeing *Gaman* I too felt like the protagonist, taxi driver Ghulam Hasan, driving my pen's taxi in the city of Bombay.'

Poetry danced like shadows of the leaves of the imli tree, at times gleaming in the moonlight drizzle, at times aflame with the fire of unrequited love. Its resonance touched the sky, and its meaning lulled one to sleep . . .

> *Ham aagahi ko rote hain aur aagahi hammien*
> *Va raftagi-e-shauq kahań le chali hamein?*
> *Vahshat ne vo bhi loot li dam bhar mein dostoń,*
> *Jo muddatoń mein aayi thhi shayastagi hamein.*

(I moan of awareness, awareness moans of me,
O my quest for wanderlust, where are you taking me?
Madness has deprived me in a flash of a moment
Of all that refinement which took ages for me to be.)

—Javed Kamaal

Javed Kamaal's real name was Wajid Khan. Behind that formidable exterior of the don of Library Canteen, he was a soft poet, lyrical and sensitive, deep and vulnerable. Those days, poetry impacted me so intensely that in one hearing I would remember an entire poem,

Ham zarra zarra dhoond chuke mauja-e-sarab,
Har qatra qatra dhoond chuki tishnagi hameiñ.
Aayi thhi chand gaam usi bewafa ke saath,
Phir umr bhar ko bhool gayi zindagi hameiñ.
(Each particle of every wave of the mirage, I looked,
Every drop of thirst was in search of me.
It did come a few steps with that unfaithful beloved,
Then in this quest this life of mine lost track of me . . .)

You can imagine the impact on a teenager's mind in the dead of the monsoon night, tossing and turning with such poetic imagery in an alien bed at a hostel in Aligarh. You needed a friend to share this feeling. It was an intense exploration. I sketched these feelings into abstract lines. It opened my mind to more intense poems, more complex idioms. As the exams drew closer, we boldly said to ourselves,

Kaghaz ki kashti meiñ darya paar kiya
Dekho hamko kya kya kartab aate haiñ.
(I crossed the river in paper boats
See how many tricks I have up my sleeve . . .)

—Shahryar

Aligarh prepared me for a larger role in life. Political, personal and professional. When the Babri Masjid was brought down in 1992, Shahryar rang me up very late one night and said, as he often did, *'Lo sher suno.'*

Har khaab ke makaañ ko mismaar kar diya hai
Behtar dinoñ ka aana dushwaar kar diya hai.

(Every abode of dreams has been shattered
Chances of return of better days are forever lost.)

Shahryar became a lifelong partner in my creative life, writing the lyrics for most of my films. I discovered characters through his poetic feelings and in the course of time gave new dimension to his poetry.

Aligarh taught me to see the world poetically and lyrically. It taught me to feel that imli tree through the four seasons, giving it new meaning with the passage of time. I was made to feel the poetry of life, its many *manzils* (milestones/destinations) felt by many a *rahi* (traveller). He had described himself as Ghulam Hasan, a writer driving the taxi of his pen, and me as the windblown boy with a *manzil-e-benaam* (destination unknown) in his eyes.

I sat under the imli tree connecting two distant milestones with Rahi's couplets,

> *Ye charaagh jaise lamhe kahiñ rayegañ na jaayeiñ*
> *Koī khwaab dekh daalo koī inquilab laao . . .*
> (Don't let these glowing moments go waste,
> See a dream, bring in a revolution . . .)

The refreshing breeze takes one to another milestone as the imli tree stands denuded of its lush leaves.

> *Hamari aabla payi ka zikr kar dena,*
> *Thaka hua jo tumhe koi inquilab mile.*
> (Speak of my blistered feet,
> If on the way you meet a tired revolution.)

I share Jazbi's couplet with this generous tree,

> *Duniya sune to qissa-e-gham hai bahot taveel,*
> *Jo tum suno to qissa-e-gham mukhtasar bhi hai.*
> (If the world wants to know, endless is my tale of woe,
> And yet it is brief in case it is you who wants to know.)

* * *

Aligarh stands as a backbone of my creative journey. Understanding life, expressing life, both directly and indirectly. Understanding pain and death. The cycle had become my best friend. It was constantly by my side. I had begun to see a new world of imagination in people. What their art could do to others. But my days in Aligarh had a deep undercurrent of turmoil. On the one hand, my mother's illness was growing irreversibly worse. I would come home to Lucknow to pain and apprehension. On the other hand, my brother Manjhu Mian's state was not improving. Both suffered from incurable ailments. My mother's being fatal and my brother's lifelong.

It was in the middle of this pain and anguish that Aligarh was happening to me. It was making a man out of me. A soft man of steel, who would wield his sword with his heart. I was her unrealized dream. I would go back to Aligarh with more pain than I could rise above. Till one day, on 19 February 1964, coming up from Agha Mir Ki Deohri in Lucknow on a rickshaw from the railway station, I saw my father drive down from Medical College. My mother's body was in his car.

Lucknow was never the same again. Gone were the lively ladies who had enthralled us with stories. Gone were all my knife-carrying and gentle, feudal La Martiniere friends. The fancy cars were all jacked up on bricks in garages. Lucknow was silenced. Only whispers of the past were heard. Abba Jaan was a shattered man. He spent his life with Manjhu Mian, looking meaninglessly out of that window. Yet he continued to pound on his typewriter, setting the world right in his own way. He was still young. He could have remarried but decided against it, because of us. Kotwara House was a joint dream. And one dreamer had gone.

Poetry began to make a different sort of sense. I failed in my BSc semester that year and had to repeat my class. I lost a couple of classmates but found some new ones.

Aligarh had seen many like me. No one ever showed off. I, too, had to be known for what I was and not my background. The post-Independence Aligarh had taught us this. Its poets had made us humble and concerned. *Ghazal Mere Shahar Meiñ* (Ghazal in My City), composed in Salma Agha's voice, was my tribute to four poets of Aligarh— Shahryar, Rahi, Javed Kamaal and Khalilulrahman Azmi. My romance with the poetry of

Aligarh continued even as I moved towards Sufi poetry. Later, I composed an album, *Raqs-e-Bismil*, in the voice of Abida Parveen. This featured one ghazal by the same Hasrat Mohani who had beckoned me to Aligarh eleven years after he was no more.

> *Roshan Jamaal-e-Yaar se hai anjuman tamaam*
> *Dahka hua hai aatash-e-gul se chaman tamaam . . .*
> (With the beauty of my beloved the congregation came aglow,
> The garden burnt bright with the flaming flowers . . .)

As I hear this ghazal I recall the *shaam-o-sahar* (the mornings and evenings) of Aligarh . . . and the beauty that exudes from the garden of love and learning to the Realm of the Heart of 'Jahan-e-Khusrau', our annual World Sufi Music Festival, held at Arab ki Sarai in Nizamuddin, Delhi.

Aligarh gave us all a gift of *zamana shanasi* (understanding the world). It created a collective psyche of appreciation that needs to be cherished with great design and detail, to pursue all that is beautiful and wonderful. But alas! Maybe just the tarana of Majaz is enough, yet far from enough. There is too much barrenness for the clouds that rise from here to irrigate the parched world.

Chapter 5

Charbagh to Chowringhee Road

'*Kalkatte ka jo zikr kiya tu ne ham-nasheen*
Ik teer mere seene meiñ maara ki haiy haiy . . .'
('When you spoke of Calcutta, o my friend
an arrow pierced my heart, and how . . .')

—Mirza Ghalib

I walked into Calcutta with my lost Qaiserbagh inside me in 1966, journeying along the same Hooghly that had taken the British East India Company upstream to set up cantonments along the Ganges, brought Wajid Ali Shah as an exiled prisoner and Ghalib, to plead for his pension. I too had come to find a job to eke out an existence. This was to be my home. Why, I don't know. I didn't have a job or a friend in the city. I stepped out of the Howrah junction into an unknown world.

A Mecca of migrants, Howrah received not just people from Lucknow's Charbagh station—which sees millions cross its threshold, often never to return—but from every stop on the train tracks created by the British: Eastern UP, Varanasi, Patna, Cuttack and every part of poverty-stricken, jobless Bengal. It was like rivers meeting the ocean. A strange mix of colours, sounds, languages and odours assaulted my senses as the bridge over the Hooghly took me straight into a maze of streets and through layers of civilizations. Calcutta will never be short of people, no matter how inhumanly they may have to live. At that moment, I was one of the lot.

The taxi from the station wound its way through unknown streets on to Writers Square, then down Chowringhee Road, where I would end up staying one day, turning left on to Park Street, where we passed Murshidabad House and entered Park Circus. That was the address of Abba Jaan's friend, the son-in-law of an eminent barrister, the late Chaudhari Haider Husain from Lucknow. Chaudhari Sahab had built a mansion in Lucknow, overlooking the historic Aminudaulah Park. His wealth was a recent acquisition, the result of handling feudal disputes like many other lawyers in the city at that time. In fact, it was seeing this that my father had locked himself up in 1952 after the abolition of zamindari and emerged as a law graduate. I remember often seeing the elegant barrister drive into Kotwara House in his sleek black Packard. I had recently returned from Aligarh when I found a Ford A parked in the porch and Chaudhari Sahab's son, Ashar Husain, parked in my bedroom. He had just returned from England, and talked and behaved like an Englishman. There was a dispute among the brothers after Chaudhari Sahab's demise and, finding a sympathetic listener in Abba Jaan, Ashar had moved in with us along with his Ford. I wished he had come in his Packard but by then the Packard had already found its way to a *kabari* (junk dealer).

Ashar was a very funny man, straight out of a P.G. Wodehouse novel. He kept my father and Manjhu Mian amused as he sailed in and out of the house reciting Shakespeare. Soon, we started calling him 'Sindbad the Sailor'. Ashar would sail through Hazratgunj in his open Ford, clad in a silken Tootal scarf and Harris Tweed jacket, a Charminar cigarette in his mouth.

Soon it was arranged that I would stay in Calcutta at the home of Chaudhari sahab's son-in-law, Qamaruddin Ahmad. He was an engineer who had studied in Aligarh and was working in the Calcutta Port Trust. Like doctors from Lucknow, engineers from Aligarh were a dime a dozen—if you were a graduate from Aligarh you had to be an engineer, an issue I was to face for some time to come, till I reached the point where no one asked me about my qualifications any more. This was one reason I never picked up my degree from AMU till very recently, and that too only for archival records! Like many other things I write about here, I don't recommend that anyone do this.

At Qamaruddin Ahmad's home, I was the family's most immediate connect with Lucknow, and I felt most wanted in the house. There was a vivacious girl, with a beaming smile, of about my age there, who added to the feeling of being welcome. Naaz was her name. She would cover her head every time at the sound of the azan (call to prayer).

Park Circus was a Muslim area, with excellent street food and a sense of joie de vivre on the streets. People lived for the day, and you were surrounded by a vibrant sense of humour. People from UP, Bihar, Orissa and Bengal mingled seamlessly, connected by gastronomy and the azans, which echoed melodiously five times daily for a couple of minutes to cleanse your mind of the mundane chores of the day. As the sound relayed through the streets, it embraced you with the reassurance that He was indeed great and was present everywhere.

* * *

Calcutta was a city fluent in the language of money, very different from my Lucknow, which didn't even know its spelling. The mansions belonged to those who were part of the emerging mercantile colonial machinery that had replaced the erstwhile feudal culture. Wandering through the *baris* (traditional residential buildings) of the northern parts of the city was like moving through the decaying majesty of a world that Satyajit Ray showed, a contrast with the monochromatic reality of poverty.

Though romanticized in Ray's films, Calcutta, as I saw it, was a weapon of subjugation, of tyranny and exploitation. Yet, I was lost in its faded and ineffectual charm. Only traces remained of those who had played their games here and had gone. The Bengalis were fabulous storytellers who lived in the past and dreamt of the future. This made them very alluring, particularly when they wrote or sang or made films. I was there to take it all in, a ready prey for every shade of culture that was Calcutta.

In some ways, I felt like Gauhar Jaan, stepping into Calcutta with the advent of recorded sound. A nineteenth-century courtesan, Gauhar had moved from city to city, with Calcutta being her wonderland. She learnt to make friends with this new technology through her romance with the arrestingly good-looking Nemai Sen, the zamindar of Behrampore. He bridged his knowledge of art with a sense for technology. His response to each note, each word sung by Gauhar made her transcend her expression. She conquered not only the city but the country by unleashing her courtesanship through her voice on everyone who was without the means of gracing her company.

On an evening at an aristocratic home, I saw a shadow of Gauhar, a little less over-the-top but in no way any less talented. She wore a diamond nose ring, which pierced whoever she gazed at. There was Lucknow in the air. '*Koyalia mat kar pukaar, karejwa laage kataar* (O nightingale, don't call, it pierces like a dagger through my heart).' The nose ring was like a *kataar*, a dagger. It hit me where it was meant to. She obviously knew Abba Jaan and softened up with gentle sentences that could only come from where I came. She was Begum Akhtar. The diamond nose ring reminded me of my mother. An adornment used by women of influence. A decade later I was to use it for Rekha in *Umrao Jaan*. I have seriously thought of making films on both these people, Gauhar and Begum Akhtar, but it has yet to happen.

Calcutta had seemed like a natural next step after the progressive and scientific world of Aligarh. I did not wish to pursue geology, botany or chemistry. The poetry of Aligarh had opened a new world for me and inculcated in me a reverence for art. Those were poets who had dreamt of a renaissance as they waited in the wings to illumine the new and free India. I had begun to feel the plight of people who were just waking up from the nightmare of colonial darkness; from the oppression of foreign exploitation and their Indian agents. Calcutta had all those dreams and more. It was a blend of the old and the new, the British world of managing agencies and Marwari companies taking over slowly, and then the multinationals changing their corporate identities to become Indian, such as Hindustan Lever, the India Tobacco Company and even the Gramophone Company of India. And this was the world of Gauhar Jaan, where they rose to Olympian heights, while she died a pauper. Such was this Calcutta and its lingua franca of commerce.

Calcutta brought with it a strange hangover of a legacy which I discovered as I walked around, a past which bore similarity to Lucknow. It was the Calcutta of a wily Clive that was to swallow the Murshidabad legacy, leaving no trace behind except the frail world of weavers and embroiderers that one sees now. The Battle of Buxar, fought in 1764 between the joint forces of the mighty Mughals and the nawab of Bengal with the British East India Company, and funded by the largest banker of the world, Jagat Seth, had finally sealed India's fate. The wealth of the Mughal emperor, banked with Sethji, was now free to be used in the interest of the British East India Company against the Indian forces.

Rising from the ashes was a cultured Calcutta which survived with time. There was classic writing and poetry, there was the legacy of the world of Nawab Wajid Ali Shah, who spent his last three decades on this soil in exile. His innovations in, and patronage of, kathak and thumri, even in his days of distress, had touched the soul of the city.

One of the first people I met in Calcutta was the beautiful Attia Hosain. She came from the taluqdar family of the Chaudharis of Gadia. Her brother, Chaudhari Rishad Husain Kidwai, was my father's childhood friend. Attia was a novelist from Lucknow, and also a broadcaster, journalist and actor, as well as a muse for many a creative soul. An accomplished blend of intellect, beauty, grace and imagination, she was a bridge between the East and the West—one moment you felt she was completely English and in the next she was someone who had stepped out of the *parikhana* (fairyland) of Nawab Wajid Ali Shah. She appeared like a character in *Gone with the Wind* but could represent a modern Lucknow of the 1930s. She embodied the zenith of the gracious, generous, pre-Partition feudal world. I wished I was thirty years older; or that she was that much younger. But nevertheless, she was great company.

Attia Aunty was living as a guest in Park Mansion on Park Street. Her permanent base was supposed to be London, but like the phoenix she would sweep across the East—Delhi, Bombay, Calcutta, Karachi and Lucknow. Her visits came packed with stories that connected various families in the subcontinent. She would reminisce about the days before I was born, telling me stories of how Abba Jaan would take her for drives in his magnificent Isotta. which he brought back to India upon his return from Scotland for good. There were others in Calcutta that my Phuphi Jaan talked fondly about on her visits to Lucknow from Karachi, where she now lived. One of them was about her dear friend Kona Das and their touching farewell when Kona went to see Phuphi Jaan off at the station when she finally departed for Pakistan. Years later, Phuphi Jaan told me that she had a premonition that this would be their last meeting. And sure enough, it was. Kona died in a car crash soon after. Phuphi Jaan had a deep bond with Kona's children, Brinda Karat, Radhika Roy and Junie Bose, and she would always see them when she came from Karachi, an emotional reunion I encountered several times. Through Junie I was introduced to the English theatre world of Calcutta. Her husband, Tutu Bose, and I often wandered in Mullick Bazaar, where old car parts were sold. We picked up a sports Wolsley Hornet, which lay in Tutu's home for a while and then one day just vanished.

Calcutta gave me a new way of looking at life, my art and myself. I did not want a commercial job. I wanted something that bridged art and commerce. Advertising was the obvious answer. Attia Aunty could sell anything to anyone, unconditionally and without a price. She could have been in advertising, but she was already in an emotional realm of art. She knew everyone who was worth knowing in the social milieu of Calcutta and opened doors for me into the world of advertising. She was now to sell a youth from Lucknow whose journey was limited to Aligarh and who had never heard of a career in advertising. Without knowing more about it, I wanted to be in it. The first call and I was in service.

Through Attia Aunty's circle, I landed myself a job as one of three trainees in Clarion McCann Advertising Services, earlier known as DJ Keymer. At Clarion McCann, I saw a world where the consumer was king and where selling was the greatest of all arts. This was a compromise many an artist had made to exist—live a less mercantile existence in an otherwise commercial milieu. They were near the world of 'words' and 'moving images' that they needed for their soul. Satyajit Ray was one of them. Clarion McCann was a melting pot of these strains, servicing clients of all hues.

Clarion McCann offered me a salary of Rs 150 a month; I closed my eyes and accepted it. For Rs 125 a month, I got myself a small cabin room in Birkmyre Hostel. Here I found a small admiration society of wannabe 'Boxwalas'—smart young men or women from well-to-do families who had studied in public schools and graduated from good universities, preferably English ones. Intelligence and marks were not so important. They were impressed with my taste, my ties and cufflinks, all inherited from my father's Edinburgh wardrobe after he had vowed to wear handwoven khadi till the mills in India were nationalized. The 'Boxwalas' usually worked in managing agencies with heavy perks.

Meanwhile, I had vowed not to take help from my father as he was not in favour of my job in advertising, given that I had obtained a degree in science. With the remaining Rs 25 in my pocket, I would walk to my office at 5 Council House Street every morning and window-shop as I walked back in the evenings.

In Calcutta, I was exposed to a wide range of styles that would always live within me—from the very down-to-earth film-maker Mrinal Sen to the highly sophisticated Arshad Farooqi, a dashing, pipe-smoking uncle whom I discovered at Clarion. Like Attia Aunty, Uncle Arshad could sell any idea to anyone through his aura. So he never had to work much. He reminded me of another uncle from Muradabad, Captain Rashid, who lived by his style and the gift of the gab. One of the captain's marriages was to Durga Khote, a legend of the silver screen before Bombay became Bollywood.

Those who had returned from the West after education carried their formal and semi-formal tweed attire with great aplomb. I was reminded of a few of my teachers at La Martiniere and their choice of ties, shirts, shoes and cufflinks. I would stare at those who dressed well, and I am sure they knew that I was silently admiring them. Since my childhood I have admired the art of dressing, and I had many role models, my father being the best. I was mesmerized by a good dress sense. In Aligarh, black was the bottom line of style, and it was inconceivable to step out without a black sherwani over the kurta. I recall Arjumand Ali Khan, an aristocrat from Hyderabad whose flamboyant personality and wardrobe had impressed me greatly in Aligarh. But no one could compete with my father, who had by then given up on Western clothing but not on style. There was something very enigmatic about his khadi suits and sherwanis that made him stand apart. 'The clothes say you respect me, and I will respect you,' was one of his many one-liners to guide me through life.

In three months, my salary was increased to Rs 500 per month, and I could afford to rent a small room at Auckland Square in South Calcutta. Just off Moira Street, it was a large enough room on the ground floor, with old, colonial double windows with shutters, overlooking a small pond. I bought three pairs of beautiful, handcrafted Chelsea boots by Chap Hing on Chowringhee Road for Rs 100. The moment I walked in, my admirers fell for the shoes. Among them was a boy called Nanda, working in a managing agency, who had the same shoe size as me. I immediately sold two pairs to Nanda at double the price! From then on, I developed a fetish for shoes and a renewed confidence in style. Nanda reminded me of

Wolly, but with a little more taste and aspirational values. This little sale gave me a sense of self-reliance; if nothing else worked out, I felt, I could live on the business of style, clothing people and making them look great. To date, I am of the firm belief that there are next to no clothiers in India who know how to dress a man.

I sent for Tahir, my cook from Lucknow, and he stayed with me in that room. For a while, another friend from Naini Tal, Yusuf Ali Khan, shacked up with me. The house belonged to a very old lady, Mrs Yakchee. She was an Armenian Jew, and grew very fond of me and wary of Yusuf. He was extremely fair and often pretended to be an Englishman, but would be caught in just three sentences. Anyone on whom he tried that trick ceased to trust him.

Down the road lived another friend of mine, Askari Imam, whom I had met in Naini Tal while I was still in my early teens. He was tall and handsome, and I loved his brown corduroy pants and naughty sense of humour. He would make Naini Tal come to life. He had a way with girls which I lacked. He now worked with Balmer Lawrie, lived in a one-bedroom flat on Hungerford Street and had a black Fiat, 1956 model with a centre light. He was married to a very attractive lady, whom I had only seen from afar initially. I wondered if she looked down on me, as I was a very junior accounts assistant and she a copywriter with Bensons.

Askari would give me a lift to work. A penny saved was a penny earned, plus there was the fun of being with Askari, with whom I had connected after almost a decade. I would walk up from Auckland Square after having Tahir's khaagina and roghni roti for breakfast. Often, I had to wait for half an hour to an hour before Askari and his wife would appear from their bedroom, looking fresh as daisies. While I waited, I imagined the romantic time they must be having together. Their appearance always proved I was right. The attractive and aloof lady was Syeda Imam. Syeda continues to be a part of my life, while Askari is no more. I saw them a lot socially till he passed away. He was the life of the evening, talking about the politics of Bihar, where he hailed from. His mother was a member of Parliament. I often wonder why Askari didn't step into politics. Maybe he took it too lightly. Syeda was working with Contract, and she has been an important part of the Jahan-e-Khusrau branding and marketing strategy since its inception at the turn of the millennium. She was later invited to become a part of the Rumi Foundation, headed by Dr Karan Singh, with me as its secretary and executive director. She continues to play an active role in the foundation and has helped in structuring our journal, *HU: The Sufi Way*, and the coffee-table books published by us.

It was around this time that I went to shop for some nice clothes for meeting clients. With most of my salary gone, I had to plan the rest of my monthly expenses carefully. But the next day, there was a theft in my flat, and all my new clothes were stolen. I had no choice but to buy a second-hand jacket, which actually hung very well on me. Apparently, it was some English brand. I have never told anyone this secret. If I had gone to the market a week later, I would probably have found my own clothes up for sale! That theft was a big setback, and I realized that it was not safe to stay on that street any more, even with the attraction of a very pretty Muslim girl from a well-to-do family as my neighbour. I had asked Usha Gupta, who had joined as a trainee with me at Clarion, to make friends with that girl so she could eventually introduce me to her. This never worked out, as I was too down-and-out financially in the eyes of her parents. Usha's father was the chairman of the ICI at the time, one of our biggest clients. Usha claims that a few years later I saw through her at the Sea Lounge, one of the most popular rendezvous spots in Bombay, when I was with Air India. I don't remember that, but she certainly has become a part of my life in Delhi in the present. She is now Usha Soni, married to Gautam Soni, whom I knew in Lucknow and Naini Tal. His father was the chief conservator of forests of undivided UP, which included Uttarakhand.

After this theft, I moved to another old-world house on Chowringhee Road, a magnificent stretch that went past the Victoria Memorial, Birla Planetarium and the Academy of Fine Arts, where I would exhibit one day. It was a flat with just one room but with a view of the most magnificent garden. It was just about 10x10 ft, divided by a cupboard with a narrow bed for me on one side. The other side of the cupboard was Tahir's domain—his little gas ring and sleeping area. Tahir continued to cook and look after me. He stayed with me till he died and was my greatest public-relations person in every conceivable way. I knew that Tahir's talking well of me was the only reason those who worked in the building started acknowledging me with a respectful smile. When I began to ask a friend or two over for dinner, Tahir would create the most fabulous Lakhnawi meal possible, and my guests would go back raving about it. His shaami and galavat kababs took you beyond the streets of Lucknow. They were fit for the *dastarkhwaan* of a raja. His dopiaza, kate masale ka qeema and biryani were to die for. Armed with this menu, I was ready to conquer the world, be it Calcutta, Delhi, Bombay, Srinagar or Kotwara. The secret was that Tahir cooked with his heart. Whether for a friend or the whole unit of a film, he cooked with the same love and dedication. It was Tahir's cooking that made me realize that food cooked lovingly could win over anyone. From the Bombay of my Air India days to the three decades of my film days, he survived it all. He brought up my children and witnessed all my marriages. He faced everything with a ready smile and an endearing twitch in his eyes, as my strength to face any adversity, sleeping on the same floor in tough times.

Another colleague at Clarion who had joined at the same time as me was Prabir Sen, né Bantu, the son of the exotic Lota Sen, who hailed from one of the most sophisticated Bengali families. They lived in a well-appointed flat in an old-world mansion.

* * *

Calcutta opened a world I could not have imagined in the wildest of dreams. I made inroads into various cross sections of societies. Film-making was the new art that emerged out of the arrangement of a medley of moving images in the sombre darkness of a projection hall, and it made me see reality differently. Satyajit Ray was the art director and vice chairman where I worked, and his inimitable spirit showed us a new light. Each day of my life at that time held some treasured moments with him. He opened my mind to the culture of cinema, to global cinema being born out of the milieu of Bengal—the real and fading Bengal. The renaissance of Bengal. It was the same as what had happened to me when I was in Aligarh. In Ray's own words, 'The most distinctive feature of my films is that they are deeply rooted in Bengal, in Bengali culture, mannerisms and mores. What makes them universal in appeal is that they are about human beings.'

Stimulated by these influences, I made up my mind to paint in my little room in Chowringhee. In the creative world of Calcutta, all I had to speak through was my art. To take my resolve further one day I bought a canvas and some paints to start painting. Each day I would return to my room to this blank canvas looking me in the face. I would speak to the canvas in poetry. It didn't respond. I suppose this was what meditation is all about. It expected more from me. It was about emptying your mind, which was full of things. I would try to empty it. It had to be a blank mind facing a blank canvas. But blanking out Calcutta was no easy task. Poetry would touch me and go.

I became bolder and bolder in this medium, and I could feel the poetry of Aligarh begin to speak through me—Rahi and Faiz in particular. Their romantic lyricism found a melody in colours and rhythm in my strokes. Ever since, poetry has throbbed in my soul when I traverse the visual world. I was a poet in flight without any command on poetic structures, which, in hindsight, was also good. I found myself in the service of poetry, which has continued till now. Poetry softened my heart; it put life and history into a context and became a powerful tool to inspire parallel forms of creativity. Had I become a poet, the purpose and effect of poetry may have been very different for me! In fact, it was Asghar Wajahat, my closest friend in Aligarh, who had cautioned me, 'If you can get good poetry to hear, don't attempt to write yourself.' Maybe he was right, and these are the few things I have lived by.

However, I don't promise that I will never write! Still, I realize the need for translation in English, and I have done that with poems I choose and use. I am glad that I am poetry-driven, and I hope there will be a day when our country will become poetry-driven, because poetry is a deep reflection of oneself in a larger milieu. It is through poetry that I understood the angst of Lucknow, the pain of love, the intensity of separation of Wajid Ali Shah, who himself, one gets the feeling, was inspired by Krishna leaving Radha and his beloved Braj. It is this that I have found mirrored in my work, and I have intensely felt and laboured in great detail to share it.

As I chart my course, I see a subtle criss-crossing of the tangible and the intangible. Of arts, craft and spiritualism, all speaking a language of their own, like animals, none of which I understand, yet I am deeply conversant with them. I have lived this life in the abstract language of symbols, with a prayer and a hope that the world will one day be sensitive to this phenomenon of the hidden and the revealed. Unfortunately, the numbers are not large enough to make democratic sense in our society. Yet, it may play a balancing factor if we are open-minded. It is here that being global makes good sense.

As a painter, I have evolved to understand textures of life. Of time, feelings and relationships. Often, I enter a labyrinth of situations plagued by conflict and contradictions, which I end up resolving in unusual and creative ways. They empower me with a new energy to find beauty in adversity. An instinct God has blessed all of us with.

The moment you begin to see it as a realm of art, the world immediately becomes different. Starting from a haze of bewilderment, things start to become clear. As a painter, I began to see things with a different vision.

This happened to me in my junior class at La Martiniere. I was not good at studies and was amazed at those who could understand and recall. Neither was I any good in sports. I admired those who could sprint, score goals and hit sixes. But I knew I couldn't settle with that perception of myself. So I picked up a pencil and began to look at things from its sharp, brittle point, and put them down on the matt texture of the white surface of a drawing book. I used to gently stroke the surface as if it was some sacred ritual before making the pencil point glide on it. Heady with an unknown fragrance, I kept sharpening the cedar wood-clad graphite. I began to capture shapes and forms on paper, shading them in my own childlike way. The sharpened pencils of varying hardness began to reveal unknown mysteries, which one day I would leave far behind. I would often put my left cheek near the drawing book and unleash my mechanical imagination. That child in me saw everything through the fine tip of that graphite. From then on, life began to show me things differently. The pencils became coloured, turned to crayons, transformed like a wand into a watercolour brush, and the paper became a canvas . . . And I never looked back.

Subjects glided past faster than my perception as an artist. I saw more than I could capture. The mountains and trees, the lake and landscape . . . from Lucknow to Kotwara to Naini Tal—I was absorbing images in the piggybank of my mind to decode decades later. Then I abandoned art to take up science, as many people did to secure their future. But this could be anyone's story. What was so different in my case? I was born in Lucknow around the mid-1940s. So were many others. It was a time when India was becoming independent and divided into two. Was that the big story?

Yes and no.

The story was that I was born to my particular parents who had certain concerns, which made the difference and determined what the future held in store. This was the story that drove me on to think and feel the way I do. These picture postcards kept being sent to an unknown address. An address I would discover and rediscover at unknown times all my life. Characters kept emerging, forming and disappearing, often becoming larger than life, like in a film. What would be erased and what would get distilled into art was anybody's guess. In what form things would reappear was the wonder of my existence. At all times a fixed deposit would mature and pay back dividends. I realized that as an artist everything was a lifelong reflection. Today, I find myself in a lost, bygone yesterday. In Lucknow, I would be in Kotwara. In Kotwara, I would be in Naini Tal. The trigger of associations of ideas became stronger, and with it emerged a sense of nostalgia. Today, the scent of cedar takes me back to so many sunrises and sunsets over stately trees and broken columns, reminding me of Attia Hosain. With these triggers I was becoming a little more than a visual artist.

Kabhi roshni ki talaash meiñ kayi manziloñ se guzar gaye,
Kabhi raat aisi daraoni ki ham arzu se bhi dar gaye.
Rahe dil pe tere khayal meiñ kabhi teergi kabhi roshni,
Kabhi vo sukoot ke alamañ kabhi karwaañ se guzar gaye . . .
(At times, in search of light I transcended many destinations,
At times, the night was so terrifying that it froze all intentions.
Your thoughts in the path of love, at times in pitch darkness
and in blinding light at times.
At times an alarming stillness and at times I crossed many a caravan
station . . .)

—Rahi Masoom Raza

Painting began to emerge from the romanticism of abstraction, like secrets of nature, like geological formations, the hidden and the revealed. A dialogue with verse.

I began to feel this with music and poetry too. Aligarh had opened my mind and heart to a romantic notion of revolution. To think and feel change, yet not be a part of it. To empathize with the human predicament in a free country. There were poets a decade and more older than me who were part of the freedom struggle and who showed me the way that can lead one out from the world of the heart and the mind. Those who opposed the two-nation theory contrived by the visionary divide-and-rule policy of our colonial masters. It struck a chord because my father was a vehement opponent of the same.

People became black and white. Right or Left. I went with the Left. Exploitation of man by man went against my grain. The metaphors of change were so romantic in Urdu poetry. The likes of Faiz had taken revolution to mystic heights. The beloved became the soil, and love became freedom. Urdu became the most exotic language of change in the world. So much so that it demanded translation. In this process English, too, followed in its footsteps of the romance of change.

I was not a poet and was far from being a film-maker. So, in my small room on the fourth floor in the old colonial building on Chowringhee Road, I painted and painted, and showed my works in 1968 for the first time in Calcutta. I was part of many worlds in Calcutta. I had known of the Calcutta where Nawab Wajid Ali Shah was exiled in Matia Burj. Calcutta began to unfold like a made-in-heaven, massive Persian carpet with an amazing intricacy of a startling chiaroscuro blending seamlessly through the fading shades of the cultural tapestry. Persianized aristocrat Raja Rammohan Roy stood tall in the midst of this rich carpet. He was the forefather of Tagore and lived ahead of his time. He wrote a book in Persian called *Tuhfatul Muwalhdin* (A Gift to Monotheists) and published a regular journal in Persian called *Miratul Akhbar* (Mirror of Intelligence). He founded the progressive, monotheist, liberated Brahmo Samaj. This was carried forward through his son and grandson, Rabindranath Tagore.

Many Westernized intellectuals and artists belonged to this fraternity in Bengal, of which Satyajit Ray was a part. Then there was the very traditional Hindu–Bengali world and its exact opposite—the leftist world. There was the Muslim world, the British managing agency world, with their clubs, and the feudal world of Burdwan, Murshidabad and the likes. There was the 'Boxwala' theatre world, of which Amitabh Bachchan was a part. He was tall and skinny, slightly differently proportioned than me. I think his legs were longer than his torso, and his jackets sat loosely on his narrow shoulders. Not the best material for a superstar. We worked on the same street, and he would come to see me during lunch, often to borrow my portable tape recorder, which my American girlfriend had given me before returning to the US. That quarter-inch tape recorder had changed my life. I had recorded all the poets who had moved me. All the poets who became recurrent characters in my life. Rahi, Khalil-ur-Rahman Azmi, Shahryar. Our very humorous copywriter Jack Dante, who lived in the Christian quarters in the Free School Street area, would secretly pop his head from the frosted glass partition and, in his usual catchy-headline style, whisper, 'Coat on the hanger is here . . .' He meant Amitabh.

My paintings cut across the entire length and breadth of Calcutta society, and were my humble calling card to this creative city. It is a gratifying feeling to meet people who have lived with my art of 1968. Anthony Mayer, an English creative director at Clarion, wrote a moving introduction to my work which deeply resonated with the people of Calcutta.

Antony, better known as Tony, was married to Jyotsna, the daughter of the maharaja of Burdwan. They had a very sweet son, Toby, whose company I enjoyed very much; and I often drove him to the zoo in their tiny two-seater MG Midget. I made a painting for him, *Toby in the Zoo*. It still stands out vividly in my memory.

I married Geeti Sen, an art historian who studied art history at Bryn Mawr in Philadelphia and did a PhD on the paintings of the *Akbarnama* in 1968. She came from an illustrious Brahmo Samaj family. Her grandmother was Charulata Mukherji, whose life was full of tragedy, seeing all her children pass away before her eyes. From Air Marshal Subroto Mukherji to Geeti's own mother, who died when her sari caught fire. Geeti was a creative person, and her deep sense of art was inspiring. We got married in the simplest possible way, in the Brahmo Samaj tradition. Her father, Dr Budha Sen, was Rabindranath Tagore's doctor, and it was Tagore who had given Geeti her name.

My father was enamoured by the Brahmo faith, and he wrote an interesting article on Brahmo Samaj and Islam. A distinct quality of Abba Jaan that kept surfacing was his ability to find commonalities in faiths. It was around this time that he joined the Indian Humanist Union, which he cherished with a handful of people till his last days. Ours was the first intercommunal marriage to take place under aegis of his Indian Humanist Union. In fact, it is from Abba Jaan that I have acquired the knack to find commonalities in faiths and cultures. There is a book of notes in which he has compared the similarities between Advaita and Sufism.

I did crayons and oils, and started selling a few paintings. My subjects were abstract. I had seen a world within a world through my sojourn in geology. The outside and inside of rocks. This emerged from my oils and crayons, and since then the rocks have persisted in my art. Sometimes barren, sometimes clad with long cypresses. Poetry began to peep through rocks.

The essential thing is to understand the possibilities of the medium. Every medium has its limitations—one experiments to transcend them. If you know the viscosity of water you will know exactly how it will flow, where it will go on the ground . . . similarly with linseed oil, you must know how it will accept or reject turpentine. The materials used have an inert energy which has to be activated to bring out their intrinsic character.

—Excerpt from my diary of 1968

My art had begun to make sense. A dialogue had begun between the empty canvas and my empty mind.

'I work with a sense of revelation . . . as the painting crystalizes it develops an equilibrium between one's experience and its transference to canvas,' said my diary as I prepared for my exhibition in Calcutta in 1968.

One of my early buyers was Indar Pasricha, who runs a reputed art gallery in London even today. Then others followed, mainly from the British fraternity of Calcutta—Peter Leggat, Antony Alexander. I made a little money and could afford to spend a little here and there. The way I am describing my economic predicament, I am sure you must be calculating how it was to survive each day! But don't worry; it never showed on my face; I continued to look my father's son, way above what I had. Money never made sense or mattered to me. I wanted to live creatively each moment and seek creative beings with an open mind and heart. And Calcutta had them in large measure.

Given the opportunity, I would relive my life in Calcutta. But where will I find another Tahir or another Ray? Layer by layer, I could see a film emerge on paper and in my mind—crystal-clear, with its music score, frame by frame, through the long fingers of my friend Subhas Mukhopadhyay, on his piano. Subhas Da would accompany me to Ray's home on Bishop Street, and his very soft words in Bengali crafted images of subtle beauty. I was in love with the language and those who spoke it, and there could be none gentler than Subhas Da. These were simple people, always on foot, always with the common man, one of them yet rising above them, though dreaming for them. Another bridge character was Barun Chanda, who was my colleague at Clarion. He, too, was tall and lanky. Though a copywriter, he had his heart set on films. He was extremely lighthearted, with a very Bengali, *bhadrlok* style of speaking English. He was always writing copy as he spoke. He somehow landed up with a role in a film by Satyajit Ray, actually playing someone like himself, an advertising executive. He is my living link with Calcutta.

Today, I often wonder if I could be a Ray or a Subhas Da to a person like myself in quest of a dream!

The answer is yes, if you read between the lines. It is all about finding that me in you and you in me. The world is facing change, and we have braved the change and gone against the wind. Some went with the wind and reached sky-high.

On 20 September 1968, I was ready with a good body of work for an exhibition at the Academy of Fine Arts, to be inaugurated by Lady Ranu Mukerjee. Tony Mayer wrote in the exhibition catalogue:

> . . . and it is his love of the innate characteristic of material—the coarseness of jute, the oily spread of turpentine on pigment, the sharp delicacy of a charred edge of canvas—that characterizes the artist's work. But while there is no rational analysis of mood and very little obvious symbolism—Muzaffar, like the forerunner of Abstract Expressionist Kandinsky, is a non-objectivist—there is a special expertise which dictates the selection of the interest in material. Muzaffar had no formal training in art. He did however take a degree in Geology, Botany and Chemistry and his study of the processes of chemical and organic change is apparent in his work. You will see on these canvases the record, actual or implied, of the fundamental processes of growth and erosion. Science and art coming together at a point of creative expression.

And what is to me especially interesting is that this record, while it is a record of fibers of an existence common to all men, has an outward shape which is specially Indian. In the same sense that the outward shape of the landscape of Bihar or Rajasthan is unique to those areas, while the geological processes which formed the landscape are presumably of a more general nature.

'The morning's White Sun—the generating source of light which brings colour and form to the world, itself drains white in the process,' spoke one of the paintings about itself. It acquired a language of poetry through the metaphor of science.

Murad, my eldest son, was born on 20 September 1969, exactly a year after my first exhibition opened, at St Elizabeth Nursing Home, Dongersy Road, Malabar Hill, Bombay.

I lived in Calcutta with these works of art which needed no elaborate interpretation and my lost Qaiserbagh inside me till 1969.

Chapter 6

Endless Horizons

'Kuch nahiñ khulta ki kyuñ mere qadam jaate haiñ
Aisi manzil ki taraf jiska pata kuch bhi nahiñ.'
('I don't know why my feet pull me
towards ways that have no end.')

—Shahryar

My faithful black 'M.A. Zaidi' trunk moved with me from city to city—
Aligarh, Lucknow, Delhi, Calcutta, Bombay—often in unreserved
compartments of trains. Geeti and I moved from Calcutta to Delhi in
1969. I had begun my series of migrations.

A short spell here with Advertising and Sales Promotion Company
(ASP), belonging to the Birlas, gave me a new perspective on both
advertising and art. Many painters had begun to make their homes in
Delhi, and the city became a centre of modern art. I came in close contact
with several of them, Tyeb Mehta and Husain being the ones I was closest
to. I admired them and they, in turn, made it seem very romantic and
meaningful to be a painter. Within a few weeks of joining ASP, I was sent
off to train in Bombay.

It was during my training period in Bombay that I fell in love with a
Jaguar Mark VII. It belonged to a legend of the advertising world, Peter
Fielden, who had looked after it lovingly. The smell of old leather reminded

me of my father's Isotta, which I had played in with the other children in Kotwara. But this was new, and it moved like a real Jaguar on the open roads of Bombay. One day, I was driving to Pune with Arshad Farooqi's family. We were touching nearly 100 miles an hour when suddenly there was a burst of steam, and the car sputtered to a stop. How we got back to Aderbad Sethna, the eccentric Parsi mechanic at Apex Garage in Haji Ali, from whom I had bought the machine, I don't know.

Aderbad was an impatient and intolerant man who was always very upset with everything. He had added rail tracks sticking out of his jeep and would not hesitate in slashing through the sides of cars if he found anyone misbehaving or breaking traffic rules on the roads. He would just pull in and rip their sides apart! So, when I took the car to him, I was scared out of my wits. But there was no one else to turn to. That day, he was unexpectedly calm and unlike his usual self. We became good friends. For fifteen long days, I spent hours at the garage while my car was restored back to life. I almost became a mechanic. I have always nursed a passion for workshops. It all started during my schooldays on Abba Jaan's insistence that come what may, each person should know what happens below the bonnet; the Kotwara library had a full section on how and why things work.

On the tenth day, I got a telegram from Jog, my boss in the Delhi office: 'THROW CAR INTO SEA AND REPORT BACK TO OFFICE'. But I was hell-bent on getting the car back on its wheels before my very own eyes. And equally determined was I to drive back to Delhi. And so, I did. Aderbad had grown so fond of me that he offered to drive down with me! I learnt more with Aderbad in fifteen days than I had learnt in the months of training. In that journey, I acquired a taste for the adrenaline rush of long-distance driving. Over the years, I must have driven to Lucknow from Bombay over twenty times. I know the routes and the landmarks by heart, and can still see the landscape framed in the car's windshield—the ghats, the Shivpuri forests and the hills . . .

It was a Monday afternoon when the dusty Jaguar Mark VII pulled into 1 Ratendone Road (now called Amrita Sher-Gil Marg) just as Jog was driving out! Thank God for that. The car said it all. I walked out with a gleaming smile on my face, instantly reciprocated by Jog, who couldn't help but come out and admire this swanky old machine. They don't make them like that any more—neither Jogs nor Jags! I was not a very useful

fellow, and ASP would not lose a penny by my absence. Why I was there I
didn't know myself. Maybe Jog saw how I brought out the best in others.
I had learnt the art of 1+1 equals 11 and not 2. This made me mistrust
mathematics, much to my father's dismay. He used to say, 'You trust
people blindly'—something my wife and daughter still say.

* * *

It was in the early 1970s in Delhi that I saw an advertisement in the
newspaper for a deputy publicity manager in Air India. It seemed perfectly
tailored for me, and I applied forthwith, without really expecting anything
to come of it.

At that time, I was living at A-35 Nizamuddin East, in a house that
belonged to one Raj Kapoor, a migrant from what is now Pakistan. An
ex-aristocrat, he looked down on people who were not of his status. He
grudgingly rented out his place to me, rubbing in the ex-aristocrat angle
every now and then, and talking of what he had left behind. There was
something in him that rang true, but I didn't see the need to talk so
much about it. But when you understood what he and his ilk must have
been through, you could justify it. He was reasonably impressed with my
two-tone Jaguar Mark VII, which stood impressively outside his home.
Then, one day, my father arrived. That made his day. Abba Jaan's regal
demeanour, his way of addressing people and the wisdom of his age swept
Mr Kapoor off his feet. He had finally met the first one of his kind after
leaving Pakistan. Suddenly, I was not the same Muzaffar Ali who worked
on a paltry salary with ASP. I was my father's son. And that was the first
time I realized the true value of being my father's son in an alien city like
Delhi. Mr Kapoor still lives in Nizamuddin, aristocratic as they come but
with nothing to show for it. He lives by himself with real-estate vultures
eyeing his property, waiting for him to drop like a ripe old fruit any day!

It was Mr Kapoor who handed over to me a nice crisp envelope with
the Air India logo embossed on it. I had forgotten that I had even applied!
My joy knew no bounds. It felt great to be wanted. I was thrilled that I
had been called for an interview without knowing anyone. It was a step
towards building my self-confidence.

I had by then developed a unique style for clothing. I took to khadi,
wearing fine checks with khadi ties inspired by Abba Jaan's eclectic style
that I imagined bridged the best of the East and West. I walked into the

most magnificent office I had ever seen. Perched on the seventeenth floor of the brand-new Air India building, the room looked out at the endlessly blue Arabian Sea. There was an expansive mahogany table in the centre, across from which, in an equally impressive chair, sat a diminutive man in his late fifties. He was dressed in a dark suit and a bright tie with a big triangular knot, and had an aura of power and mischief.

This was Bobby Kooka, the commercial head of the most stylish global product of India—Air India. He had designed the Air India Maharajah and handpicked and trained each cabin crew that came in contact with a client, to the degree that you could say that each of them was a clone of Bobby Kooka himself.

He was a man of wide-ranging pursuits and was really interested in what I was all about. From clothes to cars, one thing led to another. The Isotta tickled his fancy, and he spoke passionately about his two-seater Invicta sports till he realized that he had gone off on a tangent. He was only interviewing an inexperienced fool for a job, someone who seemed too young for the job and hiring whom would probably create resentment among his cadre. But Bobby Kooka had made up his mind to employ me and created a position, a grade lower than the one advertised. I felt hesitant to accept. The tables had turned. Now it was he who was luring me into accepting the job of an assistant station manager. It came with several increments and perks, he said. I would not regret it for a moment, as the position offered an endless horizon. I would be able to look far into the Arabian Sea, which I had not even seen in my dreams. And to this day I believe that it was the kind of encounter I will never have again in my life. The man knew the future as far as he could see. I don't think anyone was hired this way in Air India, before or ever after.

Soon, I was back on the shores of Bombay and walking into an eighteenth-floor office with the same view of the ocean as Bobby Kooka's. It was a small room that I shared with Uttara Parikh, who was to be my junior as a publicity officer, which she perhaps resented but, being a gracious lady, never showed. Uttara was stunningly statuesque, maybe a couple of years older than me, with many admirers in our office and in other offices.

Geeti and I moved into a small, two-room flat in Palm Springs, also on the eighteenth floor with an equally magnificent view of the sea. It was a déjà vu moment—like in my first job, my rent was just Rs 150 less than my salary! Fortunately, Geeti got a job with the JJ School of Architecture.

Our tiny apartment was most inspiring to paint in. Then, one day, I discovered a rash on my fingers. I was anguished to realize that I had developed an allergy to oil paint. I was advised to paint with gloves but that was not very effective. The allergy became worse, and I had to keep my hands in my pocket. The pus began to ooze out so much that I could not shake hands with anyone. I stood there for days looking at the blank canvas and the Arabian Sea. I just had to do something. Finally, the sea spoke. I saw brown boxes drift towards me in the sea. I pasted the 6×3 canvas with brown-and-khaki craft paper using Fevicol. Painting has its own discipline. I worked within the conformity of a canvas and was regulated by its dimensions. The structural dimension of a painting is like a chemical equation. Counterpoised masses that suggest a sense of change and yet of equilibrium. Anything that is changing is in itself in a state of equilibrium.

The passion to work overrode all material obstacles. Again, I started painting and this time it was with a difference. A new way of feeling surfaces. A series of collages began to emerge. My diary from that time reads:

> Almost a year ago paper had begun to intrigue me. I began to discover its sensitivities, its textures, shades and this simple realization found identity with my own personality, and that which motivated me visually. So I began to work with paper, a very basic material, not for commercial or industrial use, but as an end in itself. In this sense my collages became an experiment, a discovery. They helped me to explore the subtle realities camouflaged between the subtle membranes of existence. I attempt to bring alive the character of paper and the transparency of colours. By analogy they may appear to you like fungus on the walls or texture of leather, the complexion of paper. They mean to me many more things that arise from the world in which I live, that explore for me the magic phenomena of existence. But finally they are themselves paper, retaining an inherent character and resilience which I try to preserve intact.
>
> 2 May 1972

In 1972, I had an exhibition of my collages at the Pundole Art Gallery and, fortunately, sold many of them, including one to the National Gallery of Modern Art, one to the Taj Mahal hotel, and a 6x3 canvas to none other than the passionate collector Jahangir Nicholson. Impishly, he said, 'I want this because it is bigger than myself.'

There was no looking back. A new phase opened. And as Kooka had said, the sky was the limit. An endless horizon awaited me. The waters of the Arabian Sea engulfed me from sunset to sunrise to sunset.

Air India and its sheer scale presented a new world. My tourism publicity experience in Delhi came in very useful. As an advertising executive I had learnt the art of packaging the little I knew into something invincible. I had been handling a fabulous campaign for the Department of Tourism with ASP, headed by Jog. Jog was an institution in his days and had put together the most glamorous and talented team in Delhi— Mickey Patel, Bim Bissel, Sunita Kohli, Shekhar Kamat, Fatima Al Talib. The campaign, 'Welcome a visitor, send back a friend', was an institutional campaign for the Ministry of Tourism, Government of India, to influence the members of Parliament on the social, cultural and economic impact of tourism on society. We saw the campaign work in strange ways. With a bold, typographical layout, and simple, stylized sketches by Mickey Patel, the art director, the campaign became the talk of the town. For me it was an eye-opener.

ASP had exposed me to a new vocabulary of drawings and sketches, something I had seen with Samir Sarkar at Clarion in Calcutta. ASP introduced me to AMUL, Bisleri, Limca and the lot, through an intense period of training in Bombay. Advertising was opening new vistas in consumerism, and between these three cities one could feel the winds of David Ogilvy and Marshall McLuhan blow across the Indian subcontinent, creating the likes of Sylvester Da Cunha, Frank Simoes, Kersi Katrak, Bal Mundkar, Eustace Fernandes, Mohammad Khan, Syeda Imam, Arshad Farooqi, Shyam Benegal and Saeed Mirza. The advertising world of Bombay was suddenly as important, if not more exciting, than Calcutta. Delhi was more laid back, with nothing to prove except how arty you could be, and Jog was the king at that, a larger-than-life godfather who felt challenged by Bombay and therefore despised it. 'Morons' was his favourite term, and he used it freely, even for those he loved. Today one can safely say, without losing an account, that clients are usually all 'morons' of the highest order.

Jog never had a table or a chair. He worked out of a well-appointed drawing room, designed by Shona Ray, and was my early exposure to contemporary interiors. Shona was an aunt of Geeti's, and she was indeed extremely creative and opened a new vocabulary of art, craft and textiles in utilitarian ways. There was a new aesthetic renaissance taking place, and she was a forerunner in the field. Finally, one could see good Indian taste emerging after two decades of independence. Pupul Jayakar and Kamaladevi Chattopadhyay were giving a new meaning to the warp and weft of our culture. Great institutions like the HHEC, Cottage Industries Emporium and ITDC were coming up. There was a national space being created in the world of tourism and design in Delhi, and Jog had positioned himself firmly in the midst of it. It was a period when many down-to-earth movements were spearheaded, one being Fabindia by John Bissel. He created a working model which gave opportunity to the likes of Riten Mozumdar, Ratna Fabri and probably many others.

There were minds like Mulk Raj Anand, Khushwant Singh, Joseph Allen Stein, Ebrahim Alkazi, Charles and Ratna Fabri, Ramesh and Raj Thapar and Romila Thapar, who set a tone for the exploration of what the new India needed to be. It was here that the global minds from Aligarh were mingling with those from Delhi, and one could see a huge relevance in their thought process—minds like Dr Moonis Raza, the founder of Jawaharlal Nehru University. A rational approach to humanism and society that stood head and shoulders above our neighbour Pakistan, which had lost the plot to their own petty, divisive politics.

I was a fortunate learner mentored by so many people, exposed to so many happenings and touched by diverse minds. I was happiest being humble, having come from the enriching world of Calcutta. Jog was very partisan to Bengalis and would any day speak in Bengali rather than English, though he looked every bit an Englishman. He was partial to me for a few reasons: first, my being married to a Bengali; second being Tahir's food and last, because of my being my father's son. I was not of any other value, I realized, to any cause or purpose. I was still in a training phase, which, I suppose, I will remain in all my life.

But to come back to Bombay. My sojourn with Aderbad had made me love this new city and a new lot of people—Bombay and its Parsis. When I came to Bombay in 1970, we stayed with Keko and Khurshid Gandhi at their grand Parsi home, Kekee Manzil, standing tall overlooking the Arabian Sea at Bandra Bandstand. Their son Adil was a friend from my Calcutta days, running an art gallery called Chemould and their Framing Shop on Park Street. Parsis were a breed apart, and the fact that I was in Air India, *maro* (my) Jahangir's airline, hired by maro Bobby Kooka and working with maro Jal Cowasji was enough of a passport to be part of their world.

The Parsis had unusual traits and were known for keeping their things well, particularly cars. Even their homes nursed nostalgia. Bobby Kooka kept his mother's room the way she had left it when she passed away, till he died. There was Adi Dubash, who slept with his 8-litre Bentley, which lay open under his bed in a building I used to visit to meet Chidananda Dasgupta, Aparna Sen's father and film critic. His landlord was a Parsi gentleman who read *Time* magazine cover to cover, and there was always a few years' backlog. One day we heard a scream. 'Kennedy shot, Kennedy shot dead!' This was five years after the incident had happened!

As I write this, I feel like the Parsi gentleman hearing the news that Tata has bought Air India! Delighted yet finding it hard to believe.

In the vicinity were the Jeevan Jyot apartments, overlooking the coastline of Cumballa Hill. Here lived a friend of mine, Francis Wasciarg, with whom I have been associated for decades on many projects. We ran a shop together in Delhi's Khan Market, the Kotwara-Neemrana Shop, and directed an opera in French, *Le Fakir de Benares.* It was at his flat that my painting exhibition was previewed, preceding my show at Pundole Art Gallery in 1972.

Those were the days I had begun to buy art for Air India. Art with a difference. Not what Jal Cowasji, my immediate boss, patronized. I bought Gaitondes, J. Swaminathans, Nasreen Mohammadis, Tyeb Mehtas, Husains, etc. Today this art must be worth more than the entire building.

Jal Cowasji was a portly Parsi famous for owning and driving the Rolls-Royce that once belonged to Lord Brabourne, the governor of Bombay in the early 1930s. Jal introduced me to the old-world charm of Chor Bazaar, where he would stomp in, literally like a maharajah, with every shopkeeper paying obeisance to him. He had a fabulous collection of inkwells and old clocks. By the time I came into his life in 1970, he had sold the Rolls and bought a 1939 burgundy Chevrolet coupe. Those were the days of old cars making their grand appearances down the Malabar and Cumballa Hills on to Marine Drive. He looked fabulous driving down Little Gibbs Road and Chowpatty before gliding into the Air India basement. I was a part of this pageant with my odd fleet of oversized toys. I had left my Jag VII for Jog and acquired a Jaguar Mark V—which I still have and is in good shape—along with an MG TC 1948 and a Lagonda Le Mans replica. I remember once driving down in the MG, from the Air India building to the Taj Mahal hotel, to see an exhibition of paintings. I was passing the Sachivalaya building when suddenly my peon Dhondu, who was in the car with me, screamed, '*Sir, pahya kaisa jaa raha hai* (Sir, there goes the wheel ahead!)' The front wheel of my car had come off and was speeding before me. It hit the pavement with a vendor right in its path, jumped over his head and landed on the roof of a minister's car with a blinking red beacon. My own MG landed with a huge screech and a thud, grazing the road with sparks. Three calamities could have happened that day but were fortunately averted.

I have had many such romantic and memorable escapades with old cars. Another I hold close involved driving ten times in one night between the Air India hangar in Santa Cruz and Malabar Hill in my Jaguar Mark V. I had collected about fifty-odd friends to model for an inflight-service photoshoot, and I had promised to take them back. In those days, there was hardly any traffic, particularly in the dead of the night. I loved driving the Mark V, its wooden dashboard reminiscent of my Isotta. It was a dream to drive, as it purred at a speed of 100 mph. Gliding through the city one felt that the journey was both endless and timeless. I enjoyed this dropping off bit more than the actual shoot. The last to be dropped was my photographer, Jahangir (Jangu) Guzder, a legend in his lifetime. We did a lot of work together over the years. I still remember his parting compliment: 'This car has taken all the fatigue out of me.'

My sense of the old came from a mix of many things. The Parsis, regular visits to Chor Bazaar with my boss Jal Cowasji, my Isotta Fraschini, old books and postcards from Kotwara, and my paintings. I basked in Jal's reflected glory, more often than not agreeing with his taste in things. I was quick on the uptake, which allowed me a lot of free time to dream in this massive city. I discovered many diverse things—from the romance of the past to the heartbreak of the city, from collages to finding expressions in moving images.

Bombay was a textured, multifaceted human experience that sharpened my perceptions as an artist. I had a penchant for open roads and, at the drop of a hat, would drive off to Lucknow. I wanted to feel that the Bombay I was in was not a trap. Driving gave a fillip to my thoughts. I enjoyed music and talking while I drove. My perception became sharper, and I remember many remarkable landmarks on this extensive highway, including magnificent trees. It was sheer poetry. Today, as I create my collages, I draw on this memory piggybank of landscapes. 'Romance of the Open Roads' emerges as a theme looking at the future and the past through front and rear windshields. In those days, air-conditioning in cars was unheard of, and I drove in my soft-top jeep totally unmindful of the heat and dust. Very often I would drive off to Lucknow.

I was too romantic and adventurous for any one person to accept me. I was wild in a different way and would be attracted to people for a variety of reasons. I was a people person, and was very accepting and tolerant of them, finding a great sense of humour in each of them, forgiving them their errors, unless it was mean and egoistical. Geeti was short-tempered, and there was a conflict between her and Tahir. She would lose her cool beyond control, leaving me disbalanced for days. It would be unnerving to absorb myself in work that needed inspired teamwork.

* * *

Air India offered new vistas of opportunities and imagination. It was an unimaginable challenge to arrive in the midst of an organization that was so people-oriented. Civil aviation was nothing but people serving people in the best state of mind, and Air India did this across five continents in the most caring way possible, making passengers feel like kings. From the tangible to the intangible, it was a human engagement for which a training of a different sort was designed and imparted. Though professionally I was in the publicity department, emotionally I was drawn to service. With minimal resources, we made the maximum impact. Being Indian had to be reinvented, and we had to draw upon our legacy of hospitality to make us stand abreast, if not ahead, of the American giants. I had experienced their might and presence in the Indian advertising world and seen a number of brilliant Indian minds dwindle away before them. Fortunately, Boeing was looking at expanding frontiers, and therefore it was in the larger American interest for every country to have their own national carrier. So, our future was secure! Though Air India had been nationalized by then, it still had the stylish elegance of a competitive corporate organization, with J.R.D. Tata and Bobby Kooka at the helm.

Promoting destinations traffic became a major commercial mandate. Willy-nilly I found myself in the world of the 'Red Sherwani Maharajah', a diminutive character bending backwards to please you. He was informing, teasing, entertaining and often being cheeky in matters of current affairs, beyond his domain to meddle with, but not beyond Kooka's! The Maharajah garnered attention at the cost of getting Kooka into endless trouble. With just two billboards he had wrapped up the entire city of Bombay. But there was more to the airline than what met the eye.

That was the time I went to Seattle to do in-flight photography of the first 747 Air India purchased. It was the same Jahangir Guzder, the very talented photographer of his time, who accompanied us with a group of fifteen cabin crew handpicked by Bobby Kooka, including the glamorous Coleen Bhiladwala and Jaqueline Proudfoot. Those were the days when being an air hostess with Air India was no less than being a star in the movies. I had already got an overview of what the Air India corporate needs for advertising were, having had to deal with agencies across the world—from the UK, USA and Europe to the Middle East and Far East.

At that moment, a unified campaign on the new, customized 747— with its exquisite upper deck lounge, the Rajasthani costumes of its special hostesses and the colourful Bandhini saris of the other girls—had to be photographed beautifully and sent across the system for publicity. I often didn't agree with their aesthetics. We had to create point of sales, cutouts and a 747 brochure, along with so many other details for in-flight use, and for our offices and lounges. It was all about 'INDIA CALLING'. Air India was truly India's calling card to the West, and I wanted to be true to it in every detail possible. It took us almost a month to photograph the entire gamut of in-flight services, since the engine was also being tuned simultaneously, which could only be done when the wind blew in a particular direction. Often, the photography would come to a stop due of the vibrations passing through the fuselage.

This gave me ample time to explore Boeing and its people. We were no ordinary clients and got VIP treatment everywhere we went. It was during this time that I got a budget to make a half-hour film on the 747. It was to be a seminal film presenting new-age technology in an old-world way, true to the ethos of India and to the way I was slowly moving to project our national airline. I wanted to feature all the services I was shooting in moving images at our offices in Rome, Paris, London and New York. The culture of India and the modernity of our cabin crew. *To Serve Is to Love*: this was to be the film, and I got Zafar Hai, an eminent and a meticulous film-maker, to direct it. The film got Zafar his bride—*To Serve Is to Love* made Coleen Bhiladwala into Coleen Hai. Merchant Ivory, the well-known international film producer of Indian origin, was brought in as the line producer for the international aspect of the production. The film remains a visual treat. Through the language of moving images, I found a romance around our national airline which I felt could take us places. It was no less than the concept of the Maharajah.

A couple of years ago, on an Air India flight to Udaipur, I was most saddened to see the armrest of my seat taped down to conceal that it was broken. Within minutes of taxiing for take-off, we had to turn around as one of the doors was not locking. It is indeed very disheartening to see that the Indian public sector could not rise up to meet the challenges faced by growing economies in a rapidly changing world. I recently finished a seven-year tenure as a member of the Prasar Bharati board, the body under which both Doordarshan and All India Radio exist, and saw at close quarters how much harm limited, closed and insecure minds can do to a nation. While I am all praise for people, I am equally impatient with narrow-mindedness.

* * *

My time with Air India brought me closer to the people of Maharashtra. I began to observe Bombay more closely—the people, their lives, their habitat, their culture. I grew to love their language and their theatre. One day, while I was parked outside a *mochi's bhakra* (shoemaker's tiny wooden stall) at Opera House, waiting for my mechanic to return with the part of my car he had gone in search of, I got deeply involved in watching the cobbler stripping and shaving leather with a *raapi* (a sharp instrument to shear hide) as he created a pair of Kolhapuri chappals. It took over two hours for my mechanic to return. How those two hours flew by, I cannot describe, but in that time, I had thought of many things one could create with the cobbler's talent and the medium of leather. On an impulse, I asked him if he could make leather seats for my Jaguar Mark V. He sized me up and smiled, implying that he thought I was joking or that he wanted to say nothing was impossible. I liked his attitude and asked him if he would like to work for me and gave him my address.

I got back to office that Monday and was told that I was in charge of putting up an aviation pavilion at Asia 72 for Air India, Indian Airlines and DGCA. Asia 72 was the biggest international expo held in Pragati

Maidan, Delhi, designed by architect Raj Rewal, to celebrate twenty-five years of Indian independence. The pavilion was conceptualized by Jolly Barua, a very talented designer whom I had always admired. The slides we had shot of the in-flight service at Seattle were projected on the wall through a Kodak Carousel, which was the in thing those days. Dr Karan Singh, the then minister for tourism and civil aviation, came to inaugurate the pavilion.

Just as I was embarking for Delhi, the doorbell rang and lo and behold—whom do I find at the doorstep! Shri Bharat Waghchawre, the cobbler I had met at Opera House! He had sold his *bhakra* and taken up my offer to join me seriously. I was totally unprepared to face this challenge at that time. I had no ideas, no designs, no raw material and, above all, no space to fit him anywhere, except on my little balcony overlooking the Arabian Sea!

Both these relationships lasted several decades, in fact till the end of their lives—with Bharat the cobbler, and with Jolly Barua the graphic designer. Their contribution to my creativity is immeasurable. Jolly opened my mind to a new, simple style of graphic design and a few years later designed the graphics and posters for my films *Gaman* and *Anjuman*. He gave a sense of simple poignancy to the designs. Looking back, this was the beginning of a long design journey. Each breath is a repetition of moments. Of moments you create or those that are created for you. Design applies to both these moments. You see things as repetition of each other. I was waking up to design as an expression of a psyche, a purpose. It needed a lot of us to make this a reality. Jolly had good taste in textiles and other expressions of Indian craftsmanship, free of feudal or colonial dominance. From this association evolved a Gandhian sense of aesthetics, verging on spartan purity, as became evident in our way of living. At home I adopted the concept of a *chatai* (straw mat) as floor coverings on which one could be barefoot, and discovered the elegance of wearing a *mundu* (lungi) from Kerala with Kolhapuri chappals.

Meanwhile, Bharat began to cobble up some bags to justify his presence. I asked my friend, Ashrafa Sattar, extremely dexterous with her hands, to help. Between the two of us we created a successful collection of bags for women, under the brand 'Craftsmen of India'. They slowly became every stylish woman's possession, and still remain a collector's item. For twenty-odd years, Bharat and I created these beautiful shoulder bags, so sensitively crafted that they could make any woman look stunning! In New York, I discovered Tandy Leather, a miracle for my tiny enterprise. Founded in 1919, Tandy Leather created all possible tools and implements to work with leather. Bharat and I also discovered a suede which was smooth on one side, the patina of which became better with use. My journey with Bharat was extremely stimulating, except he would not teach anyone his art, and his only son refused to learn. He moved with me wherever I went and finally settled in my house in Mandar Society in Juhu, where I still live. Bharat is no more, and very few samples of his work survive. Looking back, I should not have lost track of this work in leather.

The rise of Air India continued with Bobby Kooka and went on till the time of Nari Dastur, who was the Air India regional director for Europe. Nari took over from Kooka and remained true to the legacy. I had by then moved from publicity to tourism and managed to convince Nari to give me independent charge of a new section altogether—Congresses and Conventions—to promote India as a venue for international meetings. While people vied for foreign postings, I never wanted to leave Indian shores. For me, building my airline was building my nation. I would often go to New York and return by the next flight after the meeting!

The concept of Congresses and Conventions was a fabulous one and we all worked hard to kick it off. Bidding for it was a virgin field in the late 1970s. We needed active and precise promotion and marketing. I got a film made by Malvika and Tejbir Singh to promote India as a venue and created an exhaustive brochure spelling out the facilities offered in each city and region. Then I took special training as a professional conference organizer. It opened another new world and helped me define a strategy to address the Indian situation. The Congresses and Conventions division in Air India would assist an Indian delegate going abroad to attend an international conference to bid for India as the next venue. Once the bid was successful, the office bearers of the Indian chapter would help in organizing the event and facilitating travel to India.

Statistical data at the Union of International Associations in Brussels indicated that 90 per cent of these meetings were held between April and October, with most attended by under 600 people. I realized that we did not have a venue for those months to create an all-year conference season in India. I came up with an idea: Why not Kashmir? I put it down in the form of a page-long note to Nari Dastur, who immediately responded by writing on it 'Go Full Steam Ahead!' He was a step ahead of Kooka in terms of adventurism, and I realized that I was reporting to the right boss!

I wrote a concept note to J.R.D. Tata, and he immediately asked for a page to be drafted for Sheikh Mohammad Abdullah, the then CM of Jammu and Kashmir. This was a much bigger challenge. I had to present an idea that the chief minister could not turn down. I was reminded of a story Abba Jaan had told me about his maternal grandfather, Mir Muzaffar Ali Aseer, a great poet and the ustad of Ameer Minai. He began his career as an apprentice in the court of Nawab Wajid Ali Shah. One day, the nawab, in a fit of anger, dismissed his favourite minister, Raja Jai Lal. This act weighed heavily on the nawab's mind, and he went into serious depression. He summoned his *wazir-e-qalamdaan* (minister of documentation) and gave him the challenge of addressing this crisis. He said, 'Give me a letter addressed to the raja, which, while it should not appear that the nawab is calling him, should make him feel that he will be more than welcome if he came back to court!' The wazir, in turn, briefed his apprentices and soon returned with a draft. The nawab read the draft and exclaimed loudly, 'Who has written this?' Fear gripped the wazir, and he begged pardon, passing the blame on to a junior. The nawab thundered, 'Call him right away!' And in walked the young Mir Muzaffar Ali Aseer! 'Hand over your charge to him,' the nawab commanded the wazir. I was named after Mir Muzaffar Ali Aseer, and I began the draft with this inspiration!

I spelt out four reasons why being the centre for international conferences would change the face of the valley. Firstly, Srinagar would go down in the history of whichever specialization's conference took place there; every significant discovery or development in that field would be associated with Srinagar. Second, a conference delegate spends three times as much as a normal tourist. Third, a conference tourist provides scope for varied skill development and employment potential. And finally, this conference centre, with a capacity of 600 delegates, would fill every hotel in the valley.

The letter went to Sheikh Abdullah duly signed by J.R.D. Tata.

In less than a week, Sheikh Sahab arrived in Bombay, and a meeting was scheduled at the Raj Bhavan, presided by the then governor L.K. Jha. It was really like going full steam ahead. Air India became the nodal body for the project. We were given the freedom to choose our team of designers with no compulsion to use any government-accredited local architects.

But it was design that concerned and bothered me. Design was the larger purpose of doing something and the inner purpose of doing it well, and in detail. I wanted to realize my dream beautifully and perfectly. I did not want any unprofessional ugliness to creep into this project. This intent was very clear to all concerned. I wanted the right consultants from day one. I was a member of the ICCA (International Congresses and Conventions Association), of which all airlines, tourism boards of different countries and consultants in the field were also members. I brought John Moreu to visit the valley to guide me as to which would be the right agency to do a feasibility report. After a week-long look around, he suggested Donald Hellstedt of Stockholm Convention Bureau, who had worked on similar destinations and projects of this scale.

To cut the red tape, Air India picked up the tab. And in came Donald. We repeated a similar orientation for him, except in more detail, and in a month came his crisp and clear report as a brief to the architect. Donald and I had bonded well during this period, and he unofficially mentioned that if a feature film could be made on the valley integrating the beauty of its four seasons, the valley would be sold forever worldwide.

The Kashmir project was now my responsibility and concern, not just to see through but to see through with a visionary eye, with taste and in detail. Srinagar was the single biggest concern in my head. I did not want an inch of cement and concrete to scar its beauty for all time to come. My prayers were answered when I met Joseph Allen Stein in Delhi. Each moment spent with him was spent in celebration of nature, discussing its wonders and marvels. I could see our dream becoming a reality: a 600-seater conference centre, with a 250-room hotel. Fortunately, he had Sheikh Sahab's ear, so I had to only battle the ugliness of taste of the Hotel Corporation of India, a wholly owned subsidiary of Air India. Though the Tatas were interested at that time in having the Taj take over this hotel, I was determined to get the project for Air India. By then the fate was sealed, and the project was divided between the Government of J&K owning and building the conference centre—which came to be known as the Sher-e-Kashmir International Conference Centre—and Air India owning and building the hotel—which came to be known as Centaur Lake View Hotel.

My job done, I stepped back. My takeaway from all this was a love for the valley and my friendship with Joseph Allen Stein, who, till his last breath, kept thinking of how to bring peace to the valley. Whenever I visit the India International Centre, I am reminded of Stein and his corner in the lounge from where he must have seen the building unfold. He gave me two books which I will always treasure. One is *Small is Beautiful* by E.F. Schumacher and the other, Le Corbusier's *Creation Is a Patient Search*.

A new chapter had opened. I began to look at spaces as feelings.

I was born amid the spectacular architecture of Lucknow, but it was only through Stein that I felt its dynamic relevance to societies and cultures. I had begun to realize the importance of an architect who could take your dream beyond you. If I were to do anything besides what I have been doing, it would have been architecture. Architects shape spaces and lives, and make dreams come true. They create harmony between people and nature, with spaces that display a reverence to both. I feel buildings should bow to man, and a beautiful exemplar of this aesthetic was Hasan Fathy, better known as the architect of the poor. Architecture should celebrate the unity of man, a complete negation of feudal, imperial and mercantile cultures. I realized an architect was the most godly person on earth, given that she was required to think how to leave a long-lasting mark on His earth! Empowering people's aesthetics is a challenge for the future in which both films and architecture will continue to play a role.

* * *

I spent eleven years with Air India, years that saw me through tumultuous and trying times. My marriage to Geeti ended. I married Subhashini, a Communist leader whose parents, Colonel Prem Sahgal and Captain Lakshmi Sahgal, were from the Indian National Army. I had to leave my flat and move to an Air India colony in Kalina. In 1974, my second son, Shaad, was born. Soon after, we bought a place in an Air India society in Juhu—Mandar Society. Mandar was in the heart of the film world.

There was a lot of interest in my Isotta Fraschini, which was still parked in Lucknow. Not a day went by without someone ringing me up regarding the car, which I had nursed over the years and restored just enough for it be road-ready once more. There was global interest in the car, and agents were on the prowl to get it from me. It reminded me of some sort of a thriller with more than one person playing cat and mouse with me. Since then, I have developed a sad distaste for situations where the car has been pulled away from where it rightfully and historically belongs. In fact, it was a *Gaman*-like situation, with a scheme in place to take the car from me, a fact I came to know of later. There was a car dealer, Ian McRoberts, representing two big parties from England who were both trying to lay their hands on my Isotta. He was playing one against the other for a better offer.

One of the potential buyers was Peter Grant, manager of the band Led Zeppelin, who then ruled the music world. It had become fashionable for celebrities in the West to own rare old cars with a lineage. Ian offered me a very small price of Rs 50,000 for the Isotta and never allowed any other dealer to come near me, telling everyone that the deal had already been struck, though I had not yet agreed. He took the car and parked it at Walsingham Mansions, where he stayed with the old English lady who owned the mansion. He was very charming and posed as a grandnephew of one Mr McRobert, who had built the McRobert Hospital in Kanpur, where my mother-in-law worked. He also met my father and wooed him surreptitiously, exploiting the Scottish Edinburgh connect, all the while pretending he never wanted me to sell the car and that he believed it was important that it stayed with the raja of Kotwara.

I was not selling the car but was going through tough times myself and felt sad to see the car deteriorate. One day I succumbed to the pain of seeing it decay before my eyes and fell right into Ian's trap. I asked him to get the car restored for me. Ian got a beautiful job done, and I realized that I could never afford to pay him back for the restoration expense. All through this game, Ian pretended to be a great friend, keeping close tabs on my life, waiting for the right moment to strike, and one day it came. I was in a great crisis. Ian appeared with a draft of Rs 50,000, saying that all my troubles would now be over and I would owe him nothing. The Isotta was no more mine.

The Isotta was the last car to leave the shores of India before they were declared heritage products and all export was banned. I would dream that the car was still with me. I became so obsessed that I started to track it down, to buy it back somehow. I came to know that Peter Grant was no longer the owner and that the car was parked somewhere in a garage in England. Each time I went to England, I would go to dealers like Coys of Kensington, in search of the Isotta, knowing full well I would never be able to buy it back.

These cars were an era, a time, a people. The taluqdars of Awadh had had some of the finest automobiles, and they were the first to let them go after the downfall in their fortunes. I remember my father talking about his friend Raja Saadat Ali Khan of Nanpara and his fleet of cars, among which was a nickel-plated Rolls-Royce. It made heads turn as Raja Nanpara went for long walks with his dogs and the car purred behind him, following, in case the raja got tired and needed a ride. Another coveted car from his fleet was the open Hispano Suiza, which he took for drives into the Terai forests. All those cars ended up languishing with *kabaris*.

There was the Mahmoodabad Minerva, lost in the aftermath of the abolition of zamindari. History was playing a cruel trick, and the nouveau collectors were having a field day! All this induced a lot of sadness within me. Fortunately, Subhashini, who was the new fire in my life, made me see the romance of the 'Left'. A romance that was there in both poetry and real life. She resonated with my father as a comrade on the path. This also imparted a sense of meaninglessness to these symbols of ostentatious living. Isotta or no Isotta, it made no difference. These ideas were paving the way for my first film, *Gaman*.

Gaman had been taking root in my mind for a while. It was a slow process. There was more than what met the eye in the rambling metropolis that Bombay was, which sucked in millions of people each day into its fold. People with dreams and people with no dreams, all entered into the trap of the gargoyles of the Victoria Terminus, never to return to their far-off homes in rural India. They would never be able to free themselves from the shackles of the slavery of a mundane job. This human helplessness tugged at my heartstrings, even though I sat perched on the eighteenth floor of the Air India building, in the comfort of the ultramodern infrastructure of the Bombay of that time. In India, we always live in contradiction and have learnt the fine art of balancing. We say one thing while we mean another. We set double standards—one for you, one for me. A series of questions emerged wherever I went, in whatever I did. In poetry and folklore, in music, which resonated with the angst and conflicts born out of these imbalances. Would such conflicts not interfere with one's creativity?

Chapter 7

Gaman

'Jin se ham chhut gaye ab vo jahañ kaise haiñ,
Shaakh-e-gul kaisi hai, khushbu ke makañ kaise haiñ.'
('From whom I am parted, how are those worlds?
How is the bough that bears the rose, how is the
fragrance that dwells within?')

— Rahi Masoom Raza

Making a film in Bombay is easier said than done. Bollywood, to me, was
going hugely wrong. I was comparing it with the Calcutta of Ray and my
dream of what Awadh was all about. There were so many genres of cinema
coexisting in Bombay itself, yet I could not find them.

Working in Air India, I was perceiving India from a very different
perspective, entirely opposite of what Bollywood was projecting. There
were many Indias in the eyes of the world. I was often confused as to
which India I belonged to. I had to find my own India. An India of my
own making. An India I was made up of. An India I saw myself in and
wanted to share . . . Being in Bombay I was confronted with a larger India,
and there was no easy way to immerse myself into it.

In no way did I wish to take the short route to success. Bollywood had
literary giants, some of whom were reduced to pygmies in the hands of
the cut-throat financial minds which have survived all changes in financial

97

systems, all the way to the present corporatizing of cinema. Now it has gone into the hands of global players. Was I learning anything from Air India to add value to my entry into cinema in Bombay? I was an emotional fool and, carried away by the Isotta logo, the big IF, I called my production house Integrated Films. IF! Sounded good, looked great, but way off the mark in the harsh, callous world of the metropolis. I felt lost and helpless.

The only pockets of intense realism and truth seemed to be in the cinema of Bengal and Kerala. Nothing globally luring was coming out of Bollywood at the time. Only people like Shyam Benegal or Saeed Mirza were among the few that were dimly lit in the firmament. The Film and Television Institute of India (FTII) in Pune was, however, producing technicians who were providing a strong backbone to Indian cinema. They were not instantly accepted but slowly began to make a difference.

My first film, *Gaman*, was with a complete FTII team. Production design then was in its nascent form, though lyrics and music were very evolved and alluring. Poets had congregated to Bombay, adding a romantic charm to life, and they will be celebrated for all time to come—Sahir Ludhianvi, Majrooh Sultanpuri, Kaifi Azmi, along with composers like Jaidev, Khaiyyam, Naushad, O.P. Nayyar, S.D. Burman and others. They vied with each other to take credit for the success of a song. Was it the melody or the lyrics? This went on then as it does now.

As a child I had grown up on Bollywood films, of which today I recall very few. Dilip Kumar was indeed a giant in his own right. His refinement and passion for his art knew no bounds. His command over the nuances of the language was the jewel that adorned the silver screen, each word preserved in the cloud of the Internet for all time to come as colossal milestones of acting. A decade and a half later, I went to cast him as Ali Shah Chak, the father of Yusuf, the hero of my film *Zooni*, about the Kashmiri poet Habba Khatoon. We had the most amazing afternoon and talked of everything under the sun, except what I had come for. We ate and laughed, and as I was leaving, he said, 'The biggest problem is that I am living in a cage called "Dilip Kumar". Whenever somebody narrates a role, I fall asleep, like a lion in the cage!' He guffawed as he saw me off. 'Did I tell you that Mehboob Sahab had approached me for the hero's role of Yusuf Shah, with Nargis as Habba Khatoon, forty years back!' But he gladly became a member of my foundation TVFTNUP, a society to promote film-making in the state of Uttar Pradesh.

Today there is no one to touch those dizzying heights that only Dilip Kumar could reach, with eloquent silence or while catching his breath between syllables. He would breathe love into his co-stars, life into a stone statue. He understood poetry and became poetry. He knew that ghazal was talking to the beloved. It was for this that India saluted him. Yet everything in Bollywood is designed for low audience intelligence, impatience and little recall value in which songs and the hero's action play the biggest part. Action was often replete with elements one had seen before. But the stars who could add newness and credibility to violence and action, a new dimension to anger, began to grow. Amitabh Bachchan fitted perfectly into this mould. A new world was being invented by the people of the pen, the likes of Salim–Javed, to take Bollywood to new heights. I stood on this threshold testing my destiny.

I have only made stories based on what I have been through or seen. It was in 1976 that I began working on *Gaman* in earnest. The Sanskrit word 'gaman' means 'going'. It was a question I was posing to people who controlled the destinies of the helpless and dispossessed. Somewhere there was a convergence of the crafts at the grassroots level, and if only I could blend global design sensibility in craft and integrate it into films as the West had been doing, I believed it would change the course of cinema in India. It started off as a poem of the dispossessed, and still remains a poem of the dispossessed—a saga of helplessness as the men leave their families and their homes, thereby destroying the social and cultural fabric of their environment themselves.

In my village there was a Ghulam Hasan in every household and a Khairun Nissa that he left behind. There were endearing shades to both these characters—the helplessness of their predicament that drew you into their story, driving you to take the resolve that you would make society empathize with them. But the problems in their lives had no solutions in sight. My *Gaman* was the story of one such young man from Uttar Pradesh, Ghulam Hasan, who has little education, less land and no opportunities in his village, and has, therefore, to migrate to Bombay, leaving behind his old, ailing mother and his new bride, Khairun Nissa. With his departure, the lives of these two women come to a standstill: the present is unbearable and the future uncertain. The only events of any significance are the periodical arrival of letters and money orders from Bombay. Their lives are transformed into long, unending periods of waiting. In an Indian village, a woman or a household without a man loses all identity.

In the city, Ghulam finds refuge with his childhood friend from the village, Lallu Lal Tiwari, who is a taxi driver and a colourful character. He has completely come to terms with the nuances and contradictions of city life. He helps Ghulam first to become a taxi cleaner, then a taxi driver like himself. Lallu is involved with a Maharashtrian girl, Yashodra, and through her family are depicted the problems that Maharashtrians face as a result of the migration onslaught, especially from Uttar Pradesh and Bihar. Lallu's involvement with Yashodra builds up into the final tragedy and crisis of the film.

For me, the city of Bombay at that time was more exciting than anything I had seen. It was that story, of a journey, that I continued to paint. I began to see my collages in brown and khaki craft paper in the context of the larger socio-cultural artistic reality that I had seen in Aligarh and Calcutta. *Gaman* began to emerge: a story about why people left their villages and came to lead hybrid lives in a faceless metropolis.

It was a way of perceiving the reality of both town and country that I would be geared to feel when I stepped out of Aligarh. It was the resonance of the poetry of Aligarh that made me see social reality so differently. 'Seene Mein Jalan' (Burning in the Heart) became an expression of this anguish in moving images. It was Aligarh that would make this windblown questioning son of an 'educated villager' a poet of cinema. I remember watching *Gaman* with my father after it was completed and listening to this particular song he had gnashed his teeth, saying, 'This can lead to a bloody revolution.'

The medium of *Gaman* came to me from Calcutta, its inspiration from Aligarh, its soul from the heart of Awadh and its palette from my paintings. I had sketched out each frame of the film as it took shape in my mind. I was fascinated by khaki, from the paper of my paintings to the khaki-clad taxi driver protagonist of my film. Symbolically, as a migrant taxi driver he had no identity left except khaki, the colour of *khaak* (dust).

Gaman kept cooking in my mind, far removed from the reality of Bollywood. I was on the eighteenth floor of the cocooned world of global civil aviation, yet I came into daily contact with the harsh truth of commuting in the city. And this was where *Gaman* emerged from, as a powerful story of real-life contradictions—of going to Kotwara for Muharram each year and seeing the rural helplessness seeking ways of redemption from that exploitation. I saw hidden meanings in traditions, symbolism and culture. Yet I realized that a story should be designed and told with utter simplicity. I did not know the language of cinema, though I had been so close to it. I wanted to address it through my own direct engagement with words and images. I started taking pictures of this spectacular city, Bombay, with my dear friend Shivaji Rao II, who was popularly known as Richard Holkar, son of Maharaja Yashwant Rao Holkar of Indore. It was through these photographs that the urban canvas of the film became clear in my mind. I still have the contact sheet prints, as that was the size in which I was going to sketch the film, frame by frame, scene by scene. What was going to come out of it, none of us knew then. Asghar and Subhashini helped with the script, and the dialogues were written by Hriday Lani. The script was submitted to the Film Finance Corporation and rejected. But I persevered hard, revising and reapplying till it was finally accepted.

With *Gaman* in my soul, Bombay for the first time was emerging as a larger-than-life entity. It was a character both ugly and beautiful. It had to be felt by the protagonist to become real. There was the transient way of spanning spaces and people as a taxi driver, with the touching aspect coming from what he'd left behind in the village, like thousands of people in that predicament. There was also the aspect of the local people of Maharashtra facing unemployment, as they were not flexible enough to change as per the need of the hour. And yet, another layer of migration to Dubai was taking place. I knew it all too well, being in Air India. For us, migration and tourism went hand in hand, as markets. This was termed as the Fourth Freedom of the Air, where an aircraft registered with a country would carry citizens back to their own country, in this case India, from anywhere in the world.

What is migration? In scientific terms it is the adding of an external element and thereby the replacement of the original organic element. I saw the emergence of a *Gaman*-like world in Bombay when I moved there in 1971. The influx of people from all over was displacing the original character of the city. The making of a metropolis is the unmaking of a place. Spaces are threatened in layers, year after year, and each year it changes the aesthetics of a cityscape, rendering the earlier out of date. The enormity of this tragedy was rendering people faceless.

Kya koi nayi baat nazar aati hai hammeiṅ?
Aeina hameiṅ dekh ke hairan sa kyuṅ hai?

(Is there something different you see in me?
Why is the mirror so wonderstruck?)

—Shahryar

A question of becoming a stranger to oneself.

Bombay was becoming Mumbai, a strange mirror that reflected our past with a perspective of the future. Bombay was a series of fading mirrors that pulled one each time one saw oneself in them. Most of these mirrors find their way from sacred spaces to the crowded narrow gullies of places like Chor Bazaar. *Gaman* became a journey of changing images in such mirrors. It was the reflection of the dynamics of roadscapes, of a city which never sleeps, in the rear-view mirror of a taxi, in the eyes of a helpless driver. Spaces which are yours and not yours. A river which can never afford to stop. The protagonist of this ceaseless flow is a throbbing heart, beating, yet lifeless like a stone. Seeking reasons. Finding none.

Dil hai to dharakne ka bahana koi dhoondhe.
Pathhar ki tarah behiss-o-bejaan sa kyun hai?
(If there is a heart inside, it needs reasons to throb.
Why is it senseless, motionless like a stone?)

—Shahryar

This was me in 1970s Bombay, a city which I saw from atop the Air India building. From where for hours on end I watched the yellow-roofed taxis crawl like ants. I wondered whether under those yellow metal sheet roofs there was a man like me far away from his home. How far was his home was anybody's guess. What he had left behind was beyond anyone's imagination. The feeling was enough of an answer. Was it worthy of a film, I thought to myself. Was this loneliness our inevitable destiny—a wilderness beyond what the eye could see? On the one hand the ocean, and on the other an endless sea of humanity.

Tanhai ki ye kaun si manzil hai rafiqo?
Ta-hadd-e nazar ek bayabaan sa kyuñ hai?
(What is this destination of loneliness my friends?
Till the limit the eyes can see, why such wilderness?)

—Shahryar

But certainly, it was an emotion as deep as the Arabian Sea. It was an emotion in which I saw the fathomless tenderness of a thumri.

Each time my eyes met those of a taxi driver's in the rear-view mirror of a taxi, a truth transpired. I saw beyond what the eyes could see. I felt the piercing gaze of a loved one whom the taxi driver had left behind in his hometown, waiting for him. I saw the helplessness in the eyes of both the taxi driver and his beloved as they pined for each other. Was it still worthy of a film? What was beyond these frozen frames? There were moments of truth and more truths, of humans waiting at red lights on pavements and zebra crossings, on metal bridges across mighty rivers ferrying helpless souls packed in metal cabins. Amid this human exodus were shattered windows of glass allowing the last ray of the setting sun to play its flute on a windblown face.

> *Aaja sañwariya tohe garwa laga luñ*
> *Ras ke bhare tore nayan . . .*
> (Come, my dark beloved [Krishna]
> let me embrace thee,
> your eyes are full of nectar . . .)

It was a lonely journey. Could the loneliness of this phenomenon become a collective journey of a film? I found the words which described the emotional angst of the migrant. When Krishna leaves, do Radha's tears drown Braj? As I thought of this I felt I was near the beginning and the end. Everything was in the minds of these mindless travellers, at times bringing the odd tear when emotions aligned with the sound of the changing train tracks. But the sharp horn of the railway engine wiped it off in an instant as the morning sun rose behind the formidable Western Ghats surrounding Bombay and one was sucked into an endless tunnel. One wonders which side one is on. With the ones on the train or with those they are going to displace? I had become a *ghati* (a term used to describe people living in the region of the Western Ghats) and a *bhaiyya* (a term used to describe people living in the regions of Uttar Pradesh and Bihar) in the same breath. For many years I had been on that train, not knowing the difference between the beginning and the end of these journeys.

And hence 'Gaman', a name given by my friend Asghar to this feeling. Something I had begun to see with my inner eye. But *Gaman* was more than I could hold in one glimpse. It had too many metaphors, both vivid and fading. Khairun Nissa sniffling and wiping her nose with her *chaadar* as she extinguishes a night fire at dawn. Clothes becoming one's second skin, fading and becoming sensuous, looking nostalgic and inviting with their faint textures under the smoke-filled thatched roof turning black with soot. The soot and the smoke were not different to the soot and the smoke from the speeding train—one went towards darkness and gloom and the other towards the light at the end of the tunnel.

> *Aap ki yaad aati rahi raat bhar*
> *Gham ki lau thartharati rahi raat bhar . . .*
> (Your memories kept me up all night long
> The flame of sorrow kept flickering all night long . . .)
>   —Makhdoom Mohiuddin

One was static in a moving environment and the other moving in a static world.

> *Dard ke chaand dil meiñ utarte rahe*
> *Chandni muskurati rahi raat bhar . . .*
> (The moons of sorrow kept descending into the heart
> The moonlight was aglow all night long . . .)
>   —Makhdoom Mohiuddin

Gaman was yet to be born. And was it worthy of being a film? I asked myself again. I didn't care any more. I had begun to unearth the city called Bombay.

When I look back, I cannot see anyone else but Farouque Shaikh play the role of Ghulam. There were choices and suggestions. Dr Rahi Masoom Raza was, in a way, our bridge and guide to Bollywood. I visited him often since his stepson, Nadeem, was my cameraman. Rahi Sahab, though, wanted no part in this project, and pretended to be busy and out of reach. We were all in awe of him and admired him as a poet. He suggested that there was a new boy on the horizon whom I should consider. He said he was like him, tall and with a deep voice, and that he hailed from Uttar Pradesh and was now getting noticed in the Bombay film world. I knew who he was talking about. I had known him well while working in Calcutta. We often went to the same parties, and he would sometimes give me a lift in his Herald car, maybe because he'd borrowed my tape recorder and wanted to return the gesture. So I went on in search of this man who would carry my *Gaman* in his eyes. I went to a studio in Dadar with my bound script. The script was then handed over to the actor. He said he had given it to his poet father to read. I thought maybe it might touch a poet's heart. After a whole month of up-and-down to these soulless studios he made a very genuine confession. 'Muzaffar, I have just developed an image of a fighter and huge amounts of monies change hands in my name. So I cannot take this risk.' This was the legendary Amitabh Bachchan in 1977. I bowed away gracefully, accepting humiliation and my 'seene meiñ jalan', but his decision made great sense from Amitabh's point of view.

Parikshit Sahni, son of the great Balraj Sahni and my neighbour in Juhu, came up as the next option. But while I was still exploring, I saw Farouque Shaikh in *Garam Hawa*, a seminal film by M.S. Sathyu, and immediately, the die was cast! As it happened, he turned out to be a flight purser with Air India. But just as I was going to meet him, a huge tragedy befell him. He had gone to the Bombay airport to receive his father from Dubai, but unfortunately he had died on the flight. This tragedy was not easy to come to terms with. He accepted the role in spite of his sad predicament. He was truly a method actor and never once stepped out of his role. He remained a *ghulam* (slave) of his circumstances all through the film.

> Kotwara, the village where *Gaman* was shot appears so tranquil, peaceful and unperturbed on the surface that one could never imagine the tremendous wrenching apart and the dismembering of the social setup which is actually taking place below the surface. Very sad, but also very typical of rural India. It is a world going asunder.
> —Farouque Shaikh, 14 February 1979

Farouque got into the role of Ghulam Hasan so organically that when Rahi Sahab, the Byron of Aligarh, saw *Gaman*, he wrote a touching review in *Shama* magazine that he too, like the protagonist Ghulam Hasan, was driving his pen's taxi in Bombay!

Then began the search for Ghulam's wife, Khairun Nissa. There was no one better than Smita Patil to express the yearning through her eyes. She read the script and said, 'But where am I?' I said, 'You are everywhere . . .' She smiled and looked down, just the way she looks in the poster.

I had found my poster girl! Very graciously she consented, and was an inspiration for the entire film and its different stages—poetry, music, etc. She was the muse.

> When you start with the house tomorrow just try to get away from your past. I know it is the strongest thread, but try. It is difficult to detach yourself from it but if you evolve out of it everything will emerge. I know how much this film means to you.
>
> —Smita Patil, 20 February 1978

I made an attempt to combine the feeling of traditional UP culture and of the alienation of an uprooted individual in a city through a Bhairavi (a morning raga) which comes from the very heart of this village; a *noha* (a poetic elegy) of Muharram; a *banra* (wedding song); two very powerful ghazals by Shahryar; and a ghazal by the late Makhdoom Mohiuddin which was used to combine the parallel tragedies of the village and the city.

The music-making process was extremely romantic, and working with Shahryaar and Jaidev was a delight. I was deeply moved by Jaidev's compositions in *Hum Dono*, which had given a new panache and abandon to Dev Anand, who I felt looked great singing such touching melodies.

> *Abhi na jao chordh kar ke dil abhi bhara nahiñ . . .*
> (Don't leave me and go away, my heart still yearns for you . . .)

I was clear about one thing which often never happened in Bollywood: getting the music composed for ghazals that had already been written. I was sure of all the lyrics and some traditional compositions for *Gaman*. Bollywood always worked backwards by getting the lyrics written on tunes given by the music director. There were always conflicts between the two, as to what contributed to the success of the song: the melody or the words. Since the identifiable element was always music, the music director had the upper hand. To enter into a film project with ready lyrics was the first handicap. My own conviction is that poetry is the mother of the art, and a poet's work is not to be tampered with.

But why would a Bollywood composer share my conviction? As expected, when I went to meet Jaidev he was a little suspicious about the end product. The art film world was not held in great esteem by anyone even slightly commercial. Jaidev lived at Churchgate, in a one-room apartment next to the Eros cinema, where *Gaman* would premiere one day. It was hardly a ten-minute walk from my Air India office at Nariman Point.

The same conflict played out, but I was convinced about Shahryar, and that was a fait accompli. Those days, Jaidev was already in clash mode with the likes of Sahir, so he took the soft-spoken Shahryar, who was protected from the Bollywood breeze by staying at my home. Jaidev's other big hang-up was that these were all background songs. That no hero or heroine was going to lip-sync to them. Jaidev too took a while to come to terms with the idea that they were all background songs! The first song to be created was 'Seene Meiñ Jalan'.

I always insisted on having enough options, and after a little explanation arrived at the first of one of the most memorable songs in Bollywood. We used the soulful, haunting voice of Suresh Wadkar, which made the ghazal evergreen and unforgettable. We introduced Hariharan for the second ghazal, 'Ajeeb Saneha Mujhpar Guzar Gaya Yaaro' (A Strange Incident Came to Pass, My Friend). The third ghazal was a village woman's response to the predicament of being left behind, waiting for her husband, often a large part of their lives: 'Aap Ki Yaad Aati Rahi Raat Bhar' (Your Memories Kept Me up All Night), written by Makhdoom Mohiuddin, a progressive revolutionary poet from Hyderabad. It was about the taxi driver Ghulam, static in a moving environment and his wife, Khairun, moving about in a static environment defined by rhythm and absence of rhythm. Smita loved this song, and when she hummed it she got into the soul of Khairun Nissa. We chose the husky, grainy voice of Chhaya Ganguli. The composition had such sensitive objectives to achieve that it went through severe birth pangs. Here Smita emoted the feelings of the ghazal so deeply that she rose above the need to lip-sync, which would have distorted the simplicity of the character whose predicament the ghazal was meant to underline.

Then came the theme song of *Gaman*: a Bhairavi I heard in the voice of Hira Devi Misra from the Banaras gharana, who lived in Bombay in the hope that one day she would gain recognition like many others of her ilk. I was very keen to use this thumri, which describes Braj with Krishna away from his beloved Radhika. A soulful connect with the theme of

Gaman—migration! Jaidev did an outstanding job of using this thumri in Hira Devi's voice. Hira Devi also sang the banra, '*Bare dhoom gajar se ayo re nausha ameeroñ ka* (With such pomp and grandeur comes my rich groom) . . .' Chhaya also recited a *soz* (elegy) for Smita as her character is dyeing her clothes black for the advent of Muharram, a commemoration that often drew people back to their roots. Armed with these six tracks and my scenes, I was fully prepared to shoot.

Kotwara was to be the location of the village—a treatment that would set the emotional feel and the visual grammar of the film. We started step by step, most organically.

Karbala and communism were the symbols of freedom and signified raising one's voice for the oppressed. And in all my films black and red have always played a symbolic role. Muharram adds pain to the soul. I made Jaidev compose a *noha* before anything else to set the tone, '*Ro ro ke poonchtiñ haiñ Bano Shah-e-zamañ se* (Bano weeps and asks of Husain, the king of the world) . . .' In fact, this reminds me of Kotwara every time I hear it. Muharram has been an emotional trigger in most of my work, and I feel connected with the soil and blessed.

My father gave the opening shot, typing as he always did with two fingers on his Corona typewriter. He typed:

KOTWARA, District Kheri, U.P.

These words were imprinted on my mind with their sound forever. The click of the keys and the sound of a bird. They meant everything. An inspiration. A lifelong challenge. A responsibility, an obligation to be picked up in greater seriousness more than a decade later when my film *Zooni* was to come to a grinding halt due to rising insurgency in the Kashmir Valley.

While shooting *Gaman* I was protected from the onslaught of Bollywood attitudes. I didn't need to suck up to anyone to work with dignity. I am fortunate that my bosses at Air India took a positive view of my film-making. And I had the goodwill of the general staff. When Bobby Kooka was asked why Muzaffar was making a film, he said with diabolical Parsi humour, '*Pela sala ne puch* (Ask him).' But he was also always quick to put those questioners in their place, saying that I was doing this on my earned leaves. 'When we can have people play cricket, why not a film-maker?' After Bobby and Nari Dastur, I felt very vulnerable. I had done half of *Umrao Jaan* when I parted ways with a corporation that I sincerely loved and was reasonably recompensed for my efforts. I am happy that I left when I did. I had entered into a full-on fight with the system, of both the film world and the social world, and it was tough for a person like me to survive without resources. Just marketing and advertising acumen, with some film-making talent, was not enough.

I had a circle of film-maker friends who recognized the predicament of fighter film-makers like ourselves. We called ourselves MUKT—Marketing Union of Kinematograph Technicians—with Basu Bhattacharya as the main functionary, along with Basu Chatterji, Saeed Mirza and others. However, we could not make a dent in the system. I did design the letterhead, though hardly any letters were ever written on it. The meetings were fiery and full of gas till all of us lost confidence in each other and realized that each of us had to fight our own battles, with our own ideology and dreams. The situation has not changed since. The big fish is the only fish. There was the real-life fighter whose destiny was a lifelong fight, and then there was the reel-life fighter for whom the entire industry was always crusading.

This instinct to go against the tide was in my genes and came effortlessly. Till today, it is this strong factor that helps one withstand adversity. *Gaman* had given me a strong resolve and critical acclaim. It was released at the Eros cinema with a premiere in aid of the Taxi Drivers' Union. It was quite spectacular to see passengers and drivers flock to see the film side by side! A queue of taxis from Bombay Central to Churchgate lined up for the event. We presented the oldest driver from UP, Musharraf Ali, a memento of a watch on the occasion. He was chosen by the Taxi Drivers' Union. There was a telegram from Lucknow waiting at the theatre as I walked in. I ripped open the telegram and read, 'EFFORT THY DUTY, REWARD NOT THY CONCERN, ABBA JAAN.' This was a reference to the Gita. He had written knowing full well that I had mortgaged Kotwara House, 10 Qaiserbagh, as co-lateral with the Film Finance Corporation.

Gaman grew like normal, everyday life; it happened as we just drove around, stopped and began shooting. Most of the actors were real-life people—the villagers and taxi drivers. Even their names were real and their roles were all dubbed by stalwarts like Naseeruddin Shah, Om Puri, Kulbhushan Kharbanda. My home in Mandar Society in Raut Lane, Juhu, was a taxi adda, with the same taxi drivers who were parked outside the

Hare Krishna Mandir sprawled in the drawing room downstairs. Everyone in the entire Raut Lane, inhabited by the Rauts, became actors, and the village became a location for the film. I had a powerful Maharashtrian cast from the stage, from where I picked up Nana Patekar. Other luminaries were Arun Joglekar, Arvind and Sulabha Deshpande. The role Arvind was playing was an interesting one—a one-time taxi driver who used to drive a big Ford car and who can't adjust to the deluge of smaller Fiat vehicles and gives up. He kept looking for petrol to one day consign the Arabian Sea to flames. This he does at the end with the last can of petrol Ghulam Hasan gives him once he decides to leave the city, after his mentor Lallu Lal Tiwari's murder. The latter was played by Jalal Agha. During the making of *Gaman*, Jalal had given us a very ferocious bitch, an interesting mix between a Doberman and a German Shepherd. She did keep a lot of walk-ins away, particularly those looking for breaks in films.

Mandar had become the first and easiest port of call for the 'strugglers'. Each taxi driver and every villager in Juhu knew where I lived and were quick to guide visitors to this most accessible fool at the fringes of Bollywood. We had bought this bungalow in an Air India society in 1975 just after Shaad was born. Shaad grew up in a crazy milieu of footpath-*chhap* (street-smart) film-making, pampered by all the unit and actors who kept coming into our lives. From Nana Patekar to Buntu Dhawan to Anupam Kher—who was introduced by me in *Aagaman*—to Rekha and many others! Shaad loved peeping into the camera as it called claps. Traditionally, the person peeping would have to distribute sweets. Shaad loved the fact that as my son he could get away without sweets but received chocolates instead! He breathed, ate and slept films, often under a Steinbeck editing table in the luxury of plush dubbing studios. He would joke and make fun of my assistants, most of whom were from Kerala, where you find such filmi fiends. Suresh Pattali and Hasan Kutty were his two favourites. Suresh, after each dialogue was dubbed, would say in a strange voice, 'Zing okay.' And we never knew whether it was a statement or a question. By the end of the film, people started referring to him as Zing Okay.

The shooting of *Gaman* in Kotwara was one of the most memorable winters of my life. *Gaman* was not even remotely like a conventional Bollywood production. It was a very down-to-earth way of making a film. It was technically no less, but the production was very basic. No artiste was paid more than Rs 5000, and we all travelled second-class sleeper on trains. That was the real India from which today we have moved far away.

We had coined the phrase 'Lungi Shoot' among ourselves. It meant a camera—a big one in those days, an Arriflex with a big magazine—popping out of the *lungi* used to hide it in crowded places! We were all travelling from Bombay to Lucknow by Lucknow Express for the first schedule. I am not sure whether we all had reservations, but we somehow managed to get two enclosures into which we all shoved ourselves. The camera was wrapped in a blue lungi, handy for the shoot. Farouque dressed as Ghulam Hasan, taking his first journey from the village to the city, sat near a window where there were two seats opposite each other with an open passage through them. Facing him was the camera attendant, Gyan, from Merchant Ivory Productions. There were about fifteen of us, including my direction team comprising Buntu Dhawan and Ketan Mehta, and the camera team of Nadeem Khan and his assistant, Rajan Kothari, who later shot my film *Aagaman* and many others' documentaries.

The train was to leave at 10.30 a.m. It was already 10.20 a.m., and we had just settled down after a general 'Lungi Shoot' on the platform. Everyone was in the compartment except Smita Patil. We were counting every second, but there was no sign of her. We would be lost if she didn't turn up. Each minute was like an eternity as I scanned each person as he or she entered the vision block. Hundreds of thousands of unidentifiable images kept flowing in and out, but there was no sign of Smita. My gaze was like a fixed block with a tele lens, slowly shifting focus as people walked forward. We lost all hope that she would appear. Suddenly, I felt that we had begun to track forward, finally burying the last chance of Smita joining. The train jolted forward with a sharp whistle. Maybe she was not comfortable with this kind of adventure with us for this film. But then she could have told us that, each time I went to her top-floor apartment on Forjett Hill Road and had espresso coffee made lovingly by her mother! I thought I had made myself very clear. Or had Shafi Patel, our production controller, goofed up? Maybe that was why he was not to be seen at the station.

Fortunately, my thoughts were moving faster than the train, and before we had done a couple of yards I saw a girl waving frantically. That was Smita's best friend, Varsha Bhosle, Asha Bhosle's daughter, and hidden behind her was an unrecognizable Smita Patil in her blue jeans.

We somehow managed to pull the two in and settled them securely among the rest of the gang. Each person occupied themselves with something to do on this extremely long twenty-four-hour journey! Varsha was a loud and compulsive laugher who could not be stopped once she got going. Little things kept happening, and they were all rewarded with her fits of laughter. The entire compartment shook, and suddenly a stone hit the window where Farouque sat huddled with his migrant baggage. Luckily, the window was shut, but it got completely shattered. I thought of something, making adversity into an advantage, and pushed up the pane gently. The laughter which had suddenly stopped restarted as if this was a big joke!

Many strange things happened on the journey. The train pulled to a halt at a station, but there was another train parked between ours and the platform. The only way to get to the platform was through that train. A poor migrant was travelling with his family huddled in a corner near the main door of our compartment. He was very kind and decided to get down to buy samosas for his family. He got into the other train to access the platform. We could see him buying the samosas as his family waited. But just as he got into the adjacent train to jump back to our train, that train started moving. Varsha was quick enough to leap and pull the chain, not realizing that our train was already static and the poor man with the samosas was in the other moving train. It was indeed a moment to burst into laughter, but it was too tragic to do so.

Luckily, the man appeared a while later, although we did not ask how. The train crossed a bridge . . .

Khairun: *Kal itte khann kahañ huyyo* (Tomorrow at this time where will you be)?
Ghulam: *Pata nahiñ* (I don't know).
Khairun: *Ab raahe deo . . . mat jao* (Now forget it, don't go).

The sun was setting as the train entered Bhusaval. We readied the camera to shoot the last rays of sunset through the shattered glass on Farouque's face. This was poetry of a kind, possibly *Gaman's* first shot even before the *mahurat* (auspicious start)! For me, it was the most iconic shot of the film.

A *chaneywaala* (one who sells boiled gram) appeared out of the blue. He passed Farouque offering chana, who hesitated for a moment and then decided to buy a *dauna* (disposable container made of leaves). For that moment of hesitation Hriday Lani wrote a line for Ghulam's mother, '*Ab roti khaye lo, roti pe gussai ke ka huyye* (Why don't you eat? Why take out your anger on your food)?'

Ghulam lifts the shattered window against the sunset. Windblown, drinking tea in a mud cup and then throwing it out . . .

Farouque had imbibed the pain of separation . . . the words of the Bhairavi. '*Ras ke bhare tore nain* (Your tear-filled eyes) . . .' a refrain etched deep into his eyes.

Pain is the best medium for art and you cannot create it inorganically. Film is an organic art camouflaged in inorganic commercial trappings, where star tantrums distort that vulnerable process of finding unseen symbolism in the seen world. It is a way beyond the acrobatics of the camera and gymnastics of the human form. It is a very evolved form of spiritual art, and you have to be a seeker to even reach its threshold! I realized this, day in and day out. The same truth revealed in different forms. And this had been my journey to Rumi and Khusrau. Once again, this truth touched me when I was making my short film *Rumi in the Land of Khusrau*, for the Ministry of External Affairs. It was shown extensively all over the world, including at our embassy in Washington, DC, when we were present. That was the time when Lalit Mansingh was our ambassador to the United States and Navtej Sarna was the minister in charge of press, information and culture (he later became ambassador).

It is my humble prayer that this book will be read by everyone passionate about art, craft, design, cinema and, above all, the love and concern for the human race.

Each person I have worked with in each of these areas has opened a new world of creativity inside me, and this is what adds value to our lives, both mine and theirs. I am certain they feel the same way. These seemingly invisible vibrations are the source of beauty in this otherwise power-hungry system, which is constantly turning black into white through its hold on all channels of communication.

Working with each cameraperson has been a powerful relationship. The deep sharing of a subject, an ethos, and understanding of the grammar of light and expression, shade and movement. The cinematographer has to instantly imbibe your vision and own the moment. And you have to allow that space and accept it as part of your design expression. This is a continuous quick-paced relationship into which no one else can enter. And having done that, it is the director's job to ensure that every other element, primarily performances, is rightly sculpted into these moments called 'shots'.

My first such equation was with Nadeem Khan, a fresh graduate from FTII, Pune, an institute which gave a new lease of life to the national film world and saved the country from the unprofessionalism of Bollywood. These students were looked down upon as *jholewaalas* (a term referring generally to a new breed of intellectual film-makers, usually from the FTII). In fact, it was these jholewaalas who changed the terms of reference for national cinema and also created a new star system which still rules. Nadeem was assistant to K.K. Mahajan, another FTII product, possibly the first of the lot.

Gaman was a fully sketched out, stylized and an extremely low-budget film. It was the energy, enthusiasm and innovation that made up for the lack of funds. The entire film's budget was less than half a day's worth of any Bollywood film today! We had to create moving images that would be engraved on the mind, like an etching. Each texture speaking more than what meets the eye. This was what Sergei Eisenstein meant by 'impact value on the audience'. Those were the days of creating a 'montage', an assembly/juxtaposition of shots that would make a visual statement with a definitive meaning. *Battleship Potemkin* was like a textbook for all of us. This was what led to our concept of certain sequences in *Gaman*; though some of the sequences took the help of a ghazal or song, many tried on their own to take the narrative forward. Ghulam Hasan driving a Maharashtrian couple in his taxi; the image of a newly-wed Khairun; the Maharashtrian Lezim processions; a red-flag march with its own imagery of a *matam* (Muharram). Tradition and change coming together, giving a new meaning to urban reality.

Gaman was all about displacement, and continues to be about displacement. Its meaning had become larger than life, a prophetic truth that continues to live beyond its time. 'Gaman' is also a Japanese term of Zen Buddhist origin which means 'enduring the seemingly unbearable with patience and dignity'. The word is generally translated as 'perseverance', 'patience' or 'tolerance', 'stoic endurance'. Forty years on, nothing has changed. The plight of the migrant is the same even today as he finds his way back home to no work.

Looking back after forty years, the experience of making *Gaman* was gratifying. It received a positive response and won several awards, such as the Silver Peacock at the Seventh International Film Festival held at Vigyan Bhawan in Delhi (this was the first international competitive film festival in the third world). *Gaman* received the citation at the 29th National Film Festival as the 'most sensitive treatment of migration from rural areas to urban centres'. The film was also acclaimed in Bollywood, winning Filmfare's Best Director Award. Jaidev got the Best Music Award at the 29th National Film Festival, and Chhaya Ganguly won the Best Female Playback Singer.

My soul was nursed on the poetry of Faiz Ahmad Faiz. I was given the gift of all of Faiz's soulful similes and masterful metaphors which give meaning to the angst of today's world. All the time *Gaman* was being made, I was shadowed by the spirit of Faiz.

It was in the thick of the Bombay monsoon. I stood looking out of a multistorey building at a storm building up on the turbulent Arabian Sea. It was kept a secret by Subhashini as to why we were there. Suddenly there was turbulence within as both lifts arrived packed with guests. The first to enter was Faiz Ahmad Faiz.

> Muzaffar Ali's film *Gaman* is a poem in visuals. It's muted eloquence, it's tragic lyricism, it's deeply perceptive, it's sensitively conceived and truthfully captured the slice of reality around us; the beauty and the heartbreak of the human situation in town and country make it a sheer delight, a veritable tour de force . . .
>   —Faiz Ahmad Faiz, Bombay, 26 August 1978

There was no award or recognition that could come anywhere near this.

Chapter 8

Umrao Jaan

'Kab mili thhi kahañ bichhri thhi hameiñ yaad nahiñ,
Zindagi tujhko bas ik khaaab meiñ dekha hamneiñ.'
('When we met, where we parted ways, I don't recall,
O life I saw you in just my dreams.')

—Shahryar

With *Gaman* I had cast my lot with the film fraternity. But I had yet not given up Air India. The idea of the next step was weighing on my mind. It had to do with Awadh, of that I was sure. Subhash K. Jain, a businessman and film financer who had taken the distribution rights of *Gaman* for S.K. Jain & Sons, was a positive force in my life. He was bold and different. Sadly, he died in a car accident soon after *Umrao Jaan* was completed. I lost a strong friend in the film world. It made me realize how important it was to have someone who believed in you in Bollywood, which was like a battlefield with different camps pitched against each other. I was fortunate that I entered this battlefield with *Gaman*, otherwise I would have drowned in the 'struggle' with no godfather. Subhashini was both creative and tough, and could boldly ward off a lot of problems that I would face as a film-maker. S.K. Jain lived and worked out of Delhi, and had been financing many films in Bollywood. He was powerful enough to keep any camp at bay, and I give him full credit for protecting me in a world of wolves.

Umrao Jaan was a classic novel penned by Mirza Mohammad Hadi Ruswa in 1905. Ruswa, who had a degree in engineering from the Engineering Institute in Roorkee, was a colourful character of his time. He was born in Lucknow in 1857, a year of great turmoil for India. He died in Hyderabad on the same day I was born, 21 October, fifteen years before me, in 1931.

Based on Ruswa's novel about a courtesan of Lucknow, my film is about Umrao Jaan Ada, a courtesan in the mid-nineteenth century, the zenith of Awadhi culture and the moment when its disintegration began. The story was originally narrated by Umrao to Mirza Hadi Ruswa, who documented it as a memorable and classic novel. Woven into the tapestry of the light and shade of the period's refined decadence is the life of a woman, who, in spite of being the victim of the most adverse circumstances, evolves into a highly cultured human being, an accomplished poet in her own right.

As a young girl, Umrao was abducted from her simple and happy home in Faizabad and sold to a *tawaif*, a courtesan, Khanum Jaan. Khanum's *kotha* is a bewitching fairyland for the innocent girl, who is trained there in music, dance and letters. She grows into a beautiful woman who takes the city by storm with her poetry, singing and dance.

Umrao had a wide range of exciting experiences. Her sustained relationship with the witty Gowher Mirza; her first intense love affair with the shy and sensitive Nawab Sultan; her attempts to free herself from bondage in Lucknow; her escapade with Faiz Ali, the notorious dacoit; and many more amazing incidents. Each person she encounters leaves an imprint on her life and contributes to her understanding of her times. Each character is not only a colourful person but also a type, a representative of a social class.

It is through her poetry, her ghazals, that these experiences and encounters are transcended and translated into expressions of beauty.

While I was shooting *Gaman* in Kotwara, Smita Patil had said, 'If you feel so much about this place, why don't you do something here?' I had no answer. A few years later I made *Umrao Jaan*, set around 1857. This brought me face to face with the beauty of the feminine world of the courtesan of that time, as well as with the poetry and music, the dance and the repartee, the textiles, the craft and the way of life. I had seen these visions in my dreams and in the feminine, feudal world of my mother. The dream became more vivid, more meaningful, soulful. A journey in celluloid which would embody the frail and ephemeral beauty of Awadh.

Here again, Calcutta and Aligarh stood steadfastly behind me to unearth the beauty from the lost debris. The search reminded me of the famous 'loot' which began from the time of Clive of India after the Battle of Plassey in 1757 and went on till we gained independence. Every manuscript, every painting, every textile and every valuable artefact found its way into the homes and museums in England. But Umrao Jaan was that intangible illusion that was left behind. They could never 'loot' her, and she continued to live on in people's minds and to rule their hearts.

To make this journey from history to celluloid was as tedious as it was beautiful. The journey was so vast and expansive that everything I had seen and felt came into full play. My mother had passed when I was only twenty, leaving behind millions of unfulfilled dreams within me. I had seen the way a woman felt life, lived a culture, saw the highs and lows of Independence, and the savagery that accompanied Partition when her only brother migrated to Karachi goaded by his ambitious wife looking for a better future for their children. Her beautiful Lucknow was left bereft of love and laughter. I saw the magnificence of a culture through her eyes, through her sadness for what was lost and what we were left with. She was fond of clothes and making clothes was a constant activity in our home. This Lucknow had lived in the courtyard of Kotwara House, 10 Qaiserbagh. Each year, with the onset of winter, clothes would be sunned in its courtyard. Each time a new array of shades or textures emerged, the gentle fragrance of *itr* (oil-based perfume) wafted through the air, filling my entire being.

Umrao Jaan was being born in a painter's mind, a convergence of nostalgia and a dream for the future. This was a future where people would rise to protect the intangible beauty of the past—a past of which they had no reference.

Umrao Jaan was a very attractive subject. But it was a tough call, as we would have to assemble the jigsaw puzzle of a strewn culture, much of it lost to time. On the surface, it seemed like nothing remained of the fabled culture of the courtesans of mid-nineteenth-century Awadh. Several films on courtesans had already been made in Bollywood, but with little or no sense of any moorings of a time or place.

The Bombay film music milieu was very strong. It had romantic film directors, the best of poets, the most talented music directors and musicians, voices that would touch the soul and draw upon a background

Raja S. Sajid Husain of Kotwara, soon after his return from Edinburgh (1937)

Muzaffar Ali's parents, Raja S. Sajid Husain and Rani Kaniz Hyder of Kotwara (1942)

Muzaffar Ali (1948)

Raja S. Sajid Husain of Kotwara in Scotland with his 1929 Isotta Fraschini (1931)

Muzaffar Ali with his father's 1929 Isotta Fraschini in Delhi (1969)

Muzaffar Ali with Pandit Jawaharlal Nehru, prime minister of India, his half-sister, Kenize Murad, and father, Raja S. Sajid Husain of Kotwara, in Delhi (1962)

Muzaffar Ali with Indira Gandhi and his half-sister, Kenize Murad, in Delhi (1962)

Muzaffar Ali with cinematographer Nadeem Khan at the Kotwara ancestral mosque during the shooting of *Gaman* (1977)

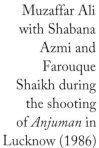

Muzaffar Ali with Shabana Azmi and Farouque Shaikh during the shooting of *Anjuman* in Lucknow (1986)

Shabana Azmi during the shoot of *Anjuman*; photo by Muzaffar Ali

Muzaffar Ali with Hanna Fischer, director of Vancouver International Film Festival, in Vancouver (1987)

Dimple Kapadia
on location in
Kashmir during the
shoot of *Zooni*

Muzaffar Ali with
his father, Raja S.
Sajid Husain of
Kotwara, music
director Khaiyyam,
vocalist Asha
Bhosle and his son,
Shaad Ali, during
the recording
of *Zooni* in
Mumbai (1989)

Farouque Shaikh
and Rekha in
Muzaffar Ali's
Umrao Jaan (1981)

Pernia Qureshi and Imran Abbas with Muzaffar Ali during the shoot
of *Jaanisaar* at La Martiniere College in Lucknow (2013)

Muzaffar Ali during the shoot of *Jaanisaar* in Kotwara (2013)

Muzaffar Ali during the shooting of *Gaman* in Bombay; photo by Mahendra Sinh (1977)

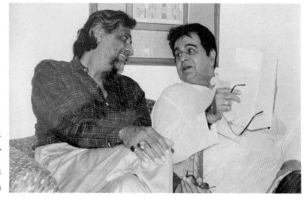

Muzaffar Ali with actor Dilip Kumar in Mumbai (1998)

Muzaffar Ali with
Mary McFadden
and wife Meera
Ali in New
York (1998)

Muzaffar Ali with Abida Parveen
during the rehearsals for the first
annual Jahan-e-Khusrau World
Sufi Music Festival (2001)

Muzaffar Ali with painter M.F. Husain and Rashida
Siddiqui at a restaurant in Delhi (1998)

Muzaffar Ali with his
wife, Meera Ali, in
Kotwara (1994)

Muzaffar Ali receiving the Silver Peacock award at the 7th International
Film Festival in Delhi from L.K. Advani, then minister of I&B, with
film-makers Ousmane Sembène, Mrinal Sen and Ben Barka

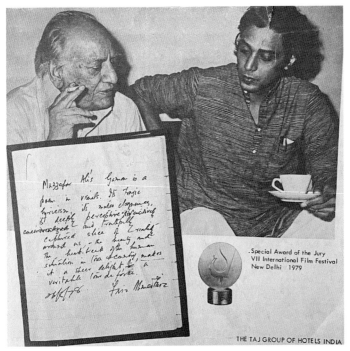

.Special Award of the Jury
VII International Film Festival
New Delhi 1979

THE TAJ GROUP OF HOTELS INDIA

Muzaffar Ali with poet Faiz Ahmad Faiz at a special screening of *Gaman* in Mumbai (1979)

A shot from the TV series *Jaan-e-Aalam* by Muzaffar Ali, with Muzaffar Ali as Nawab Wajid Ali Shah (1986)

A shot from *Jaan-e-Aalam* (1986)

Muzaffar Ali with N.D. Tiwari during the MP election where both
were candidates from Naini Tal (1999)

Muzaffar Ali with Lady Ranu Mukherji and Dr Geeti Sen at the opening of his exhibition at the Academy of Fine Arts in Calcutta (1968)

Muzaffar Ali working on his paintings for his first exhibition of collages in Mumbai (1972)

Muzaffar Ali's
Jahan-e-Khusrau
World Sufi
Music Festival,
Delhi (2005)

House of Kotwara
couture (2021)

An oil-on-canvas
painting by
Muzaffar Ali, from
his RUMI series

Muzaffar Ali with his
horse Shams

Muzaffar Ali in Kotwara (1998)

Muzaffar Ali in Kashmir
while building his set for
Zooni (1989)

Muzaffar Ali
with Prince
Charles and
L.M. Singhvi at
Parliament House
Library, New
Delhi (2003)

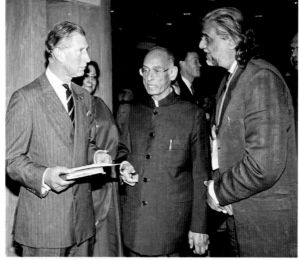

Muzaffar Ali driving from Lucknow to Bombay (1980)

of classic and folk traditions. For *Umrao Jaan*, my dream was to create a musical track that would not fall in the Bollywood mould of a 'courtesan of Lucknow'. It was not easy to do so, mainly because I did not know what to do. But I definitely knew what not to do. I therefore took the path I knew best. That of poetry. I chose to work with Shahryar, using a lyrical trajectory of his existing verse through which I could see an Umrao evolve before me. Having worked with Jaidev in *Gaman*, I saw how unconventional he was capable of being. He could create a style of music that could stand out and give an identity to a film.

Thus, my first choice of music composer for *Umrao Jaan* was Jaidev. We chose the lyrics. We even chose the singer. It was to be Madhurani. Then we arrived at the compositions. I even liked them. But something was missing. Were they too old-world and laid-back? They did not seem to hit out and arrest your imagination. We all heard them again and again on a cassette player. There was a lull. We were not certain about what we had achieved. Jaidev was completely inflexible, unwilling to change. Finally, I took it upon myself to tell him that we would have to part ways. I was heartbroken for days and decided to wait a while before looking for another composer.

Those days Shahryar was staying with me at my home in Juhu.

I was reminded of a song which I loved and repeatedly played on my gramophone in Lucknow. It was in Talat Mahmood's voice, from the film *Footpath*: 'Shaam-e-Gham Ki Qasam'. My father found the ghazal too morose. The composer was Khayyam. The name was discussed endlessly within my closed group. I was to take the final decision. By now I had realized that while certain decisions seemed collective, they started and ended with me to ensure that my vision was not adulterated. And so the choice was Khaiyyam (by then he had changed the spelling of his name, with the success of *Kabhie Kabhie*).

Khaiyyam Sahab was known to be difficult and arrogant, but I was good at taming wild horses with my mild demeanour and steel-like resolve, which would gently come into play whenever required. Mrs Khaiyyam was sharp to apprehend that moment and, with an animated expression, would forewarn her husband. Subhashini and I came to understand this unspoken language, which she would use to communicate to Khaiyyam Sahab if I did not like a melody he had created, or to me if he did not like some particular lyrics. She would hold her breath before he came out with a tune. This whole ritual was preceded by a perfectly well-brewed cup of coffee. She would then sit with a book in her hands to give rhythm to the melody that Khaiyyam Sahab would sing or just hum.

He called me Raja Sahab and indeed made me feel like one, though not a patch on my father. Khaiyyam Sahab was nothing like what he was known to be. He knew these sessions were adding tremendous value to the film. Here there was no flattery, only genuine praise and constructive criticism. It would take many sittings before a melody was ready to be shared with a singer. The decision to take Ashaji was a collective call. Khaiyyam Sahab knew that it was only Asha, the inimitable, invincible Asha, who could take the *naghma* (melodic song) as we called them, to great heights.

The rehearsal for each *naghma* was a fifteen-day process, after which it would be presented to Ashaji. She insisted on calling me 'Mr Handsome'. She might have felt that I was one of those who'd come to the film world to act and had lost his way to becoming a film-maker. There were lots of such people around, as Bollywood was all about being a star. She would call Subhashini 'Sundariji' (the beautiful one). Ashaji wanted to read the novel before attempting the songs. When a song was finally presented to her, she would sit like a humble child, head bowed low, listening to Khaiyyam Sahab, repeating the lyrics in an almost inaudible voice. She was breathing in the melody like it was some sort of *amrit* (elixir). She would then write a big 'Om' and below that the lyrics in her own handwriting. That page remained with her till the day of recording, till it became history. The recording itself was a ritual, a ceremony, where art would meet technology. Where humour, patience and perseverance would embrace each other to become a naghma, a melody to haunt one forever. Each song would be ingrained in our minds, haunting us till the next one took its place, then the next one, and so on. Recording the music was like diving into an ocean of romantic thought, and it certainly was the most captivating process of film-making.

Our sound recordist was Mr Sharma of the Bombay Film Laboratories in Dadar. He was a grand old man who would sail in around eleven o'clock after each music section had been balanced. We had more or less the same arrangers. It was Anil Mohile for *Umrao Jaan* and Daniels for the other films I did with Khaiyyam. The legendary Sultan Khan played the sarangi, Zarine Daruwala was on the sarod and Ashok Sharma on the sitar—musicians who created some of the most memorable background pieces. They all used to come separately as the music grew on them; they started travelling together, sharing their excitement on the journey to the studio. The ritual of breaking a coconut before every new song was accompanied by boxes of sweets. Hari Prasad Chaurasia played the flute and Pandit Shiv Kumar Sharma played the santoor. Then, one day, I heard they had become music directors, known as the Shiv–Hari duo who'd worked on Yash Chopra's *Silsila*. Shahryar wrote a few lyrics for them. But Bollywood did not suit his temperament.

There was another person in my musical world at that time: Ustad Ghulam Mustafa Khan of the Badaun Sahaswan gharana. I had made him my formal ustad. This did not go well with Khaiyyam Sahab and became a bit of an ego issue. But I was certain that I wanted Khan Sahab with me for some of the classical compositions. I finally had him compose and sing two songs, the *raagmala* and *jhoola*. The ustad who sang the raagmala on screen was the legendary Baiju Bawra (Bharat Bhushan himself). Khan Sahab was indeed one of the most innovative composers and singers of his time. He used to come home regularly and pray for my welfare. He called me 'Bhaiyya' like everyone around me did, and he would say that one day there will be a film factory around me. To some extent, my home in Juhu is carrying on this tradition, with Shaad making films. My elder son, Murad, is an actor, having worked with Yash Chopra, Mani Kaul and Shyam Benegal. But somehow, like me, Murad could not take Bollywood for long.

The art of screenwriting is in essence the science of holding attention. Pure and simple, it's about gaining a grip on the audience's mind, not for a moment letting go. It is the art of holding back and not saying it. The art of the set-up, the science of turning points. Then the crisis, the payoff and the final resolution. I was too full of passion to do it myself. Shama Zaidi was my screenplay writer, and the dialogues were written by Javed Siddiqui, who had a way with words. He was the grandson of Maulana Shaukat Ali of the Khilafat movement, who had performed my father's first *nikah* (Muslim wedding) to the Ottoman princess Selma Hanimsultan. Javed Siddiqui had a subtle sense of humour and a strong sense of mystery.

Once, my wife Meera and I went to meet Harvey Kietal in New York for the casting of Shams, the mentor of Jalaluddin Rumi, the thirteenth-century Sufi mystic poet, for my biopic of Rumi. As a parting shot, he said, 'There are three things that make a film.' We stood with bated breath to hear what these pearls of wisdom were going to be. 'Script, script and script!' He grinned. We left with a present, a book by Robert Bly, *The Soul Is Here for Its Own Joy*. It is part of a very selective collection of spiritual books in English, particularly on Sufism.

As the graphs of screenplay and music evolution converged, we were ready to approach the person who would be Umrao in flesh and blood. I wanted Umrao to be what she did become with time. A woman who epitomized the soul of Amiran, the essence of an ethos. She symbolized the helplessness of a girl in a callous world, a girl who would rise with each fall till she realized that no feat was impossible to accomplish as long as one had determination. She had to have a story on her face that Umrao was going to unfold.

Finding Umrao was not easy. It was her aura and faith in my dream that would make her a legend. I still wonder what the chemistry was that created this immortal legend. This was when I began to understand the power of belief. And it is this sacred belief that lives on in the world of art.

One day, I saw a pair of eyes looking at me from a magazine at a barber's shop at the Taj Mahal hotel. I picked up the magazine. It was Umrao Jaan's gaze. It sent shockwaves through me. The same eyes struck a chord with Subhashini, and then, grudgingly, with Shama, who was always difficult to please. They struck the same chord with Khaiyyam, Shahryar and, finally, with S.K. Jain, who jumped at the idea as the face behind that gaze was commercially viable! Rekha!

Why Subhashini and I took Shama with us to meet Rekha, I have no idea. Shama could never sell anything to anyone. She expected people to probe themselves and pick up the idea. Unexpectedly, something exactly like that happened. Shama's screenplay sense was diametrically opposite to the conventional Bollywood approach of first praising the artist sky-high, then the role and then the set-up. But Rekha was very intelligent. The less we said, the more she saw in it!

We came out of the meeting shell-shocked at what the three of us had achieved. Subhashini was our future interface with Rekha for most things.

Rekha was different. She was beautiful within. She came from a lineage where time stands still and makes people into gods. I was approaching a potential goddess. Urdu was a journey I did not want to rush her through. It was going to come to Rekha most organically, through everyone who was going to meet her. Somebody asked Javed Akhtar about Aishwarya Rai's sense of Urdu in the *Umrao Jaan* remake. He quipped in his typical way,

'*Khuda jab husn deta hai toh Urdu aa hi jaati hai* (When God blesses you with beauty, Urdu comes naturally).' I believed in Daagh who had said,

> *Nahiñ khel ai Daagh yaroñ se keh do,*
> *Ki aati hai Urdu zubaañ aate aate.*
> (It's not child's play, tell your friends, O Daagh,
> The language of Urdu comes slowly, very slowly.)

Urdu to me is not about using rhetoric to impress the audience, but touching souls with your breath. You breathe Urdu. It resonates within. It stays with you forever.

I always maintained that Urdu opens to you through a galaxy of teachers, each bringing their own nuances to its sounds and expressions. These exposures have to be designed based on your own experience of a culture, besides just remembering the lines. I could see Urdu being born through Umrao's smiles and tears. Each poem by Umrao opened a new window into Rekha's soul. Each couplet tore her apart like a ship in a storm. Each melody rocked her like no kathak step had ever done. Each metaphor enabled her to find new expressions to live up to the emotional lyricism. There were no words left to describe what people saw in Umrao's character.

Rekha, knowingly and unknowingly, was wading into waters that would run deep enough to drown anyone else. I was afraid that if the spell broke it would become crass and commonplace. But she went through it gracefully, true to a culture completely alien to her. She could have stopped at any moment and asked why we were doing this. But I never heard the word 'why'. Or even the word 'money'.

Rekha went the extra mile in doing a scene. She was performing for an internal force coming from within. Whatever she spoke or wore came from her soul, and there is no actor who can come close to this. Everyone wants to become a Rekha as in *Umrao Jaan*, but they have no idea what it takes to reach that level of surrender. This was a taste of living Sufism for me and for audiences for all time to come. I have felt many actors, singers and dancers come close to that while working, as long as they didn't touch the element of worldliness and commerce.

Rekha took her role to another level, working with Shaukat Kaifi as Khanum Jaan, who opened the world of the courtesan to Dina Pathak as

Bua Husaini, who gave Umrao motherly comfort. The veteran Jagirdar, as Maulvi Sahab, opened a spiritual world for her, while Naseeruddin Shah, as Gowher Mirza, introduced her to the sensual world. Farouque Shaikh was her world of love and Raj Babbar, as dacoit Faiz Ali, her spirit of adventure. But finally, it was her own mother in the film, Farrukh Jafar, who helped her tear into the hearts of people like a searing hot blade, leaving them scarred forever.

For each technician, Umrao scaled new heights of perfection. Parveen Bhat, my cameraman, never came out of the trance as he sat on the stool of the trolley, tracking back and forth. My editor, Bhagwati Prasad, was a hardcore Gujarati who had never spoken to Rekha in his life. But with each cut he would exclaim discreetly, '*Phadi nakis* (Ripped apart)!' Interpret it the way you want. And finally, my sound recordist, B.K. Chaturvedi, who went with me on the endless train journey to Madras to dub her voice at the Balaji Sound Studio. This, for me, was quintessential to creating *Umrao Jaan*.

At that time Rekha was known to dub an entire film in six hours, and she was confident that she would be able to wrap up our dubbing within one shift. But it took a good ten days to breathe emotion, Lucknow and Umrao into each frame.

Rekha came from a lineage of powerful women. Rekha's grandmother, Muthulakshmi Reddy, was born in the late nineteenth century in the princely state of Pudukottai in Tamil Nadu to an academician father, Narayanswami Iyer, and a Devadasi mother. Devadasis were women who were ostensibly 'dedicated' to temple deities and tasked with passing on the baton of the art of dance to the next generation. But in reality they were viewed as 'fallen women', often subjected to sexual exploitation.[*] Fortunately, Muthulakshmi's father gave her the power of education, and the maharaja of Pudukottai funded her study of medicine. She became the first woman to enter Madras Medical College and finally become a surgeon specializing in cancer. She spent her life establishing a cancer hospital and working on the liberation of the Devadasis. After marriage,

---

[*] Treena Orchard, 'Girl, Woman, Lover, Mother: Towards a New Understanding of Child Prostitution among Young Devadasis in Rural Karnataka, India', *Social Science and Medicine*, volume 64, issue 12, 2007, pp. 2379–2390.

she adopted her nephew Gemini Ganesan, Rekha's father. Subhashini and Rekha had an instant 'soul connect'.

I stayed with Subhashini's mother's brother, Govind Swaminathan, at the Harington Mansions on Harrington Road, of which no trace remains today. Rekha would come there to meet the Tamil side of Subhashini's family.

A few years later, I made a documentary on Subhashini's side of the family. It was called *Vadakath: A Therwad in Kerala* (*therwad* means matrilineal family system). This therwad had the most luminous personalities. Subhashini and her mother, Captain Dr Lakshmi Sahgal, of the INA, Mrinalini Sarabhai, Dr Lakshmi's sister, and Mallika Sarabhai, her daughter, and finally, Kuttymalu Amma, founder of the Congress Party in Kerala.

In the midst of this hardcore southern world, *Umrao Jaan* was being born as a Tamilian! This is the amazing beauty of India, the Constitution of which had Ammu Swaminathan as a signatory!

'Umrao . . .' The Moviola spluttered to a start as Bhagwati Bhai began to splice. *'Justuju jiski thhi usko to na paya hamne . . . iss bahane se magar dekh li duniya hamne* (What I came to seek, I never found, yet in this way I saw the world).' This was my editor's kingdom, at the Ramnord Film Laboratories in Worli. Now it is nothing but a shadow of the past. The world came to a slowdown here, where three minutes of a song on screen were stretched to three days, with a ritual invocation to different deities that guided destinies. This was the beauty of Bollywood that unified us all and will continue to do so . . . The films varied but this was the unchanged recipe for anything that moved on screen. Bhagwati Prasad was God's own man. They don't make them purer than him in Bollywood any more. He, however, didn't change to the digital way with time.

This was the India we had deliberated to put into our constitution. And Umrao was a speck in the dust of this timeless journey. Out of this speck of dust that danced in the colourful beam formed images that made the likes of Rekha into goddesses who slowly began to be worshipped. And once you were bit by the bug that snuggly dwelt in the worn-out seat that existed in the darkness of the auditorium, there was no looking back. No one could predict how different this world was going to be. *Umrao Jaan* took baby steps exploring different realms in the audiences' world.

Shaad grew with the film as he watched and felt every bump on the roads leading to the film's locations in Lucknow. Here was a young mind gathering the skill of patience, where a minute would mean a day. While shooting the opening song of the film—'Kahe Ko Biyahe Bides', sung by Jagjit Kaur—Shaad, as Amiran's brother, had to sit in the tableaux with nothing to do but smile off and on, look here and there. I had borrowed an antique *jazim* to spread on the floor on which Shaad sat. Out of boredom and idleness, he started playing with it like a puppy. Slowly, I saw one corner in tatters. He had ripped it apart. I was furious and gave him a slap. He sprang up and went out of the shot. Then, one of my assistants, Krishan Thakur, asked him in his stuttering way, '*Kya hua, Shaad Bhai, kya hua* (What happened, brother Shaad)?' Shaad replied furiously under his breath, '*Main chala gaya hota agar continuity mein na phasa hota* (I would have left by now if I was not stuck in this stupid continuity).'

The making was studded with such moments, and Taqi Hasan was my only continuity companion each day of our shoot. His mother, who died in her twenties, was my mother's closest friend. Every time she saw Taqi, her eyes would well up. She would be smiling in heaven seeing us together all the time. Taqi Hasan made sure everything was there where and when I wanted it. And the people of Lucknow followed suit. This tradition of film-making would never happen again in Lucknow, where nothing was commercial.

Umrao Jaan the book starts with a couplet attributed to her:

Lutf hai kaunsi kahani mein,
Aap beeti kahun ya jag beeti . . .?
(What is more pleasurable to hear,
The story of the world, or the story of my life . . .?)

Every film is a visual journey. Recreating the time and space of a happening; it's an art and a science, it's a method, and it's madness; it is both a learning and teaching process. My art director was Bansi Chandragupt, who had worked so closely with Mr Ray that one often took him for a Bengali. He had a Zen mind, only focusing on spaces where the film would unfold and giving just enough space to the director to move and take his shots. It was a wonderful experience for both of us—for me to see the film scenes through his eyes, and for him to see the film through my eyes. Lucknow was unfolding with a keen focus on details that people often ignore with their naked eye. The camera told a mystical truth which needed a discipline to perceive. Bansi Da and my local team spent a month looking for locations. The masterpiece was Mughal Sahab Ka Imambara, which still stands restored in its full splendour. It was the most time-consuming of all activities. Many years later I shot a half-hour film as part of my Zubaañ-e-Ishq series on Mir Anis here. The other restoration projects were in Malihabad and Amiran's home in Faizabad, which I shot in an old-world *qasba* (small township), Amethi, near Lucknow. A place from where hailed many intellectual luminaries. I found out that my own father's grandfather, Mir Muzaffar Ali Aseer, belonged to Amethi.

The set in Mumbai, which I'd sketched out, was built by Manzoor, a Bollywood art director. *Umrao Jaan* also won a National Award for art direction. I was passionate about the patina on the walls, and, like a painter, I would spend days rubbing the walls with my own hands in an effort to get the right shade of white or the correct palette of browns. So keen I was on the scale and authenticity of the doors that I went around Bombay looking for a set of twelve old doors that would open into the courtyard, along with three windows that would open on to the street below. I was lucky to find these in the backyard of a bungalow at Kemp's Corner. My production controller, Mohammad Shafi, found out that the bungalow belonged to a foreigner lady. Later, we found it was Jackie Shroff's would-be mother-in-law, whose name I forget.

The set was put up at Mehboob Studio in Bandra. For me it was a sacred space. I would always come early and sweep the floor and not allow anyone with shoes to come on the set. For the light boys we made show covers. It was in this sacred space that many tender moments would unfold—it was a temple for me. *Umrao Jaan* was a gift to me from many people; it was as though they took me across a river and helped me cross it at the right time. People like my father. I feel those children who acknowledge the goodness of their parents are blessed. *Umrao Jaan* was a blessing, not just for me but for all those who were on that boat.

While I was shooting *Umrao Jaan* in Lucknow I had met an astrologer through an antique dealer, Bichi Babu, who had a quaint little curio shop in a corner turret in the old-world Carlton Hotel, which I had made my base for the shoot. The astrologer told me that I would soon be taking on something which was also my Mamu Jaan's passion, from someone who had died the day I was born! I don't believe in these things, but what he said was too surreal to ignore. He also told my cameraman, Praveen Bhatt, to stick to me, always. While Praveen moved on, his cousin, B. Prasad, my editor, stayed with me till the day he died.

I had to move fast on this journey, meet people steeped in knowledge. Putting together the pieces of misplaced, lost cultures in this jigsaw puzzle was most important—in words, music and action. I had set aside an amount for research in the budget. It sent shockwaves in Bhaiji Pachissia's camp who were handling S.K. Jain's finances in Bombay. They felt research would make this into an art film! I could see generations converging and evolving. From my father to my son.

Abba Jaan had a strange love–hate relationship with the so-called intellectual elite of the city. He invited one Mirza Jafar Husain, who was working on a book on Lucknow, to advise me and take me to Faizabad, where Umrao was born. As we sat around the lunch table, Abba Jaan told me a story about Mirza Sahab, which Mirza Sahab himself corroborated later. There was a time when Maulana Azad had asked Mirza Sahab his opinion about two candidates being considered among the Shia elite of Lucknow for a ministerial berth in the cabinet. One was my father, who was an independent member of the legislative assembly and also its chairman, and the other was Syed Ali Zaheer. Now Mirza Sahab, in a bid to gain favour with Syed Ali Zaheer, replied in his most charming Lakhnawi *andaaz* (style), '*Huzoor Raja Sahab se behtar meri nazar meiñ koi aur ho hi nahiñ sakta. Lekin huzoor raja haiñ. Dus baje araam farma ke utthe haiñ. Phir pair daabe jaate haiñ. Aur yahi maamur raat ka bhi hai . . .* (Who better than Raja Sahab? But, sire, a raja will always be a raja. None dare to wake him before ten o'clock, and then his legs are massaged before he can face the world . . .)'

After his appointment as minister, Syed Ali Zaheer never once gave Mirza Sahab an audience. Mirza Sahab lamented to Abba Jaan that had he spoken in his favour to Maulana Azad that day, Abba Jaan's future in politics would have taken a different course. My father never once held this against Mirza Sahab, knowing as he did that there were many wily people like him in the city, but at the same time, his knowledge on the subject of Umrao could not be denied.

The people of Lucknow were indeed most cooperative in both tangible and intangible ways. From the likes of Mirza Sahab to Fakhir Husain, who translated Abdul Halim Sharar's *The Last Phase of Oriental Culture* into

English, to my own Mamu Jaan, who had written an extensive critique on *Umrao Jaan* the novel. I was lost in the romance of a culture. A romance that still lives with me. A passion for the wonder of Awadh was emerging in not me alone but in many around me.

Having lived in UP, Subhashini had a passion for history, fiction and textiles. Equipped with the experience of *Gaman* and having worked with the craftspeople who emerged from Awadh, she brought the costumes for *Umrao Jaan* to life. The costumes had to be lived in, authentic to the time and milieu in every detail not known to Bollywood till then. They had to adhere to my palette as a painter and had to be reminiscent of old-world Lucknow. They had to conform to the evocative nostalgia of the scenes. This was what made the costumes memorable and inspiring. Even today, many well-known designers admit to have taken inspiration from this medley of colour and form, cladding Umrao and a host of others surrounding her in spaces of a bygone era, exotically simulated by shafts of light.

Shaad was a key element in the making of *Umrao Jaan*, both as an actor, playing the role of Umrao's four-year-old brother, and as a 'hanger-on', having made friends with all actors and the entire unit. He would wake up at the crack of dawn, and I would bathe him and get him ready for the shoot. We would drive to Amethi, just outside of Lucknow. He would stand next to me on the seat all through the drive. Every day we would turn a sharp corner over a bump at a particular point just outside the cantonment. He would jump in anticipation, exclaiming with glee, '*Kal bataya* (Did I not tell you yesterday?) . . .' Today, when I see his son, Imaan, I am reminded of Shaad, though he is a little more protected than Shaad was then.

I had done one schedule during my paid leave at Air India. For the second schedule I had no choice but to resign from Air India, with a heavy heart. It was really hard, as Air India was like my home and its people, particularly my subordinates, were like my family. I just had no words to do so. But they wanted me to do it and I said, 'You write the letter, and I will just sign it with my eyes shut!' I still don't know if I resigned. It was like the Isotta—I still don't know if I ever sold it.

Umrao Jaan was happening on several levels. In a strange way it kept my father engaged in both research and legally battling the petty minds that kept rearing their heads with the mounting publicity of the film.

Throughout the making of *Umrao Jaan*, my father had an overarching presence over the project. One day we received a notice from a lawyer. He said he was representing a poor relative of Mirza Hadi Ruswa, who firmly believed that my film would torture Ruswa's soul if it was made. My father gnashed his teeth and said, '*Bade miañ*, you go on with your work and leave these rascals to me.' He had locked himself up in his room after the abolition of zamindari in 1952 to study law, and that had empowered him for such contingencies. He found any legal challenge exhilarating. Anything that was in the framework of common sense was legal. 'Jurisprudence' was his area of excitement, and he had topped in his class in this. He would regale my unit over a meal with law stories, which made a lot of sense in a feudal city like Lucknow and qasbas like his own.

I remember one such story about a very famous lawyer who had made a name for himself as the ghost writer of complicated judgments for several judges. His fame had spread far and wide, and hundreds of clients thronged his offices, queuing up as early as 8 a.m. to get an early appointment. His *mulazim* would enter at dot 11 a.m., bow meekly and murmur to his boss very softly, '*Huzoor, Judge Sahab ne yaad kiya hai* (Sir, the judge is asking for you).' The lawyer would jump up in exasperation saying how difficult the judges had made his life! 'Should I be drafting their judgments or attending to your poor woes?' So saying, he would slip out for the day in his Phaeton parked in the porch while his mulazim would collect the fees on his behalf. This little act always had the desired effect. His clients grew in numbers thinking that a lawyer so close to a judge could always swing the case in their favour!

Once, our meal had just come to an end. We were eagerly waiting for the dessert: shahi tukra. The meal was being served by Itwari, a Pasi (a scheduled caste) from Kotwara whose father was implicated in a murder case. Itwari had been advised to hire this particular lawyer, the only person with a reputation of saving you from the gallows. Poor Itwari. He sold all he had and hired him. When the case came up for hearing, the lawyer sent his junior instead. Itwari's father, Puttu, literally fainted upon not seeing his lawyer, his supposed saviour. When his case was called, Puttu fell to his knees and pleaded before the judge, '*Hujoor, hamka kuch araj karae ka hai* (Sir, I would like to say something).' The judge granted him the permission. '*Sarkaar, ham daam diyo Arbi ghode ka, aur hamka mila yau saar tattu. Hamri tareekh badhaye deyo hujoor* (Your honour, I paid for an

Arab horse and instead I got this mule. Please, your worship, extend my date please).'

This made us feel light about our own matter in the court. Upon some fact-finding it was discovered that Ruswa had given the rights of his novel to Banaras Hindu University. The vice chancellor was a close family friend and immediately assigned the rights to my company, Integrated Film, so that we could make the film. The case was ridiculed and dismissed.

I realized how important the protective grace of a parent could be for a project. Abba Jaan gave the clap for all my films and was always present for the opening. I remember the day *Umrao Jaan* was released in Lucknow in 1981. The theaters were far from full. My father gnashed his teeth, as was his habit, saying, '*Bloody fools, dimagh meiñ gobar bhara hai. Ek poster banao aur usme likho—Phir na kahna hameiñ khabar na hui* (Bloody fools, their head is full of bullshit. Make a poster and put it in their colonies stating—Don't you ever say we were not informed.)' The poster was made for his satisfaction and one doddering old Haider Sahab, an erstwhile royalty of Awadh, was assigned the job of pasting them all over the city. Abba Jaan held a meeting with him daily, where he would take stock of where the posters had been put up. With a roll of posters under his arm, Haider Sahab would give a detailed account. I'm not sure what really happened, but the film did pick up at the box office finally. It ran for a full twenty-five weeks, house full! It had become Lucknow's prestige and identity. Haider Sahab would smile and say, '*Ye sab Raja Sahab ke poster ka kamaal hai* (This is because of Raja Sahab's posters).' My father would wink at that and immediately, a cup of tea was ordered for Haider Sahab.

The making of *Umrao Jaan* was a cerebral process. While I might have been fighting an external battle or recording the footprints of an era soon to be lost to the world, I was internalizing the journey. Was I connecting the body with its soul? A film is a collective call, but as a maker you had to connect with the invisible. Often you lose your grip if you don't internalize each and every element of the film.

For me it was the creative journey of suffering to become an artist, a poet. What would create such poetry, and why would such poetry be remembered? This was a challenge that would even go beyond the poet and the composer, the singer and the performer on screen who will take full ownership before the audience.

The first thing I did was to record the novel in the evocative voice of Salma Siddiqui from Aligarh, married to the famous novelist Krishan Chander. She had so much pathos and expression in her voice that she often brought tears to my eyes. I wish I could find that recording. I had a nice 1961 Fiat painted in a dark greenish-black color with beige hide-leather upholstery, almost like a saddle, all done by Bharat; it was fitted with a good sound system. I would shoot off on the dot at 8 a.m. for my Air India office with the Umrao Jaan story booming at top volume. One trip up and down, and the novel was done. A customized car was conducive for creativity! So I made myself believe. Each day something new would touch me. I would slow down and salute Makhdum Shah at Mahim then at Haji Ali beyond Worli . . . I was reminded of the *Gaman* ghazal 'Seene Meiñ Jalan'. But something new was to come along. As I drove past Malabar Hill and down Cumballa Hill, Shahryar's poems reeled in my mind. The ghazal that started emerging first was:

> *Daam-e-ulfat se chuthti hi nahiñ,*
> *Zindagi tujhko bhoolti hi nahiñ.*
> *Lakh toofañ uthaye aankoñ ne,*
> *Nao yaadoñ ki doobti hi nahiñ.*
> *Tujhse milne ki tujhko paane ki*
> *Koi tadbeer soojhti hi nahiñ . . .*
> (Ensnared in love,
> Life cannot not forget you.
> The eyes threw up a thousand storms,
> The ship of memory refuses to drown.
> To find you, to possess you
> I see no way ahead . . .)

Moments started spinning, emerging, freezing. Each moment was a particular time of day, a particular month of year, a special occasion when shadows fell gently on the wall of slim *lakhori* bricks . . .

My father would send periodic telegraphic messages handwritten on post cards:

> Kerosene first came into use in 1854
> Slim *lakhori* bricks used in India till 1857
> Chemical dyes used only after 1856

Thinking back, I was amazed at how he was so keen that I get the authenticity of the film right in every angle that went into the presentation of the period. His rational and scientific approach kept authentic and realistic things on track.

Shooting a film was like going to war, fully prepared, 'proceed with due care and caution', in my father's words.

Meanwhile, my mind wandered to zones that were unseen, abstract . . .

Na jiski shakl hai koi na jiska naam hai koi,
Ik aisi shay ka kyuñ hameiñ azal se intezaar hai?
(That which has no form and no name,
I have waited for that thing since the beginning of time.)

—Shahryar

Umrao Jaan was a great learning phase in my life. It was the coming together of art, science and the philosophy of life. I was working for myself. It is only when you work for yourself that you follow your heart and arrive at conclusions that are landmarks in your learning curve. There was the art and science of the screenplay for one thing, and then there was music.

Music is a binding force in our culture. Ustad Bade Ghulam Ali Khan use to say that if classical music had been taught in each household, India would not have been partitioned! Hindi cinema was indeed a living example of India's great secular heritage. I had no idea that one day *Umrao Jaan* would become one of the most shining examples of this truth for all time to come. It was an example of acceptance without any obvious clichés.

The journey of *Umrao Jaan* had started within each one of us in our own way. Each of us joined in with our own faith and ritual, on a common path, for the film. Our God or Gods were invoked with incense, the thread of smoke curling up and drawing one into a spiritual aura which would take us towards our common goal.

Film-making in Lucknow is an emotional experience which no policy or government incentive can ever replace. The people and places spanned in my work can become part of another book altogether! One day, a girl from JNU doing research on my work phoned me from Lucknow and said, 'Where is the Lucknow I have seen in your film? It is very bleak here and I am going back.' My Lucknow is the Lucknow of poetry. The Lucknow you see today is the Lucknow of projects. Poetry is invisible, it dwells in the soul, whereas projects assault you in the face. Sadly, Lucknow became a centre of power, a victim of the policies of rulers Wajid Ali Shah onwards. *Umrao Jaan* ends where this ugly phase starts. I write this book with the earnest hope that it will trigger this emotion and highlight the finer, vulnerable, intangible aspects of Lucknow.

Thirty-five years after the release of *Umrao Jaan*, at the Faiz Mela in Lahore in 2015, there was a session on the film, and, as always, the audience was so emotionally and spiritually charged by it that it is difficult to describe. As I was leaving, an old lady came up to me and said, '*Umrao to hamara ordhna bichauna hai* (Umrao is our bedding and covering).' I walked out with tears in my eyes. The emotional journey, once begun never stops. *Umrao Jaan* is proof of this.

> *Yeh kya jagah hai dosto ye kaun sa dayaar hai,*
> *Hadd-e-nigah tak jahañ ghubaar hi ghubaar hai?*
> (What place is this my friends? Where have I come?
> Till the vision's end there is dust and haze.)
>
> —Shahryar

Umrao Jaan was an enigmatic role, and whoever played it had to breathe it mind, body and soul. It was both the choice and the commitment that made Rekha live the role in flesh and blood. The film received a spate of awards and represented India at several international festivals and forums for forty years after its release! Both Rekha and Asha Bhosle received their first awards in the industry with this film.

There was a lot of controversy when Rekha got the 29th National Award for Best Actress. The choice was between Jennifer Kapoor in *36 Chowringhee Lane* and Rekha in *Umrao Jaan*. I know now why Rekha got it. And with her there were two more winners—Asha Bhosle as the Best Female Playback Singer and Khaiyyam as the Best Music Director. This trio would rule the world for a long time to come.

There is not a day when I don't meet someone who fills my cup with the joy of *Umrao Jaan*. Strange people in strange places. I feel humbled. They tell me that I need not make another film in my life. Maybe it was difficult to create another *Umrao Jaan*, and I realized that. But I persevered. A teenage Sikh girl in London, at an event at Nehru Centre, came up to me and said, '*Umrao Jaan* has given me an identity.' There was no sign of her when the film was made, and she was not even from Awadh and didn't speak Urdu. She said she watched the film regularly.

I knew during the shooting that the film would get into people's bloodstream, but not like this. On another trip to London, while I was planning my film *Zooni*, my host said, 'Please come with me to my Pakistani butcher, who watches *Umrao Jaan* every day.' Surprised, I asked my host why he wanted to go there with me, to which he replied, 'He will give me good portions of mutton if he knows we are related.'

I know I was an instrument in the hands of a force which was beyond all property and titles, and a slave in the hands of many teachers who had failed to teach me anything. But looking back, I realize that I was learning . . . maybe from my mistakes.

Har daagh hai is dil meiñ bajuz daagh-e-nidamat . . .
(I have every scar in this heart except the scar of regret . . .)

—Faiz

Chapter 9

Aagaman

'*Abhi giraniye-e-shab meiñ kami nahiñ ayi,*
nijaat-e-deeda-o-dil ki ghari nahiñ ayi,
chale chalo ki vo manzil abhi nahiñ ayi.'
(The weight of the night has not lessened,
nor has the pain of the sight and soul,
move on, the destination, has yet to come.)

—Faiz Ahmad Faiz

Was *Aagaman* the right step? Some say no.

I would like to prove to myself that it was the right step, but it was not everybody's cup of tea. Yet it was a point to be made, a story of a colonial India that needed to be told.

The story of *Aagaman* written by one R.N. Trivedi, who had seen the saga of the sugar mills unfold at close quarters, first as the district magistrate of Lakhimpur Kheri, a sugarcane district, later as the commissioner of the Lucknow division and finally as cane commissioner. He was truly bold and outspoken. He set the story as a prequel to *Gaman*.

The year is 1933. A village in Uttar Pradesh. A one-crop village. Sugarcane is the lifeline of the village, and the joys and sorrows of its many households are bound up with its stacks piled high on the bullock carts trudging to the mill. It is at the mill gate that the destinies of the sugarcane farmers are settled. Will they be able to prepare a dowry for their daughter's marriage, or will there be more debts? Will their sons finish school, or will their bullocks be sold? For it is at the mill gate that the prices of cane are fixed and, more often than not, their hopes dashed. When the crop is good, there is too much cane and the prices are low. When the crop is bad, there is not enough cane for the returns to be substantial.

The mill's practices are geared to cheat the poor farmer, from the use of faulty weights to the shutting down of the plant, feigning a breakdown in the machinery just when a large number of cane carts loaded with produce accumulate at the weighing gates. The replacement parts are to come from England and will take at least fifteen days, they say. With the scorching sun drying up the already-cut cane, the helpless farmers have no choice but to sell at half price to the mill. This happens year after year. It is always a lose–lose situation for the poor farmer.

One such farmer, Ram Prasad, has the consciousness and courage to revolt against the stranglehold of the mill over their lives. The entire might of the mill—economic and political—is brought to bear on him, and crushes him and his fragile world. When Ram Prasad's father raises his voice, he is arrested and sent to jail—a lesson for all the farmers present. His eight-year-old son, Mohan, sees him suffer at the hands of the local mill owner and government authorities, for trying to create a union of sugarcane farmers to help them raise their voice against the misdeeds of the sugarcane mill. He goes to Lucknow and returns a lawyer. Together, Ram Prasad and Mohan give the entire village the courage to dream of their own cooperative sugar mill. It is only when an individual's dream becomes a collective's that its translation into reality becomes a possibility.

What was the predicament in which *Aagaman* was made? While colonial philosophers were defining and rejecting schools of thoughts, putting them in watertight compartments and not allowing fresh air to move through them, the Orient had so much flexibility and power to assimilate and coexist. The West did, however, understand certain stereotypes which they could use to their best advantage and reward them in their own divisive manner with titles like Rai Bahadur, Khan Bahadur, Sardar Bahadur, depending on their religion. Their own titles never had these divisions. The final journey of colonialism over the last two decades preceding Independence used all the infrastructure laid down by them, coupled with the most dependable management resource, to its ultimate advantage. Our colonial masters realized that the one thing the Indian businessmen understood was 'profit'. The feudal gentry and intellectual communities were of no value. The farmers, too lazy and spoilt by the feudal overlords, were growing nothing of any profit to the Empire, its needs or economy. The muslin trade was already decimated and so were other agro-based crafts. Our GDP was fast slipping from the time they had taken over in 1764.

Under the British, sugarcane mills sprung up all over the rich agricultural landscape of India. The railways ferried iron ore from Bihar to the shipyards, which was further dispatched to casting factories in Manchester. Here, the ore was made into machines for crushing sugarcane grown by the Indian farmer under the merciless whip of the Indian businessman. These were profit-making enterprises, meeting the surging demand of sugar in the developing Western nations growing at the cost of their colonies. It is said that the consumption of sugar in a developed nation was six times that of the third world—this by itself was a Tom and Jerry cartoon, with Tom, the Britisher, chasing Jerry, the Indian farmer, who needed to become more productive for them, with the Indian mill owners, Tom's stooges, setting the trap! The entire United Provinces back then was dotted with sugar mills, and the most effective CEOs, the Indian business community, owned and managed these industries. They were given titles of Raja or Rai Bahadur, to establish their authority in rural areas.

I remember how, as a child, I would wait impatiently every summer in Naini Tal for our ground-floor tenants to join us. They owned one of the largest sugar mills—Balrampur Sugar Mills—in Uttar Pradesh. I was more interested in their son, Kamal Nain Saraogi, who was a little older than me. I liked his flashy clothes and expensive shoes and flamboyant shirts. He made sure that he was always clad in the best clothes that money could buy. His mother was a very pious lady, and pandits would frequent their quarters daily. A fragrant whiff of strange spices, very different from our kitchens, would rise up to us on the first floor. My brothers and I would play a game of guessing what was being cooked. My in-house tutor, Syed Sahab, and one of my mother's retainers, Sibti, were like peeping Toms, prowling outside their kitchen, eavesdropping on their conversations. Their efforts finally paid off, and one day they managed to unearth a well-kept secret! Much was whispered but nothing spoken aloud. All we knew was that the cook was having a torrid affair.

Kamal always told me that Marwaris owned both 'this' world and 'that' world. I was very impressed and one day asked him to make me a Marwari too. But he retorted rather haughtily, 'You cannot become one. You have to be born one.' Several decades later, in the 1990s, we met again in Naini Tal, at the Pilibhit House, where I recounted this incident. Saroj Prasad, the rani of Pilibhit, said that if I were a Marwari, I could never have made *Umrao Jaan*. The Prasad family from Pilibhit were also Marwari sugar barons, given the title of raja by the British.

There was no looking back. Mill after mill was being made in England and shipped to India to make the farmer grow what he needed least. The water table was going down and pollution was going up, while the roads were getting worse carrying overloaded truck after truck of sugarcane. The stench and physical pollution, as always, was pushed under the carpet. All major commercial enterprise that mushroomed in the sugar belt belonged to the mill owners. It was this that was the cause of *Gaman* and needed to be addressed in *Aagaman*, which means 'arrival' in Sanskrit. Its time had arrived. *Aagaman* was a bit too close to reality and was boycotted by the theatres which belonged to these mill owners. The film, however, ran for twenty-five weeks in Lucknow's Odeon cinema. We realized soon enough that a sugar mill was the mother of all businesses and key to political lobbies.

The story of *Aagaman* is set just before and after we gain our freedom from the British. For after Independence the stooges were ready to step into the shoes of their erstwhile masters. They knew the administrative machinery like the back of their hand and the tricks of twisting it to their advantage. Seeing the winds of change, the stooges had joined the freedom movement and, afterwards, continued to control the system, crushing all the 'Jerrys' on the way! They ruled over everything that could usher in Gandhi's true swaraj, self-reliance. While on the one hand the likes of the Birlas were pandering to Mahatma Gandhi, they were destroying the enormous market of his khadi dream with the might of the Century Cotton Mills. The nation was unknowingly celebrating its independence with the bonfire of all the spinning wheels of the country, barring a few destined to gather cobwebs in museums and showrooms. It was this that drove my father's resolve to give up his English and mill-made clothing for handspun and handwoven clothes until 'the mills are nationalized'. He felt that as an independent thinker, with a mind of his own, he could justify such a stand.

Aagaman was a landmark in documenting this aspect of our colonial legacy, which smoothly bridged the past with the future. The film depicts the entry of the businessman into politics to hide his anti-worker/ anti-farmer activities. The question asked in *Gaman* was answered in *Aagaman* in 1983.

Putting together *Aagaman* was as exciting as my earlier films. The dialogues had to be real and full of local humour, of the kind we had experienced growing up. I asked Asghar Wajahat to write the dialogues, and he did a wonderful job of it. Subhashini helped with the creative screenplay and styling. The costumes were an interesting mix of a colonial, pre-Independence style and handwoven khadi. Textured beautifully, the clothes were almost like a Ralph Lauren countryside collection of tweeds and serges. We loved frequenting the khadi shops for that one in a hundred perfect weave they made by mistake!

Set in the Awadhi winterscape of the sugarcane season, *Aagaman* came to life under the subtle and artistic cinematography by Rajan Kothari. He was Nadeem's assistant in *Gaman* and had learnt my way of seeing things. This was his first film, as it was Anupam Kher's. The film did the rounds of Bollywood as a work showcasing their talent. It certainly did pay off in both cases. Anupam Kher landed Mahesh Bhatt's *Saaransh* after *Aagaman*, but the world still considers the former his debut work! Rajan, who went on to become Bollywood's ace cinematographer, worked on many of Shyam Benegal's films, including *Hari Bhari, Well Done Abba, Welcome to Sajjanpur, Netaji Subhas Chandra Bose*; with Prakash Jha on *Hip Hip Hurray* and *Damul*; and with Rajkumar Santoshi on *Ghayal*. Sadly, Rajan passed away at the age of sixty.

Casting the character of Mohan's father, who, as a young man, had the fire of revolution in his belly and, as an older man, the angst of disillusionment, was the main challenge. I cast Suresh Oberoi, who was older than Anupam, as the son, Mohan, with Anupam as his father. Make-up did the rest.

Working on Anupam was a dream come true. He was like a fabulous horse responding to each command beyond expectations. I remember the time in Kotwara, when he wore a dhoti and used a blanket as a shawl for the first time. I was taken aback. He looked like an American 'Hare Krishna' devotee. I told him to keep wearing the dhoti and lie on the rough charpoy under the sun for a week, wrapped in the coarse blanket.

What came out was a character sculpted in a body language that could not be explained or taught. He had a great degree of surrender, and it is because of this characteristic, this willingness to learn, that he is a force to reckon with today. Later on, his present wife, Kirron Kher, too, faced the camera for the first time in my thirteen-episode serial *Jaan-e-Alam* as Sabz Pari, the Green Fairy, who disguises herself as a *jogan* (woman mendicant) and appears before Raja Indra, Wajid Ali Shah, played by me.

It was during the making of *Aagaman* that I was approached by Indian Potash Limited to make a rural entertainer. I worked with Niaz Haider to create a one-hour film, *Laia Majnu Ki Nayi Nautanki*, starring Anupam Kher as Majnu. The legendary Gulab Bai and her group helped me in putting the film together, including the *nautanki* casting and music, which I recorded in Lucknow with Jaiswal, in his recording studio at Burlington Hotel, an old-world lodge entirely encroached by random outfits. *Laila Majnu Ki Nayi Nautanki* was shot in Filmistan Studios, Mumbai, using real nautanki artistes along with some Bollywood ones. The sets were interestingly designed, with painted backdrops and a quaint upright harmonium with pedals, played by my favourite V.N. Mishra. Gulab Bai and her daughters, Madhu and Asha, who played Laila's part in the film, travelled from Kanpur to Bombay. I am not sure what they went through, but Laila and Majnu played their part well both on and off screen. Imtiaz, Amjad Khan's brother, played Laila's father and Sulabha Arya played Laila's mother. Sudhir Pande and Madhu played the Natt and the Nattni (the male and female bards).

The music of *Aagaman* was composed by Ustad Ghulam Mustafa Khan, who had worked on *Umrao Jaan* as well. He was the perfect choice and truly brought the lyrics of Faiz Ahmad Faiz to life. The opening song—'*Nisaar main teri galiyon pe aye vatan ke jahan . . . chali hai rasm ki koi na sar uttha ke chale* (I sacrifice myself on the streets of my country, where one cannot walk with head held high) . . .'—and Khan Sahab's voice brought an earthy sense of revolutionary pain to the fore. The arrangement for the music was done by Anil Mohile, who had also worked with me in *Umrao Jaan*.

'*Ham tak nahi pahonche ga agar jaam hamara, saqi tere sar ayega ilzaam hamara* (If my cup does not come to me, O cup-bearer, the blame will fall on you) . . .' This ghazal was composed beautifully in raga Bhupali by Ustad Fayyaz Ahmad Khan. The nautanki song in *Aagaman* was written by Hasrat Jaipuri for Anju Mahendru: '*Chhune na doongi sareer, najjariyoṅ se ji bhar doongi* (I won't let you touch my body, but you may fill your heart with my looks) . . .'

Each composition was a different shade of the same sense of pain.

In all, there were four songs, two sung by Hariharan, whom I had introduced in *Gaman*, and another by Anuradha Paudwal, her debut, a *mujra* composed in the nautanki style. Hariharan was also a student of Ustad Ghulam Mustafa Khan. Khan Sahab is truly a giver. He was like a composition factory, churning out melody after melody, each one superior to the previous one, a refreshing change free of Bollywood clichés. He made me his student and brought me a scale-changer harmonium, which I still have.

From film to film, I was growing in my understanding of music, of its impact and effectiveness on the screen. The sound and the words added to the cinematic impact and structure of my films.

The casting of *Aagaman* was extremely innovative, with the village folk of Kotwara interacting with stalwarts like Saeed Jaffrey and Bharat Bhushan, whom I combined with newcomers like Sudhir Pandey, Anjan Srivastava, Javed Khan, Masood Akhtar and Rajendra Gupta from the IPTA. Back then, the theatre world of Bombay revolved around Prithvi Theatre in Janaki Kutir, which had become a great place for finding talent. Dilip Dhawan, my assistant in *Gaman* and later on the star of *Arwind Desai Ki Ajeeb Dastaan* by Saeed Mirza, was the second hero in *Aagaman*, opposite newcomer Deepa, who was cast as the heroine. Later, Deepa assisted me while I was making *Anjuman*.

The nautanki song in *Aagaman*, 'Chhune Na Doongi Sareer', was written by Hasrat Jaipuri for Anju Mahendru. My art director, Ramesh Darji, who had recently resigned from the Taj to join me as a designer, was deeply bit by the acting bug. I gave him the role of a lecherous man who had to make lewd gestures at Anju while she performed her mujra. With Shaad on his lap, Darji got into full character, ready for the shot. At the climax, Anju was supposed to slap him, at which Shaad was to jump with joy. And what a slap it was! Ramesh rolled down from his chair with the impact, ready to walk off the set. Shaad had to remind Dariji that he was stuck in 'continuity' and therefore could not leave the film.

Making *Aagaman*, for me, was more than making a film. It was living life. When I look back and even see Kotwara and its region today, the lines of realism and cinema get blurred. Everything is the same, except trucks have replaced the oxcarts, just as rubber tyres, also called 'Dunlop', have replaced the wooden wheel. It was same the 'Dunlop' which towed my Isotta Fraschini from Kotwara to Lucknow. The same Isotta in which my father campaigned during his first election in 1935. The light and dark green colour of the Isotta, with its sandy canvas top, made the car merge magnificently into the romantic Awadh landscape. My father often narrated the story of his going to a village one day for canvassing. There was a huge excitement in the village as all the children came out to welcome the entourage of the raja, led by the magnificent, fiery Isotta. As my father stepped out of the car, he saw a little boy's face drop. He exclaimed in dismay, '*Arre jao to admi hoeñ* (Oh! He is only a man)!' The poor boy had imagined a raja to be some superhuman monster.

Somehow, elections were a part of that region's nostalgia, as I too went on to fight four elections, two from there, one from Lucknow, against Atal Bihari Vajpayee, and one from Naini Tal, against the state's sitting chief minister, Narain Dutt Tiwari. Election was a dynamic game, and different types of people came to play it, highlighting their community traits and individual quirks.

Aagaman is about being part of a hidden, exploitative machinery in full movement, never breaking down and crushing the farmer slowly and steadily. The farmer is living beyond his means and entrenched in debt, till one day he flees to a metropolis like Bombay, Calcutta, Delhi or even Lucknow in search of menial labour. They would live their lives on someone else's terms.

The Saeed Jaffrey–Anjan Srivastava duo was hilarious, as were several other cameo roles, including that of the *munshi* (accountant) at the mill gate, played by V.N. Mishra, my all-time favourite actor. '*Anshan karo, dharna dharo, jo jo ji mein awaye karo, yau mill naahi khule wal hai* (Fast unto death, demonstrate, do what you may, this mill is not going to open).'

I remember the pack-up shoot was at Belrayan Cooperative Sugar Mill, on the border of the Dudhwa National Park. I had a Mahindra van in which I would take these endless journeys to Singhai day after day for the shoot. It was the bumpiest ride ever, the fate of all cane roads in the district. One thing I learnt in film-making is, when the going gets bad, look for the funny side. I drove to the rhythm of these bumps, switching on the cabin lights at the crest of a bump—soon, we were in sync with the road, and we roared our way with laughter all along the three-hour-long harrowing drive.

When we reached Belrayan, the staff of the mill guest house would be waiting with open arms, and there would be an orchestra of mosquitoes buzzing and humming around.

> *Junooñ ki yaad manao ki jashn ka din hai*
> *Salib-o-daar sajao ki jashn ka din hai*
> *Tamiz-e-rahbar-o-rahzan na karo aaj ke din*
> *Har ik se haath milao ki jashn ka din hai*
> *Vo shorish-e-gham-e-dil jis ke lay nahiñ koi*
> *Ghazal ki dhun meiñ sunao ki*
> *Jashn ka din hai . . .*
> (Revel in memories of passion
> It is a day to celebrate
> Adorn the gallows and the crucifix
> It is a day to celebrate
> Don't differentiate between
> The guide and the brigand
> Shake hands with both
> It is a day to celebrate
> That plaint of sorrow
> Which has no beat
> Sing to a poem's melody
> It is a day celebrate)

—Faiz Ahmad Faiz

I still reel in the melody of this song whenever I hear it. Hariharan stirs a *Gaman*-like nostalgia . . .

Certainly, it was time to celebrate the last scene of the shoot. In any case, we were not going to get any sleep there for sure. My production manager whispered something in my ear and disappeared. Soon enough, the unit was the happiest I had seen in a long time. He had got each one a bottle of rum, which lulled the mosquitoes to sleep as they bit them.

Shooting *Aagaman* was like an intensive course in living in a cane-growing district. In fact, every district magistrate should be shown this film in the IAS Academy. But it was the poetry of Faiz Ahmad Faiz, used in *Aagaman*, that truly gave it the desired pathos, created by the poet out of the angst and oppression of his time.

'Faiz' means spreading goodness and blessings around you. And that was why he chose it to be his pen name. It was from *Gaman* onwards that Faiz became an intrinsic part of my creative journey and spurred my imagination in situations which were entirely human, knowing no boundaries of place or culture. Faiz's work reflected the exploitation of man by man in the most moving poetic metaphors. I found parallels in 'Sheeshon Ka Masiha' and the Bhopal gas tragedy, which I made into an hour-long film. Faiz featured prominently in my two-part music album *Paigham-e-Mohabbat*, which I composed and compiled on the occasion of fifty years of India's independence, where I made Sukhwinder Singh and Kavita Krishnamurthy sing his ghazals. It is this dedication to Faiz that has taken me to the Faiz Mela in Lahore several times. It is this 'faiz' of Faiz that makes the city bloom with the fragrance of the soul and the mind. A few years back I started working on another series of compositions of Faiz's ghazals in Abida Parveen's voice. It is Faiz that brings us all together and allows us to celebrate a culture that should not have been severed by colonial designs. He will continue to bring this sentiment to the fore for all time to come.

I cannot justify *Aagaman* as a success or reject it as a failure. A film needs to speak to you over time to be understood and felt. Not all films have the same characteristics and journey. What were *Aagaman*'s, I do not know. Maybe it will never be known.

> *Youñhi hamesha ulajhti rahi hai zulm se khalq*
> *Na unki rasm nayi hai na apni reet nayi.*
> (The populous has always stood up against oppression
> Neither are their ways new, nor are our ways of holding out.)
> —Faiz Ahman Faiz

The opening song of *Aagaman* resounds thirty-eight years later in the camps of the recent farmers' protest, bringing to life the eternal conflict between the exploiter and the exploited. The protest of 2021 was against three laws that had loosened the rules around the sale, pricing and storage of farm produce—rules that the farmers felt had protected them from the free market for decades.

For me, the highest honour for a film is its relevance to the times.

Chapter 10

Anjuman

'Zard pattoṅ ka ban jo mera des hai
Dard ki anjuman jo mera des hai.'
('A forest of yellow leaves that is my land
A congregation of pain that is my land.')

—Faiz Ahmad Faiz

Anjuman had brought me to a crossroads. It was more than a film. It opened some doors and closed some. I didn't know which way to go. I felt like a poet at a loss for words. I wished people would believe in me. I felt more global without the resources of going global. Maybe I should have left the country then, to make a breakthrough into world cinema, which many people I knew had done. Ismail Merchant for one, Mira Nair another.

That was the time when we had much to do with Shabana Azmi, and I was in and out of her house. One evening I walked into her flat, and there was a party on. I went into a room overlooking the sea, where a number of film-makers, including Javed Akhtar and Mahesh Bhatt, were having a drink. They fell silent as I walked in. Mahesh had cast Anupam in *Saaransh*, having seen *Aagaman*. He was working with Shabana in *Arth*. Seeing me, he shouted at the top of his voice, 'People like you should not be allowed to make films.' I was taken aback, both aghast and speechless.

It was then I realized that Bollywood was not what it appears to be. How alcohol could turn absolutely normal people into demons or morons, whatever genes they had in abundance. The next morning, Shabana sent me an apology on Mahesh's behalf, saying he was sorry about last night and did not remember anything!

The idea of universalizing one's roots was not so easy. On the other hand, Bollywoodizing one's art was equally tough. Was Mahesh Bhatt right?

All films, and many other creative arts, are partnerships of trust. Relationships that outlive time. Ismail Merchant and James Ivory. James was the creator and Ismail was the fighter. Slowly I began to realize that I was both. I was following my heart, determining what the world needs to see, what it needs to be.

A tough thing to do. I was trying to make a journey within. I was not the normal film-maker people could understand. I was being drawn into the world of poets. Exploring their inner fight like my own. I was working through the poet to create a world that would be prophetic in a context of simple journeys, journeys that were without end, not easy to realize. Today, whatever I do is a realization of these journeys. Maybe I'm a dreamer, but not the only one. I want people to dream, but I also want them to fulfil their dreams. I wish to weave dreams while helping craft their lives with them . . .

A dream was being born within me which was beyond the limited mind of Bollywood. Would *Anjuman* take me to this threshold?

'Anjuman' is society. Anjuman is Lucknow. Anjuman is a young girl of old Lucknow. A young girl who dares to dream of changing her life and the lives of those around her.

Anjuman lives with her family—a mother who has been deserted by her husband, a younger brother and a sister. Helpless and alone, they have no choice but to move in with her mother's brother. It is a life of genteel poverty made all the more difficult by the constant barbs and stings from her aunt, who resents the burden Anjuman and her family place on the frail economy of her household.

Anjuman and her mother are both chikan workers and are paid a pittance for their painstaking embroidery, which takes a terrible toll on their eyesight. Their world is a world of hundreds of women like themselves, poor, insecure, helpless. It is a world of narrow streets, suffocating houses and black burqas, of being constantly smothered by stifling conventions and ruthless exploitation. But it is also a world of strong cultural traditions, colourful festivals and much humour. Anjuman endures the hardship within her home and outside it as an exploited craftsperson. Anjuman is helped in her struggle against the chikan merchants by a young eye doctor, Suchitra, who sees a spark in the girl and succeeds in fanning it.

Romance enters Anjuman's life with Sajid, a handsome young aristocrat, the roof of whose house adjoins hers. But it is more than walls that separate them, and Sajid lacks the courage to fight social barriers.

Disappointed in love, Anjuman continues her fight for fair wages for craftswomen. She takes up the fight to such a level that the trader community has to resort to fanning the communal divide between Shias and Sunnis to break their unity and shatter the strike. Ultimately, her courage inspires not only the women around her but Sajid himself.

Anjuman, a movie depicting the exploitation and struggle of the chikan craftswomen, was inspired by Faiz, who had always stood up as a poet of the downtrodden, the oppressed, upholding the unity of the working classes. It reflects the vulnerability and neglect of a city. The plight of the unorganized sector, of its craftswomen, the apathy of the middle class towards the oppressed, and the helplessness and decay of its cultural ethos.

The film opens with a dedication to Lucknow in the words of Faiz:

Aaj ke naam
Aur
Aaj ke gham ke naam
Aaj ka gham ki hai zindagi ke bhare gulsitañ se khafa
Zard pattoñ ka ban
Zard pattoñ ka ban jo mera des hai
Dard ki anjuman jo mera des hai . . .
(Dedicated to this day
Dedicated to the anguish of this day
The anguish of this day, indifferent to gardens in bloom
A forest of yellow leaves is my land
A congregation of pain is my land . . .)

The film ends with another poignant poem by Faiz, to celebrate the unity and coming together of the weak and the oppressed chikan craftswomen.

It was beautifully composed and sung by Khaiyyam and his wife, Jagjit Kaur, with deep anguish in their voices.

Kab yaad mein tera saath nahiñ?
Kab haath mein tera haath nahiñ?
Sad shukr ki ab in ratoñ mein
Ab hijr ki koi raat nahiñ.
(When are you not in my thoughts?
When is your hand not in mine?
A hundred thanks that in these nights
There is no night of separation.)

Anjuman was set in the Lucknow of the 1980s, torn between the old and the new. It was set in an area of the city where the buildings were as frail and delicate as the *chikankari* the craftswomen did to keep themselves financially afloat. It was a craft dying and living at the same time. This was a place where lanes reeked of a world gone by, leaving the streets to rot and die. The post-1857 ire of the colonial masters had led to its neglect, and all development continued to elude this region. The people continued to hate their new masters for what they had done to their beloved Wajid Ali Shah and the city he loved. They resented for decades all that was English, particularly the language. This made it even more difficult for progress to penetrate this vulnerable fortress. It was only craft that made it tick.

> A film is born out of many conflicts, much courage, faith, inspiration, doubts, uncertainties, perseverance . . . it is born out of sanity, out of madness and it is the rhythm of all these feelings that brings people in this medium together and also makes them drift apart. *Anjuman* is the coming together born out of faith that has been sustained through assassinations, cyclones, gas deaths . . . and so many other lows in life. It is the certainty and faith in every moment that makes a film. A film has a strange concept of the past, a wonderful illusion of the future and a delightful uncertainty about the present. *Anjuman* is one such coming together of the tenses.
>
> —Excerpt from my diary, 7 December 1984

Anjuman, played by Shabana Azmi, is the dreamer in this citadel of helplessness. Shahryar added a new dimension to her dreams—of change, romance, disillusionment and resolve. A similar trajectory like Umrao's. Except *Anjuman* begins with a dream and ends with a resolve.

> *Har dareecha muzmahil, darwaze haiñ kumbhlaye huey,*
> *Aaj ki aañkhoñ meiñ hai kal ka dhuaañ is shahar meiñ.*
> (Every archway is dilapidated, each door is singed with fire
> The smoke of the yesterday fills every eye of today.)
>
>   —Rahi

When I look back, *Anjuman* is about engagement with people whom you have seen closely and wish to share with others. You hear their story, you get absorbed in them. Through *Anjuman* I was absorbed in Lucknow. Through its characters one understood the city's history, and through its well-crafted dialogues a culture became timeless.

Two films were being played out at the same time. The people in the film who became real, and the real people who became unreal, including Mohazzab Sahab. Each day we explored this reality of the passing of time through people and places. My eyes were the camera, recording each brick, capturing each smile.

The climax of the film is the coming together of women defying the curfew resulted by the riots orchestrated to break their unity. It was not the Lucknow of our dreams. Social disunity had spread like poison, with vested political and commercial interests.

It makes one realize the relevance of Wajid Ali Shah, then and now, as well as Rahi's, who wrote his epic book in 1857. The last poem in this book titled *Gomti*, after the river which flows through Lucknow, was enacted as a play designed and directed by me for the inaugural Wajid Ali Shah Festival, instituted by Rumi Foundation's Lucknow chapter in 2013 in Lucknow.

The shooting of *Anjuman* brought the good, the bad and the ugly of Lucknow into focus. Firstly, the homes and those who dwelt in them and the bubble within which they existed. I had sketched everything frame by frame, scene by scene, character by character. I was trying to find the people of my dreams and places of my imagination. To create a labyrinth of a city that was going to change beyond recognition. To figure out how each character would become an organic part of a city and its soundscape.

Naya Mahal, a traditional home in Kashmiri Mohalla which served as Anjuman's home, was a miraculous find. With its gentle, old-world rooftops, and with the most magnificent view of a quaint mosque, the sound of the azan wafting across magical sunrises and sunsets, Naya Mahal served as the single most inspiring location for the film. While its northern entrance was at the same level as the street, its southern entrance was accessed by a flight of steps, raised as it was two floors above the street. This unusual access added to it its cinematic appeal. Its Imambara and the central courtyard were the main architectural features of Naya Mahal, laced as it was with intricate Awadhi floral stucco work, like the Bada Imambara. Today, Naya Mahal holds on to its existence, frail and decrepit, dwarfed by tall buildings that have sprung around it like wild mushrooms, ruining the romantic skyline of the *mohalla* (enclave). This was where Kashmiri Pandits affiliated with the Awadh court had also resided. Some still do. Within its courtyard was an old pond with a fountain, the sound of which had often lulled me into a meditative mode while shooting.

The soul of Naya Mahal was Janab Mohazzab Lakhnawi, the likes of whom Lucknow will never see again. I am glad I spent a lot of time with him and sad that I did not record him. His fourteen-volume dictionary of Urdu phrases is the greatest functional tribute to the language. When I met Mohazzab Sahab for the first time, he had almost lost his eyesight but not his sense of humour and memory. He was a *marsiakhwan* (a reciter of elegies), and it is said that Mir Anis, the great poet of the early nineteenth century who wrote extensive elegies on the martyrdom of Imam Husain, Prophet Muhammad's grandson, had recited in his Imambara.

Shooting in Naya Mahal, my haven of peace, soon became a nightmare. Neighbours and passers-by became agitated at being denied entry to see the shooting. The refined Kashmiri mohalla changed into an unruly, unrecognizable monster. The rowdy crowd would hurl brickbats, once hurting one of the artistes. In this chaos, talking to Mohazzab Sahab was like a healing balm. Each statement was a story, linked with more stories, more statements, the kind we don't have time for. Each night was full of stories, nestling in memories, in the darkness of Naya Mahal's parapets and corridors. The very architecture was designed to hide tales, and these tales were passed on from generation to generation. People changed little, lest they lose track of the footprints of the time gone by.

Taveel hone lagi haiň isi liye raateiň
Ki log sunte sunate nahiň kahani bhi . . .
(The nights are becoming excessively long
As people no longer hear or tell stories . . .)

—Shahryar

Stories are the art of interweaving time and life. Today, the art of storytelling is playing out big on the small screen as we engage with characters. We spend most of our waking time glued to watching what they do to each other, at times with the magic of design, of light and shade, or just the simple unfolding of crass moving images. The challenge is to get people addicted to this art form that eats into their time and life.

All my characters were either born in Kotwara House, 10 Qaiserbagh, or had drifted in and out of there sometime in the past. I was reliving all these Lucknow characters in my films. I had seen them with a detached slant and found them endearing, enchanting, vulnerable, invincible in mind and spirit, despicable yet intriguing. The vocabulary of my feminine feudal culture of Lucknow came alive in *Umrao Jaan* and *Anjuman*. My fascination for Lucknow grew beyond the nostalgia that drew people to the city.

Nostalgia, I realized, had to rise above being subjective, to becoming a driving force for social change. Nostalgia was an interesting ingredient for recreating beauty, but one should not get buried in that trap. It was needed to put history correctly in its human context. There are two kinds of history. One written by the powerful and the other, a parallel history of the oppressed. Their roles may change in time, but the framework for perceiving human history is eternal. Muharram is one such instance, when one helpless man stood against the might of a very powerful man. One man positioned himself to erase the history of the essence of humanity, and its pride in truth and poverty. However, the two histories have always coexisted. The role of Sajid, played by Farouque Shaikh, was a mirror of this change. He was a taluqdar with a traditional upbringing, who upheld the old-world values and at the same time was progressive and futuristic. He was fascinated, awestruck and supportive of Anjuman, much against the wish of his mother, the dowager rani. The history of old Lucknow was being rewritten, and Sajid was a testimony to this.

Dr Rahi Masoom Raza, who had done his PhD on *Tilism-e-Hushruba*, knew this art. An art where the power of the spoken word expanded into a gamut of many interrelationships. An art of words that Rahi Sahab had mastered.

Meri poñji haiñ yahi lafz, yahi thode se lafz . . .
Muft ka maal samajh kar maiñ lutata raha is daulat-e-be-payañ ko . . .
Jis tassawur ke liye ek hi lafz kafi thha, usse sau lafz diye . . .
(These words are my only asset, just these few words.
I squandered this wealth, as I thought it came free.
I gave a hundred words for a thought for which one was
enough . . .)

—Rahi

Rahi's poem goes on and on to describe words as toys, as unlimited ideas, both meaningful and meaningless, their power and their futility. From being infants, ageing and passing away, and finally, a lack of words when you have a lot to say . . .

I did not miss this opportunity of a lifetime to get Rahi to pen the dialogues for *Anjuman*. Each word spoken was worth its weight in gold, each character true to type and life. Rahi opened a new game of chess, using each character as a pawn in his hand. Each day a new game, each game a new day. A few years later, in 1991, he wrote the unforgettable dialogues for B.R. Chopra's *Mahabharat*. Today would have been the right time for Rahi to have been alive.

Rahi was a joy to work with. He told me very openly, '*Bhai, ye tumhare log haiñ, tumhare Lucknow ki zubaan hai . . . maiñ to sirf inse maza looñga* (My friend, these are your people, it is the language of Lucknow . . . I will just have a good time with them).'

He and I had a wonderful time with the characters: Chuhiya Begum, who works with the middleman in exploiting the chikan craftswomen; Nau Bahaar bua, the eunuch; Raunaq Jahan, the small-minded aunt of Anjuman. The compulsively romantic pseudo poet-turned-petty politician Bankey Nawab's expression of his love for Anjuman from excerpts of *Zahr-e-Ishq* literally made you weep and laugh in the same breath. His flunky, Habib Bhai, who later taught Dimple Kapadia Urdu for my film *Zooni*, was a brilliant counterpoint to Bankey Nawab's hilarious histrionics spewing out of his paan-filled mouth. A host of other cameo characters came alive with Rahi's words. Each major character was built up by the juicy dialogues of the minor characters supporting them.

Rukhe pur shikan ke hami leiñge bosey . . . ye baasi siwañyyañ suvarat kareiñ ge.
(It is only me who will kiss this wrinkled face, only I will get to eat this stale, sweet vermicelli.)

This is how Rahi introduces Chuhiya Begum in the film through a street urchin, played by a boy who had run away from his village with a resolve that even if he had to sweep the floor it would be in the house of a film director. He had been bitten by the bug. To date, his name is saved in my mobile as Saeed Acting *Keeda* (insect).

Shaukat Apa played the role of Chuhiya Begum. A *kutni* (a conniving middleman or middlewoman) of sorts. She was one of my characters who walked from the real into the reel world. As I remember, the original Chuhiya of my childhood wore a Begum Bhopal-type half-burqa, under which was a Bhopali *ghuttanna*. On her feet were Bata canvas shoes, later replaced with *hawai* chappals. She was agile for her age. She claimed to be a poet with the pen name of 'Noor Chashm Chuhiya'. Kotwara House and my mother's company were a regular routine in her life. She would gather cigarette packets from the streets and had set up a little corner in the courtyard of Kotwara House as her workshop—she would open these packets and repurpose them into plain, sliding boxes to store homeopathic ointments. (Calendula for one . . . since then I have sworn by Calendula ointment as a healer for all wounds!) Chuhiya sang to herself about herself, lost in her own world!

When Kaifi Sahab saw *Anjuman*, he said in his inimitable sarcastic way that had he seen Shaukat in the role of Chuhiya before marriage, he might not have married her! During the making of *Anjuman*, I got to know Kaifi Sahab intimately, meeting him in Bombay and Lucknow. I also got to know the dreamer in Shabana. Poetry was in her blood, and with it, a sense of *sur*.

Anjuman was the new muse in this film about a city ablaze and left behind by the river of time. Casting Shabana was a vital choice which would give a new meaning to this fire, a purpose to the river. Shabana had been discovered by Shyam Benegal and had been crafted exquisitely as an actor by masters like Ray, Mrinal Sen, Gautam Ghosh. She was also a part of the Bollywood mainstream, having worked with directors like Mahesh Bhatt. Opposite her was my favourite actor Farouque Shaikh, his third time in my film.

Anjuman, like *Umrao Jaan*, was a poet's film, pouring out the dreams of the protagonist in song and verse.

Maiñ raah kabse nayi zindagi ki takti huñ,
Har ik qadam pe, har ik modh pe sambhalti huñ . . .

Kiya hai jashn kabhi doobte sitaroṅ ka,
Kabhi maiṅ ik kiran ke liye bhatakti huṅ,
Kabhi falak pe chamkti huṅ nur ki soorat,
Kabhi zameen par gul ki tarah mahakti huṅ.
(I wait for a new life, at every turn,
At every step I stumble, fall and brace . . .
I have celebrated the falling of the stars,
At times I have longed for a ray of light,
At times I am the glowing light in the sky,
At times I bloom like flowers in the soil.)

—Shahryar

The songs spanned her dreams and illusions . . . her desires and longing for a just world, the heartbreak and the energy of union.

When Khaiyaam Sahab sang out these *naghmas*, I saw the glow and pain on Shabana's face. I could not see anyone else sing these songs on screen. It had to be only Shabana. She imbibed them body and soul. Khaiyyam Sahab endorsed this wholeheartedly. A new chapter opened up, with much talk and publicity. Why hadn't anyone thought this magic would work? I had a partner, Shobha Doctor, on the project, and inspired by the idea of *Anjuman* we had set up a new banner for making films, Collective Films. She had made her name with a serial, *Khandaan*. She was open and supportive of this idea. And so it happened. Shabana sang these songs for the screen, sounding indeed like it was Anjuman herself humming in her simple, old-world, nasal voice!

Before casting Shabana, I had thought of taking Salma Agha for this role, hearing her voice and seeing her typical Lucknow features! I had just recorded an album with her, *Ghazal Mere Shahar Meiṅ* (Poems in My City), with poets of Aligarh. She sang with her soul, and I felt she would repeat the magic. But somehow this didn't happen.

My cinematographer, Ishan Arya, was an alcoholic on a self-destructive track. During the making of *Anjuman* he was under pressure not to hit the bottle. He helped me use the vocabulary of textures and faces as effectively as it could be done, besides adding constant humour on the sets with Yunus Parvez, who was playing a eunuch in the film, as the butt of our jokes. Next in line to Yunus was the frail Ishtiaq Mohammad Khan, playing Anjuman's maternal uncle Jahandar Mirza. Ishtiaq Bhai was from the Pathan pocket of Qayamgunj and had studied at Aligarh Muslim

University. He had composed the famous 'University Tarana', written by Majaz, which we had sung with full sincerity and gusto while at Aligarh. Ishtiaq Bhai was one of my all-time favourites and had also played the role of Farouque Shaikh's father in *Umrao Jaan*.

There was a scene where the burly Nau Bahar Bua had to embrace Jahandar Mirza. As a joke we told Yunus Parvez to squeeze him so hard that he would scream. Yunus Parvez took our suggestion so seriously that Chuhiya had to add a line, '*Aye haye chhod muey, kya uski pasliyañ tod dega* (Leave him, you cursed soul, you will crack his ribs).'

But behind Ishan Arya's innocent and mischievous smile and amiable nature was a complex and hurt individual, out to put an end to his own life. How could such a creative soul be so utterly destructive?

Anjuman was chosen as India's entry into the International Vancouver Film Festival in 1986, after being part of Indian Panorama earlier that year. Panorama screens Indian films chosen for the National Film Festival. Bim and John Bissel hosted a dinner for us in Delhi at their home in New Friends Colony to celebrate the occasion. Bim had always been a great support in whatever I did. That evening, she also invited Mary McFadden, the American couturier. Little did I realize how that meeting would change the course of my life. Mary and I would become a lifelong influence on each other. At the time, Mary was a part of the Golden Eye Festival, which had been held in 1985 in collaboration with the Cooper-Hewitt Museum in New York, and was driven by the potential of Indian craft and design. She saw *Anjuman* with Satish Gujral. They both pronounced it the best-looking Hindi–Urdu film they had seen. Satish could not hear and Mary knew no Urdu.

I reached Vancouver with *Anjuman*. The festival director, Hannah Fisher, seemed delighted to have me. Urdu cinema was coming of age. The beauty and expressiveness of the language lent itself to cinema, to an experience that allowed one to understand the film without knowing Urdu. I secretly congratulated myself for having chosen Rahi to write the dialogues and having hired people from the real-life Lucknow milieu to dub for most of the actors. These were experiments that were paying off, and a new genre of cinema, with a genuine urge to understand cultures and people through languages, was being born. On the other hand, designers like Pupul Jayakar and Martand Singh had created an interest in the Indian idiom of the visual arts. The appeal of Indian art and aesthetics was at an all-time high. We were riding that wave. Cinema was to be the in-depth medium giving expression to those cultures.

Vancouver was beautiful. A good-looking Sikh man would appear in a bus to drive me around the city. Just him and me on a whole bus! He would even enter one-way streets with an enthusiasm propelled by my hurry to get somewhere for a meeting. There was a stunning lady, dressed always in black gowns, who would drive me in her Maserati sports on the coast-hugging roads along the steep mountainside. She was a veteran actress who continued to look devastating even in her sixties. I met her at the festival during the screening of *Anjuman*. Unfortunately, her name eludes me now.

Between the bus and the Maserati, I saw most of Vancouver. Somebody would leave a hundred dollars in my name at the hotel desk every night. I discovered much later that the hundred dollars waiting for me every evening came from the same Sikh bus driver! He had seen *Umrao Jaan* repeatedly for months on end. It had brought him close to his roots so far from home, and this was his way of paying his humble tribute to my efforts. Vancouver was truly magical—the place, the people and their emotions. There was a lovely photographer, Eliza Massey, who would take me around the city, constantly taking photographs of me to remember the city by. The importance of photography had begun to dawn on me, like Richard Holkar and Mahendra Sinh in *Gaman*, and Stephen Waide in *Anjuman*. One phase in my life which was not filled with photos were my days in Aligarh.

Life is a series of messages linked with each other, leading you from one milestone to another, often bringing you face to face with a gigantic landslide blocking the road ahead. But in this, too, was a message. The time beyond *Anjuman* was full of messages. Each day. Though these messages were spiritual, they did not show me the way ahead, but gave me light where I was. People began to take shape beyond their socio-economic predicament. They were what a Sufi would see in them or what they would show a Sufi. This energy was beyond any measure of success or failure. They were gentle and human, like a sunrise or a sunset. Things would seem like toys that would spoil people, much of them I have talked of earlier, but a new phase would show me things differently, except the human effort would be underlined by a sharp sense of beauty, visible to the inner eye. I would be meeting more characters, more people, forging more relationships, within and beyond my films. Maybe beyond Smita, Shabana and Rekha. I would find a different poetry, different music . . .

I would understand the beauty of surrender. The emergence of the way of the Sufi would come with its own message. It was this quest that would show the path. I had begun to see the world as a big game played by minds who dealt in a different currency. I saw people beyond region and religion, beyond colour, caste and creed. I saw similarities everywhere. It was here that my father's humanism showed the way, and I saw in each religion messengers predicted by the Holy Prophet. I saw an Islam which emerged from peace and beauty which had the power to manifest in every act of man as a Divine message of Truth. In Muhammad I saw human in the form of man. And in human history I saw the history of mankind.

For me, *Anjuman* was the coming together of Lucknow, Aligarh, Calcutta and Bombay. It was a painter's film. Satish Gujral, the famous Indian artist who had also designed Mayawati's Lucknow, always maintained, as I have mentioned before, that Indian films and Indian architecture were India's biggest '*himmaqat ka namuna* (examples of stupidity)'. And his telling me that *Anjuman* was visually the most beautiful Hindi film meant the world to me. He and I continued to bond till he passed away in the dreadful COVID year of 2020.

While *Anjuman* will continue to lead me on, Lucknow would continue to inspire me. The women of *Anjuman* will continue to weave magic with their nimble fingers. And Anjuman, the protagonist, will continue to remain the face of that innocence and resolve, that precision of the needle and thread, to which the world will always bow.

Gar baazi ishq ki baazi hai jo chaho laga do dar kaisa
Gar jeet gaye to kya kahna haare bhi to baazi maat nahiñ.
(In a gamble of love, why fear, gamble away all you have.
It's great if you win, and you've lost nothing if you lose.)

—Faiz Ahmad Faiz

Chapter 11

Zooni: An Unfinished Poem

'Yahi shauq thha hameiñ dam ba dam
Ke bahar dekheiñ ge ab ke hum
Juheiñ chhute qaid-e-qafas se hum
To suna khizañ ke din aa gaye.'
('With every breath I had only one desire
To see the spring in bloom
Just as I was released from prison
I was told autumn had come.')

—Bahadur Shah Zafar

I returned to India from Vancouver via New York, one of the greatest cities of the world where art, design and commerce converge. It was a city where things were created. Art was in the look, in the eyes of people walking the streets. There was an energy on the streets. It was a time when people were looking beyond. That was the time when Bernardo Bertolucci's film *The Last Emperor*, based on the revolution during the time of Aisin Gioro Puyi, the last emperor of China, was released to packed houses. I watched the film with Mary in New York, and we both felt that the time had come for India, the greatest culture of the Orient, to present its magnum opus to the West. It just needed the right group of people.

Having been a marketing executive in Air India for eleven years, I almost always positioned myself as a producer. A producer in control of the destiny of his art, essentially through the power of advertising. This was what I had learnt from my professional life. It gave me confidence to create and conquer markets, dream big. Air India had been my learning ground. It had liberated me from the typical petty Indian businessman's outlook of not allowing art to bloom for itself but instead treating it as a commodity to speculate on. This was the bottleneck of artistic endeavour, which made Indian artistes like lost souls not being able to ascend with their art. I wanted to liberate art. Through cinema, I wanted to create a sense of human history and not a ruler's history.

Mary could see this restlessness in my eyes, and she had the vision to help me create a global product, and when I told her that India needed its own classics like *The Last Emperor*, she understood. I made her see her own role in this as a 'designer' in the widest sense of the word, from the idea to the product, sets and costumes. I shared with her the true sixteenth-century legend of Zooni, the last Chak empress of Kashmir. As the story goes, Zooni was a peasant poetess who composed simple, heart-touching lyrics as though she was talking to nature while grazing her sheep. Crown Prince Yusuf Shah Chak sees her thus and falls madly in love with her. Seeing her freedom-loving nature and the gossip of the womenfolk around, she is married off, against her wish, by her parents to an insensitive carpenter, Aziz, who has an unbearably harsh mother. They, too, cannot stand her free-spirited soul, and she is locked up frequently in a sheep pen as punishment.

One day, while filling water from a stream in her earthen pot, Zooni is enthralled by the sound of the Sufiana kalam wafting through the woods. She lets go of her pot and dances with abandon to the music. Aziz, who was in the habit of following her secretly, is incensed upon seeing this and beats her up. Her pot is carried downstream and is smashed to pieces against the rocks. Her husband's cruelty knows no bounds, and she is subjected to frequent torture by both Aziz and his mother. One winter morning, while collecting firewood in the forest, she chances to meet Yusuf, who had been searching for her, unaware that she had been married.

Aziz follows Zooni into the woods again and spies the two together. He beats her within an inch of her life, leaving her for dead in the snow. Bruised and battered, a barefoot Zooni makes her way to her own mother's home somehow. From here begins another fight, a fight for freedom. She seeks divorce through *khula*, a seldom-exercised option where a woman seeks divorce as opposed to a man giving divorce. But the male-dominated society refuses to grant her khula. Zooni is forced to appeal in the court of Sultan Ali Shah Chak. It is here she realizes that Yusuf is actually the crown prince! Zooni is finally granted divorce, and soon Yusuf and Zooni are married and she is given the title of Habba Khatoon.

But this marriage leads to acrimony within the nobility. The Sultan is murdered while playing polo, and Yusuf, a poet at heart, is crowned sultan. Resentment continues to simmer within the court. In the meanwhile, Mughal emperor Akbar has made inroads into the valley with the help of certain factions within the Chak court. Yusuf is forced to ride out to battle to save his kingdom, where he is defeated and taken captive. Exiled to Bihar, he dies there. Zooni writes lyrics, penning down her anguish. She sets out in an eternal search for her beloved till she is finally united with mother nature. She dies in the snow.

The legend unfolds to touch upon freedom and subjugation, tyranny and exploitation, and, in its midst, the celebration of nature through the dramatic changes of the valley's four seasons. If there is anything that expresses Kashmiriyat, it is this. I was reminded of Donald Hellstedt's comment on how a feature film integrating the beauty of the four seasons of Kashmir could make the valley popular forever. Mary immediately saw the bigger picture that a film on the last Chak empress would be a game changer for Kashmir, for India and for Indian cinema. All we needed was the right script.

My mind was already ticking. Make people fall in love with your dreams. The dream, in this case, was Kashmir. We thought that a modern, imaginative, young New Yorker who was willing to live in Kashmir and surrender to its ethos would be the starting point. Mary was very in with the fashion print media and knew of all the upcoming talent. James Killough, a promising young writer, surfaced in the search. A smart, enthusiastic dreamer ready to try out anything different and challenging. He appeared a bit cocky, too sure of himself, but surely it was a risk worth taking. Years later, I realized I was not so wrong. He ended up as the editor-cum-designer of *SUFI*, a magazine published by Jawwad Nurbaksh of the Khanaqah-e-Nimamatullahi. He could empathize, live and create characters. He could become one with cultures. We explored every restaurant in New York as the film took shape and decided to ask James to write one sample scene for the film. He asked for a week. New York was a destination of world dreams.

Meanwhile, we were wondering what to base the aesthetics of sixteenth-century Kashmir on. There was no visual reference of the valley from that period. Kashmir has always been a paradise in perpetual trouble. A place where good souls go when they leave this world. God had made it before its time! So many dynasties alien to the valley ruled after Habba Khatoon that the continuity of its culture was lost to the world. This was the period just before the Mughals had set foot in the valley and left their imprint in the form of monumental gardens and chinar trees. Ours had to be a Kashmir not known to the human eye today. This excited us and became a mission in itself. Mary asked Stuart Cary Welch, the famous art historian and collector, to guide us. Stuart, too, found this an exciting project and disappeared in research for a fortnight.

With Mary all doors opened. We went to the Metropolitan Museum of Art to look at textiles and crafts, particularly of the Islamic world where the formless sense of unity in aesthetics emerged in each element. Everything was same yet different. We were in search of that difference. As a painter I saw a global picture of an aesthetic which was similar in essence yet different in its manifestation.

Then, one day, I got a call from Mary that James Killough was ready with his scene. We met at Mary's apartment in Manhattan and heard him with bated breath. The bug had bit him. It was him or no one else. Before my return to India, Stuart Cary Welch too had come to his conclusions. We met him again at Mary's apartment, and, step by step, he narrated the history and influences on the valley leading up to the time when Mughal emperor Akbar conquered Kashmir. Iran had become an important influence from the time of Shaikhul Alam Nuruddin Wali and his contemporary Shaivite mystic Lalleshwari; with Sultan Zainulabidin and his stay in Iran; and with the coming of Shah Ali Hamadan to the valley in the fourteenth century. All these references led to the Safavid period of Iran being the main influence in the court of the Chak emperors. The paintings of the *Shahnama*, on which Stuart Carey Welch had done a publication, could serve as a starting point. I was excited laying out the *Shahnama* on the Kashmiri landscape. What fun! Only in New York could I find such answers. Mary was like an excited child dying to lay her hands on the rich textiles which were reminiscent of that period. We decided to call the film *Zooni*. Mary was convinced that short names with a 'Z' always worked. 'Zoon' also meant moon.

I stopped by in London on my way back to India. I carried with me the energy of Mary's excitement and James Killough's enthusiasm with a sense of responsibility of making this dream into a reality. I felt it would be a good idea to take an Iranian cinematographer to create the old-world Kashmir set in both its rich and earthy reality of the time. I connected with Behram Manocheri, an ace cameraman from Iran, for shooting *Zooni*. He was definitely worthy of being a part of this dream team. I had come back with a dream larger than life, enough to lift the spirits of a commercial Indian financer. But they were not sure about having Mary or James or Behram on board. They wanted it done the usual way. All they wanted to know was, 'Who is the "Hero"?' I realized with deep sadness that they would never be able to give *Zooni* the wings it needed to become a global product.

I thought of the Government of Kashmir to initiate the idea as they would be the biggest beneficiary in this. We would be promoting Kashmir as a centre of art and science, of learning and communication, of craft and tourism. *Zooni* would globalize Kashmir. Pakistan always had its eye on Kashmir and, by 1989, had started promoting insurgency in earnest in the valley. This was based on their notion that India was divided along communal lines, whereas India, with nearly 20 per cent of the Muslim population left behind after Partition, had taken a secular stand, much like the India of pre-Partition days. It was in the interests of world superpowers selling arms to both the countries to keep Kashmir burning.

Slowly, the Kashmiri youth was being radicalized. Slowly, I was finding my way into the frying pan. I met Farooq Abdullah, who had come to power, and was able to convince him that *Zooni* was the need of the hour. He knew of my existence through my role in the SKICC during my Air India days, and *Umrao Jaan* had won his heart. He asked me to find a bank that would finance the film and told me that the government would stand guarantee. It was a tall order, and how I pulled it off warrants a whole book in itself.

Mary McFadden arrived, delighted that our dream was finally coming true. Soon James Killough followed. My home in Bombay became a hub of activity. Raavi Khan, my faithful executive producer, also moved in, lock, stock and barrel. His actual name was Abdul Rahim Khan, and he was originally from Jaipur. He must have been quite good-looking in his days, when he'd left home for Bombay to become a star. He had given up his name to become Hero Khan. He did a role in a film, but the film never worked, so he became a producer and called himself Raavi Khan. He was a cool operator who could make the impossible possible. He was a man of very simple tastes and few possessions, with one-liners that would endear him to my sons Murad and Shaad: 'God makes man and tailor makes a gentleman.' About me he would say, 'Muzaffar Ali is my Laila!'

We began with the music by signing Khaiyyam and calling Shahryar from Aligarh to write the lyrics. The idea was to make a bilingual movie, in English and Urdu. There would be a common negative portion for non-dialogue scenes with separate negatives for the two languages. We got another executive producer, Martell, to join us from London to work on pre- and post-production. The Urdu version would have Urdu lyrics with music by Khaiyyam, and the English version would have the original Kashmiri lyrics of Habba Khatoon, composed by Mohan Lal Aima, a Kashmiri composer who had done outstanding work in the field of music with All India Radio. We approached the Oscar-winning composer of *The Last Emperor*, Riyuchi Sakamoto, to give the background score. Riyuchi spent a day in Bombay with us discussing the music and agreed to be a part of the project. This was to be kept a secret from Khaiyyam, who might have exploded at the thought of sharing credit. Shahryar came and penned the lyrics based on the phases of Habba Khatoon's life. In all, we recorded seven songs in the voice of Asha Bhosle for the Urdu version. To me these songs were truly moving. At that time, I did not know they would remain with me as a closely guarded secret.

Initially, I had cast Meenakshi Seshadri as Zooni and Jackie Shroff as Sultan Yusuf Shah. I took extensive pictures of her, and she did look like Habba Khatoon. By then, the music had begun to take shape, and I thought deeply of its highs and lows. Somehow Dimple Kapadia seemed a more mystical option for Habba Khatoon. I wanted a person who could be an inspiring muse. Certainly, Dimple was. This was a project only Raavi Khan Sahab could achieve. Get Dimple and cut Meenakshi. The former was easy, but latter was tough and painful. Much later, having recorded all the songs, Dimple would say when she saw Khan Sahab, '*Mujhe lag raha hai ki Khan Sahab mujhe cut karne to nahiñ aa rahe haiñ* (I was afraid that Khan Sahab was coming to cut me out of the film).' Strange how a harmless gentleman like Mr Khan could seem a threat to some people.

With the music in hand, we moved to Srinagar. We hired two idyllic houses near each other in Nishat Gardens on the hills. We also got an office space in Centaur Lake View Hotel and the Sher-e-Kashmir International Conference Centre. Mary set up her studio, at first at Rashid Mir's office and then moved into the SKICC. The film was finally becoming a reality. In the attic of one of my homes, we set up an embroidery, tapestry and papier-mâché unit. We were creating musical instruments, rababs and santoors, the sultan's throne, embroidered costumes and many other objects. The film was to be like a palette of a faded *jamewar*, with the subtle colours of Safavid art. I felt like a painter wielding a massive brush. A brush, I realized much later, that was held by divine hands.

The script evolved slowly as James got immersed in the ethos of the valley, becoming more human and endearing with every page. You could feel that Zooni was getting trapped in her sad, fateful life. Was this the Kashmir we were trying to weave out of the life of this poor girl? Was it this girl that had lived deep within every Kashmiri girl for the last 400 years and would continue to do so for all time? Such were the verses of Habba Khatoon. But a strange harshness was creeping into the people, and I could feel the tenderness of this girl pushed against their hardening stance. One day, the landlord of one of our guest house, where James stayed, came to see me wearing a black shirt; he was mourning the death of General Zia-ul-Haq in Pakistan. A few days later he wore a red shirt on Muharram, the day of the martyrdom of Imam Hussain commemorated as a period of mourning, where most people traditionally don black. Red is especially avoided as it is a colour of joy. These were the signs of Wahhabism penetrating the inclusivity of Kashmir's culture, where Muharram was observed by all Hindus and Muslims of the valley.

I met Ghulam Ahmed Batt, who was a class-III employee in the commissioner's office, where I would go to get permissions to shoot in the valley. We struck a bond, and he became my link with the valley. He leased me a small plot of land with the view of the snow-clad Mahadev mountains to build a set which would serve both as Zooni's home and her husband's home. Batt Sahab was a person of outstanding looks and an even more outstanding character. We would drive around the valley to pick up crumbling old woodwork for the Zooni house. He had oddly learnt to see Kashmir through my crazy eyes, which amused him no end. He retired during that period and joined me full time in the production.

One day, I took my Gypsy and drove out with Batt Sahab and my friend Saeed Sattar, who used to work with me in Air India. I had invited him for intellectual stimulation, and he stayed with me for several weeks. Saeed was a great storyteller, and, with a bidi in hand and a giggle half hidden, he would keep us amused with funny stories about people who had worked with us during our Air India days. The giggle would build up into an uncontrollable laughter, hysterical and infectious. He would suddenly punctuate the narrative with a Gujarati sentence spoken in a distorted Parsi accent. With Saeed, nothing was predictable, unless he plunged into a depression, which was not too unusual for him. But slowly, he would revive with a giggle, narrating an awkward, funny moment he had left frozen in his head—often a Kooka joke.

We were looking for a location where Zooni fills water from a stream. Suddenly, we saw this lovely stream in the midst of a forest. We cut across the water towards it. I thought to myself that with the Gypsy in four-wheel drive, it would leap across the stream, which was full of big, round boulders. The Gypsy sprang like a tiger and stumbled just short of the other end on a huge boulder, and stalled with a groan. Something terrible had happened to the vehicle as one felt the vibrations of the torrent under the floorboard. There was no way out. Batt Sahab left on foot to look for help, wading carefully through the threatening waters. We waited till it became dark. The water seemed to be rising and the current getting stronger. The car reeked of bidis, which, by now, were finished. I felt sick and desolate. Saeed was desperate for a smoke. '*Zara utar ke dekhein kahiñ bidi mil jaye* (Let me go look for a bidi).' Batt Sahab had been gone for over three hours. We could hear strange animal sounds from the forest and were beginning to get a bit scared. '*Yaar Saeed, kisi bhalu ka nashta na ban jaana* (Saeed my friend, don't become breakfast for a bear).'

I kept Saeed with me because he was a great stress buster, one you needed for shattered production spaces. Soon, the dark overcast skies were pierced by a shaft of a gentle sunlight. Then we saw the most welcoming sight, of an army jeep, with its strong headlights, groaning on the bank of the stream, trying to inch its way towards us. It came and stopped near us and out popped Batt Sahab. We left in the army jeep, leaving my Gypsy midstream. At the army base we had a cup of tea with the sergeant in charge, who had seen *Umrao Jaan* and offered to get his one-tonner to haul my Gypsy out of the water and sent to Srinagar. A little later, he took me aside and said, 'Sir, you should not trust these Kashmiris.' I was taken aback and told him about Batt Sahab and my relationship with him. He said it was his duty to warn me.

Kashmir was becoming a different place. I had to be in love with it and the people to make *Zooni*. Was this the valley that I was fascinated by? 'No,' I said to myself. Mohanlal Aima had understood my sadness and cryptically asked me for a vehicle and a room in a hotel for fifteen days. I obliged. Then I got a phone call from Aima Sahab that he was ready for me. Being a director in All India Radio, he knew every single musician by name and village. He had gone village to village in the entire valley, chasing the best of musicians and rehearsing with them tirelessly in Srinagar. He improvised new sounds from the *nutt*, the big clay pot, by stretching a rubber tube on its mouth.

I entered the room where over thirty pairs of shoes were haphazardly strewn, amid a strong fragrance of toe jam. I sat beside Aima Sahab with bated breath. Then he graciously took my permission and signalled the musicians, who all nodded in return. Out of the pin-drop silence came a deep, resounding hum from the taught rubber tube stretched on the mouth of the clay pot, which permeated the depths of my soul like never before, joined in by many voices in a harmonious chorus. At that moment I understood that Kashmir had gone into its shell not realizing the miracle it contained within. The rapid radicalization in the name of God was throttling the talent within the valley. The experience lasted for an hour, mesmerizing me till I could not control my tears. The poet Saadi had come alive at the baton of a Kashmiri Pandit who saw no difference between Lalleshwari and Shaikhul Alam Nuruddin. I had found my Kashmir. I realized it had always been besieged, since the time of Habba Khatoon. Except, in those days the goal was to subjugate women. Today, it was everyone.

I discovered that the Sufiana *kalaam* (Sufi poetry) had shrunk into *khanaqahs* (A place for Sufi gatherings). And so had the poetry of Rumi, Hafiz, Saadi and Khusrau. But at least it was alive. Today, it is more alive than it ever was. Rumi and Khusrau loom over us larger than life, much against the wishes of the petty minds of both communities.

The music had set us all in a continuous motion, with the hope that one day we would have the world in a trance.

There was a great buzz about the pre-production of *Zooni*. The design world of Delhi was in awe of Mary McFadden designing the costumes. She was a name that opened futures for Indian designers in the West. Mary picked Suneet Varma, an up-and-coming fashion designer at that time, as part of the costume team, and Sri Kulkarni, a product designer from the National Institute of Design (NID) in Ahmedabad, to head her craft development. We created a Shah Hamadan Centre for Design Development in Srinagar and invited students from the NID to work on designing props, integrating various craft forms to be used in the film authentic to the period we were trying to recreate. Joseph Allen Stein advised us on the wood and mud architecture of sixteenth-century Kashmir. We wanted to create the most authentic-looking film, and research and development was a very important part of the project.

Our little community was growing. Kashmir became our paradise. Everyone was in love with everyone. People discovered within themselves the art of loving and sharing. James Killough had a young Kashmiri boy, Meraj Ahmad, cooking and serving for him. Meraj was adopted by James, and is now in the US as Meraj Killough XIV. Mary McFadden became a Sufi and was a regular at a Jerrahathi Khanaqah in New York. James, too, became a Sufi of sorts. The Zooni House was coming up nicely. I had surrounded myself with some of the most outstanding craftspeople of the valley. Bashir Ahmed, my carpenter, could create miracles with wood. I was drawn to create my collages which I would exhibit in 1990 in Delhi and then in Paris, at Galeries Lafayette. The mountainscape began to play in my mind as artworks and spaces for *Zooni* to come alive. The fire of art was aflame like never before.

I was shuttling between Bombay and Srinagar, preparing for the first shooting schedule to start on 5 January 1989. Dimple was being tutored in Bombay in Urdu for the role. Finally, we finalized Vinod Khanna to play Sultan Yusuf Shah Chak. He would come to my home in Juhu in Bombay every night to discuss his role and drive back to town after a full bottle of Scotch, which he brought with him. He was a dream come true with his fluency in both English and Urdu. I left the script with him and, having finalized the entire casting and schedule, flew back to Srinagar. Dalip Tahil was going to be Aziz Lone, Zooni's husband; his mother's role was to be played by Shaukat Kaifi; her brother, the Maulvi, was going to be Mohanlal Aima; Zooni's mother, Sushma Seth; her father, Shabi Abbas; Zooni's best friend, Ratna, was to be played by Ratna Raina; Vikram Kaul was cast as Pandit Guru Bhavani; Mubarak Baihaqqi was Imtiaz Khan; and finally, Pran Sahab was to be Baba Khalilullah. In Kashmir, the entire cast was fitted with costumes, on which Mary and her team, now assisted by Anjum Sadiq from Srinagar, had worked with amazing detail. By now more assistants joined in. There was a Punjabi family of one Mr Khosla, living in Srinagar, who were avid fans of Begum Akhtar, the ghazal queen of India in the mid-twentieth century, and who attached themselves to the production somehow.

Zooni was a film on a woman like most of my films, but this was going to be different. In the words of Allama Iqbal:

Zan nigahdarandeh naar-e-hayat
Fitrat ou laoh asrar-e-hayat
(Woman is the preserver of life's fire
Her nature is the tablet on which are preserved the mysteries of life)

Aatash maara ba jaan-e-khud zanad
Jauhar ou khaak ra aadam kunad
(She absorbs our fire into her soul
The essence of her spirit turns the dust into human beings)
Dar zameerash mumkinat-e-zindagi
Az tab-o-taabish shabab-e-zindagi
(All potentialities of life reside in her heart
And life acquires permanence from her fire and light)

This was the essence of Habba Khatoon. Women begin to rust, tarnish; they envelop themselves in ready-mades, in traditions, and limit their dreams and desires. It is necessary for a woman to be unlimited. *Zooni* is a discovery of the soul. The recreation of *Zooni's* poetry was to be a magic to outlive time. That period of Kashmiri poetry was called 'Vacan Kaal', an era of songs that voice the feelings of the female lover addressed to the male beloved. Rohv was the popular folk dance that accompanied the song. These songs are not intellectual in concept and content, have no theme, no message, but are just utterances, simple and direct, of a woman affected by the sting of love in a world vibrating with the message of love; they often use the symbolism of flowers, turtles, doves, and the bumblebees. They embody secular love: unsophisticated, natural and human, wistful and plaintive utterances of unrequited love and longing. These were Zooni's *lol* poems of love and yearning.

It was Abdul Ghani Namtahali who introduced me to the Sufiana music of Kashmir. It was a world within in a world, in which the lol and *vacan* floated. It was he who introduced me to a range of *maqaams* that Sufiana kalaam was made of. Each maqaam was like a raga.

Abdul Ghani was a Sufi and would spend days playing these maqaams on his santoor in the khanaqah of Ahmad Shah Badshah at Chadora, on the way to Chrar-e-Shareef. We would talk at length. He told me about Ahmad Shah, who was a great devotee of Hazrat Ali. This devotion led to the resolution that he had to see Hazrat Ali, and so he sat in one place facing the mountain in the direction of the *qibla* (Kaaba). He sat through the heat, rain, snow and sleet, weathering season after season till his flesh began to leave his body. One day, he saw a veiled rider on horseback. Ahmad Shah moved towards it. His disciples followed but he stopped them saying, 'You will not be able to withstand the glory for which I have waited so long.'

This was a revealing moment. I learnt that there was no short cut to Truth. You had to gaze upon the beauty of truth to find Truth. It was this realized beauty of truth that was His Glory. It was formless and abstract. It was self-illuminating. It was like the emergence of the highest form of art, which only happens by constantly being in communion. A namaz which has a cumulative effect on your conviction. Of asking the unseen. An evolution of this conviction was finding the relevance of each passing day that brings you closer to the beauty of truth and ecstasy of this journey. In the words of Bu Ali Shah Qalandar, the thirteenth-century Chishti saint of Panipat, who also wanted to become like Hazrat Ali, '*Manam mahve khayal e ou nameedanam kuja raftam* (Immersed in the thought of You, I know not where I go).' The followers could not experience that state of wonder, but certainly they too had seen the emergence of a light, which would have one day entered and gently illuminated them, as it did with me maybe, a century later, by just being there, hearing about it.

Abdul Ghani was truly a realized soul, and I was blessed to have received this art from him. Whoever went with me to see him, saw the light. I brought him to Bombay and recorded his repertoire of Sufiana kalaam at the same time when I recorded all the *Zooni* songs in Kashmiri for the English version, in the voice of Jahanara Jaanbaz, a young singer from Kishtwar, under the direction of Mohanlal Aima. Abdul Ghani Namtahali was presented by me in Delhi and Lucknow at an Indo–Iranian concert, Tajjalli, which later became a film, *Rumi in the Land of Khusrau*.

Abba Jaan stayed with me in Bombay all the while I was recording the music. He left for Lucknow immediately after. Then, one day, I got a call from him. I remember it was the last week of November in 1988. In a broken voice he said, 'Guddu Mian [a term of endearment for a younger member of the family] is no more.' Then there was a silence. Guddu was my youngest brother. This shattered me no end. As it must have shattered him, leaving him with no energy to travel to Liverpool for the funeral. Subhashini and I took the next flight out. Sadness had gripped us.

Guddu was only in his early forties. He was a very large-hearted, loving human being. He was too young to go. He was the most amusing of us three siblings. He had the most joie de vivre among us. Without him around, there was no fun in going anywhere. He had loved calling his friends for my birthday just to get presents for himself. Once, on my fourteenth birthday, he called a sweet little Sikh friend, who arrived in a pink shirt with his hair neatly tied on top in a bun. His grandfather owned the best Swiss confectionery in Hazratganj, Lucknow, which he had bought from a Swiss lady. The little sardar walked in shyly with a present of a plastic pistol in his hand. Just before him walked in Jimmy of Jahangirabad, with a large present of a handsomely illustrated book. Guddu took the little sardar aside and pulled him up, '*Dekho Bare Miañ ke dost itna achha present layeiñ haiñ. Tum ye kya le aye* (See, Bare Miañ's friend has brought such a nice present. Why did you get this)?' His friend, looking very crestfallen, said, '*Hameiñ bata diya hota* (You should have told me).'

Whenever we went to Hazratganj, Guddu would say gleefully, '*Arre lifafa le chalein, kahiñ cake-wake lena pad jaayein* (Take a bag, we may have to buy a cake)!' I recounted all his innocent antics that were so endearing throughout the flight to London. Once he had opened a discotheque in Kotwara House in Qaiserbagh and named it Kisko Dekh Discothek. It was a complete mismatch of ideas and guest profile, and the food was served at a hefty price. He called the governor of Uttar Pradesh as the chief guest to inaugurate it. The governor was supposed to pull at the pipe of a *huqqa* for a photo op. Unfortunately, the water pipe was lower than the air pipe, and as the governor took a long pull for the camera, the water squirted into his mouth! Nooran, my mother's devoted attendant, was in charge of the biryani, both its making and selling. Seeing the strange mix of guests, she insisted on getting the money first. Lots of people got offended, and finally the biryani was distributed to all and sundry in Qaiserbagh Circus. Disgusted, my father had fled to Kanpur to take refuge with Subhashini's parents.

We arrived in the grey winter of England. It took us two days to get Guddu's body out of the morgue, as it was a case of suicide. His death by suicide was difficult to come to terms with. It left my father with no will to live. Guddu's three sweet little girls, who were like he used to be as a young boy, were shattered. I recalled him phoning me one day, just a few weeks before he died, asking me to look after his daughters if something were to happen to him. As we flew back this ghazal kept haunting me throughout the journey:

> *Kabhi ban-sañwar ke jo aa gaye*
> *To bahaar-e-husn dikha gaye*
> (Whenever he came all decked and dressed
> He brought with him the beauty of spring)
>
> —Bahadur Shah Zafar

When I reached Srinagar, Batt Sahab and the villagers of Barji held a big *majlis* (a congregation for condolence) for Guddu at the Imambara. I had never seen a gathering of so many people and felt at home with my sorrow.

I had to get back into action as the shoot was to begin on 5 January 1989. All the locations and dates, with costumes and special props, had to be lined up. The entire film was designed around the four seasons of the Valley. Starting with the winter snow was the birth of Zooni, her fleeing her husband's home, other scenes of sadness and depression, high drama and treason, the battle and arrest of Yusuf and, finally, the disappearance of Zooni. The romantic parts of the film, such as the meeting of Yusuf and Zooni and scenes of their marriage, were to be shot in spring. Autumn was reserved for all the tragic scenes. It was a complex scheduling, and the double negative and big stars added to the difficulty of achieving all.

The mahurat shot was performed at the SKICC, with Mary McFadden, Pran Sahab, Dimple Kapadia and Sushma Seth, before an august gathering. The clap was given by my father, whom I had brought to Srinagar so that he could overcome his sadness. But Abba Jaan could never come to terms with Guddu's suicide and kept saying that it was his own time to go, not Guddu's. That evening he said, 'Guddu could not have committed suicide. He was killed.'

We started the schedule with Dimple in the snow, shooting the most difficult scene of the movie first—Zooni's flight to her mother's home through a thick blanket of freshly fallen snow after being beaten and left for dead by her husband. Dimple had to slip down the steep slopes to leave the audience breathless with the scene's impact. She had to regain her composure and crawl up slowly through the fresh snow, breathless, her face blue with the cold, eyes red with tears, fatigue and humiliation. Her feet would sink deep into the snow, creating sounds that penetrated the soul. She shivered as she laboured her way through the snow, barefoot, the urge for freedom and determination overcoming hurt and anguish.

> *Jeene ki koi raah dikhayi nahiñ deti baba mere baba . . .*
> *Varna maiñ kabhi aise duhaie nahiñ deti baba mere baba . . .*
> (I see no way to live on like this, O my dear father . . .
> Otherwise I wouldn't wail like this, O my dear father . . .)
> —Shahryar for *Zooni*

Our team had swelled up to include a young photographer, Ben Ingham, from England, who stayed with us till the very end to capture some amazing images.

We went through the entire winter schedule with Dimple and Pran Sahab, but Vinod Khanna never showed up. I could not figure out why. That was one of the first setbacks for the film. We wrapped up with Dimple's performance, which went beyond expectations. The different seasons gave a texture at the outset that would set the style of the film. Vinod Khanna's not turning up for this very important opening winter schedule did scare me, and I hoped he would recognize the value of the film and not repeat this in the future.

The optimistic, large-hearted Mr Khosla was most comforting in tough times. He had an interior design business, Top Notch, making furniture for rich businessmen and government offices, and he kept our spirits high with his entertainment and dinners, where he would call a big-wig or two with some of my flunkies. These evenings were amusing, with his sons, Raghu and Robin, who had the Bollywood struggler's habit of diving straight down to touch a producer's feet, bearing the brunt of most of the jokes. It paid off, as Raghu got a small role in *Zooni* as Yusuf Shah's major factotum. We called him Fashur in the film—it was Mary's habit to say 'fashor' to every idea; it meant 'for sure'. Poor Fashur was kept on standby in full costume and make-up, on a horse designated for him, ready to shoot if Vinod landed as expected.

My home in Nishat was a piece of paradise. It was a short walk from the grandest Mughal Garden, Nishat Bagh, where I would go for a walk and experience the music of seasonal change through the majesty of the chinars. From vibrant green to a flaming variety of orange and hues of russet brown, and then clad in snow. Before the snow, I would bring home the fallen leaves as a mark of surrender, as a symbol of return to the origins. I was beginning to realize that a Sufi is born following the way of nature, in pursuit of beauty and making people realize this as a blessing: source of joy. 'Was this the way of Habba Khatoon? Was she a living soul?' I often thought to myself. I would see her in music, in streams and mountains. Was she a soul born and reborn in the Valley? Was she the shadow of Lal Ded, the naked Shaivite mystic who was known as Lalleshwari by the Hindus and Lalla Arifa by the Muslims? People saw nature in mystics and mystics in nature. What I found in common between Zooni and Lal Ded was that they both were freedom-loving women who inhabited the same part of the world. Lal Ded had all the answers any women would ask of themselves, society and the world. And one found that Zooni and many other women of the Valley derived their sense of power and freedom from Lal Ded.

I got a feeling that her soul was in the air. I had no idea what she wanted. She was definitely a protective and sensitive soul. Every time I took a shot of *Zooni*, her special fragrance wafted through the air.

The time came to go to Delhi for a few days. Mr Khosla had previously told me of a pandit, Jugal Kishore, who could predict the future, and had asked me to meet him in Jalandhar when I drove down to Delhi next. When I told him of my intent to visit the pandit in Jalandhar, he immediately warmed up to the idea and decided to meet me there. I was always intrigued by people who foretold futures and was most willing to have a stopover in Jalandhar.

I had a man Friday, Munna, deputed to me by my close friend Taqi Hasan of Salempur. I don't know if Munna was really slow or pretended to be so. He sure did a good job of being entertainingly stupid. Lighting a *bukhari* (a wood-fire heater made of metal) with a kerosene flame one winter night, he singed one side of his mustache. He came up to me with my morning tea. With half his face concealed behind a scarf, he asked me whether he should keep the other half of his mustache. I sent him away to do as he pleased. He came to wake me the next morning for my journey, hobbling strangely on his heels. I asked him what happened. He had been feeling so cold that he had put boiling water in a hot-water bottle and placed it on the soles of his feet without any protection. He woke up with huge boils on both his soles! As a punishment for his stupidity, I made him travel with me to Delhi. Throughout the journey I didn't speak to him. After several hours of silence he uttered a sentence: '*Ham sochit hain aap ek ghoda le lijiye* (I was thinking you should buy a horse).' Munna knew of my weakness for horses, knew that I was looking for a steed for the sultan in the film. He had hit upon the right chord, and this was him trying to worm his way back into favour with me. Sure, his sins were washed off with this idea, and he continued, '*Huaañ log batawat raheiñ ki Qadian meiñ acche ghode millat haiñ* (People say you get good horses in Qadian).' We were approaching Batala near Qadian. I dropped Munna at a dhaba to rest, gave him enough money for food and told him to find horses to choose from and meet me three days later.

As planned, I met Mr Khosla in Jalandhar and went with him to see Pandit Jugal Kishore, who was very respectful and went out immediately to buy sweets for me. He said that there was a shadow that protected me from all harm. He said that I had been sent to cleanse the world. I told him that I wanted to buy a black horse in Qadian and asked him if I would find one, to which he replied that I would most certainly find a horse but not a black one. My horse, he said, belonged to a girl whose name began with an 'S'. The horse would tell me to take him. Regarding the future of the film, he said it would bring me fame. He didn't say much about anything else. Neither did he say anything about Raghu's future as an actor, nor Mr Khosla's future as a producer. We left, interpreting everything as it suited us.

A few days later I met Munna at the designated place. He seemed to have made some headway and we went to Qadian, but the horses were chestnut and too commonplace. Munna could feel that he was losing my respect. Just then, someone told us about the local MLA, Sardar Pratap Singh Bajwa, who had a beautiful young stallion which he may or may not sell. Munna jumped at the idea, hoping to win back my respect. We set off to Batala and reached the MLA's heavily guarded house. Pratap Singh was most hospitable and insisted that I spend the night there, as it was not safe to travel at that hour. I talked about the purpose of my trip and said that I was looking for a horse for Sultan Yusuf Shah Chak of Kashmir. He guffawed asking hadn't the sultan died a few hundred years back! I said I was making a film and Vinod Khanna was playing the role. He thought all this was best discussed the next morning over breakfast. We talked about inconsequential things at dinner. I was wary of all this security, which was entirely alien to my life, but I suppose politicians were becoming vulnerable as Srinagar was readying itself to becoming a hotspot where security personnel would become a necessity.

Next morning, he introduced me to his little daughter, whose name was Simran. I thought of Jugal Kishore immediately, who had predicted that the horse for my film belonged to someone whose name began with an 'S'! Pratap said, 'My daughter has a horse. Ask her if she will part with it.'

Somehow she took a liking to me and said, 'If you like . . .'

I was thrilled, but I hadn't seen the horse yet. It could have been a mule. I was reminded of Syed Sahab telling me in Naini Tal, 'Never buy a horse without seeing it.'

We came out on a magnificent lawn with an old gateway at one end, through which came prancing the most magnificent stallion I had ever seen. Not black but *sabza*, a grey-white colour. A sacred colour among the Sikhs, as it was the colour of Guru Gobind Singhji's steed. The man who'd brought him jumped on him but was flung off in the next instance. I had to try riding the horse before taking a decision. He stood unbelievably docile and went wherever I took him. The decision was made. We knew that we were getting into a memorable relationship, unlike buying a nameless animal from a nameless trader. I thanked Pratap and Simran, and left Munna behind to bring the horse to Srinagar. He arrived in Srinagar at the time of *maghrib* (the time for evening namaz), and his feet touched the ground just as the azan sounded. I called the horse Shams, and he lived with me for over twenty years.

Gulla was hired by Batt Sahab to look after Shams. I rode Shams to Dachigam every morning. He was very hesitant in obeying commands. The work on horse gear had started, which I really enjoyed researching and creating—the head piece, the reins and the saddlery. An action man, Hafeez, came in from Bombay to train Shams for Vinod. The news of *Zooni* had spread far and wide through my international team.

The spring schedule was ready. We had to shoot the love-at-first-sight encounter of Zooni and Prince Yusuf Shah. He is on a hunt, on his horse, Shams, in full regalia, and Zooni is with her herd of sheep. We had chosen the most poetic orchard, with a stone wall between her and the sultan. The bulbul had come back with all her companions. The flowers were in full bloom. Dimple had landed and so had Mary. This was the season of love.

Ajab si ek khushboo
Kisi benaam shai ki
Kiye hai aisa jaadu
Meri zulfeiñ haiñ barham . . .
(An unknown fragrance
Of something nameless
Casts magic on me
My hair opens and flies around)

—Shahryar for *Zooni*

Vinod Khanna, our sultan, had finally arrived and looked stunning. But, he said, there was a problem, which he would talk about in the evening. As he went through his Scotch, he seemed to have no worry in the world. Finally, he said that he was going back a week before his time with me.

I felt totally lost. I could see my castle crumbling before me. I was too small and should have known that. Things were not going right in the Valley, and I wanted to wrap up as fast as possible. Fortunately, we were well protected and safe. The village people of Barji had created a buffer around us. Nevertheless, there was an unease.

Kashmir was in turmoil. We had taken a full circle of a year, from the day we began the shoot on 5 January 1989. We were going through the uneasy days of November. Our resources had dried up. I could only look at the russet chinar and wonder: Why was Kashmir so beautiful and so painful? This question has echoed in the valley for so long. The leaves fell from their magnificent branches and spread out like a noisy carpet.

There was no one left in the Government of Jammu and Kashmir to fulfil their commitments. The popular government had fallen, and the then governor, Jagmohan, put the onus on the earlier regime. There was talk of the governor planning a mass exodus of Kashmiri Pandits from the Valley. The Pandits were the mind of society, and the majority of Kashmiri Muslims did not like the idea of their being moved out. They felt that in order to flush out terrorism, there would be indiscriminate 'cleansing'. These were their perceptions. What the truth was, God alone knows, but such an organized exodus could not be possible without meticulous planning.

Dimple was emerging as a dream from one season to the next. There was a long gap from spring to autumn. I was scared to leave the valley. I felt it would be difficult to come back and resettle. I flew to Bombay to see the first prints. The film looked gorgeous, with a promise of better work still to come. But Vinod's absence had left gaping holes in the narrative.

We wrapped up the autumn schedule and waited for snowfall to complete the leftover of the snowbound work from the January schedule, for which Vinod Khanna, in his characteristic style, had not shown up. Things around us were getting dreary and dismal. Even the bright sunshine looked hopeless. What would happen the next moment, we did not know. Under these conditions it was difficult to breathe, leave aside dream.

Then, the grandest and the most sacred building of the Valley, the tomb of Shaikhul Alam Nuruddin Wali in Chrar-e-Sharif, was set on fire after a pitched battle between Mast Gul, the Pakistani militant, and the Indian security forces. The chances of completing the remaining shoot in the Valley were getting bleaker by the day. The anonymous threat on an inland letter—saying that 'shooting a film was un-Islamic' and that we should pack up and leave—seemed pale in front of the changing scenario. Maybe there was truth in the idea that something terrible might have befallen the Pandits if they had stayed on. We needed to look at a massive pack-up from the valley, the most depressing process of all. Kotwara was the only place which could house all the sets, properties and costumes, and, of course, my horse Shams.

I was staying in Zooni House, which we had made for our shoot with wooden lattice work. Subhashini and I were drifting apart. She was deeply involved in politics. By now we were leading different lives. She had just been elected as a member of Parliament from Kanpur, and I was torn between Kashmir, Bombay and going to Lucknow and Kotwara, where Abba Jaan was.

Living in this adobe was a world beyond the reality I was coexisting in. The sun would rise from behind the snowclad Mahadev Mountain, facing the Dachigam forest, where I would often take Shams for a ride. We would plunge into the woods and, strangely, Shams would refuse to move forward beyond a particular point! My chain-stitch and papier-mâché craftsmen would still huddle up at night and bloom in the sun on a large and high wooden bed, part of the Zooni world. They embroidered and painted flowers, from the memory of the last spring and in the hope of the next. No one knew beyond the future of one stitch to the next . . . no one could foresee its chain, yet they believed in what they did, shut out from the world. I wish I could do so . . .

> *Ab saañs bhi lene se daruñ zakhm haiñ gahre*
> *Dharkan bhi yahañ apni sunnai nahiñ deti baba mere baba*
> (I dread to breathe, deep are the wounds
> I cannot hear even my own heartbeats, O my father)
>   —Shahryar for *Zooni*

We kept meticulously planning the balance winter work, like those craftspeople who donned a hopeful, innocent smile on their lips. They lost themselves in the smoke of their huqqah, the warmth of their kangri held close to their stomachs inside their *pherans* . . . waiting to drink their nun chai from the impressive old-world samovars, again from the film. We all lived in a strange light of hope, waiting for the tide to turn. No one knew when it would happen. And how many graves it would cost.

Chapter 12

The Hidden and the Revealed

'Sarsari tum jahañ se guzre
Varna har ja jahan-e-deegar thha.'
('Speedily we went through world
Yet at every point there was world within a world.')
—Mir Taqi Mir

It was December of 1989 when we embarked on our journey through the Valley, via Zooni's own village, Pampore, known for its fields of saffron, now hidden from us as they hibernated under the freshly fallen snow. With her songs resonating in the black metallic body of my car, we plunged into the darkness of the tunnel called the Banihal Pass. At 2000 metres above sea level, it pierced through the magnificent Pir Panjal range. The Jawahar Tunnel, as it is now known, emerged at Qazikund and entered the Kishtwar Valley. The light at the end of the tunnel was still blurred and the tunnel itself, dark and dreary. We drove through Rajaouri, where, in the intestines of the Chingus Sarai, lies buried the entrails of the great lover of Kashmir, Jahangir, emperor of India, then the wealthiest kingdom in the world. It was his father, the greatest of the Mughal emperors, Akbar, who had annexed Kashmir, expanding its dominions like never before. Jahangir had died in October 1627 on his return from his beloved Valley. The drive reminded me of what happens when one is in love and how one journey leads to another. Mary McFadden joined me in Delhi, and we drove to Kotwara.

Kotwara has always been the end and the beginning of many journeys. When Mary arrived in Kotwara she exclaimed, 'Wow, this is a haven for craft!' This has forever resonated in my mind, and in spite of not having a business mind, like of those running the largest sugar mill in Asia, this thought made a deep impact on me. Each time I went to Kotwara I felt things were sliding down. To have somebody bring them back up was topmost in my mind. I had been married twice but maybe for both Geeti and Subhashini, Kotwara was too ordinary a dream to pursue. I had emerged from one shattered dream called *Zooni* to another. There were millions of people in the valley who lived nursing their own shattered dreams.

As Mary and I drove back to Delhi, we crossed thousands of buses. They were going to Ajmer Sharif, for the Urs of Sultan-ul-Hind Hazrat Khwaja Moinuddin Chishti, also known to simple folk as Gharib Nawaz. The same saint to whose grave Emperor Akbar had walked barefoot to ask for an heir to his throne of a shattered land: the same Jahangir who loved Kashmir. Akbar had walked from Agra to Ajmer and felt the plight of an ordinary traveller. He felt the thirst, he dug wells; he felt the heat and the need to rest; he planted trees and built *sarais* (inns) along the way. At the shrine of the Khwaja, Akbar received Divine guidance to go to Hazrat Shaikh Salim Chishti in Fatehpur Sikri to plead for an heir. 'Go and plead before him like an ordinary man and not the emperor of Hindustan, whose borders know no end.'

The great emperor arrived at the Shaikh's doorstep in tatters, like a mendicant. He went down on his knees and, with his head touching the ground, pleaded for a son. His plea was heard.

I had heard this story when I had gone there a few years earlier and was told to ask for whatever I wanted, which, I was told, would be granted. I wanted a daughter. I already had two sons and knew I would never have another child, as my wife Subhashini could not have more children. Still, I asked. Maybe miracles were possible, even though I had done nothing like Akbar to get what I wanted.

Those buses spoke a different language, that of dreams. These were collective and individual journeys, each no less than that of the mighty Akbar. Khwaja Moinuddin Chishti was a phenomenon unknown in a civilization which was unaware of the beauty of poverty, where thousands

were named Salims and millions named Moin. Being displaced by a
wave of separatism that had engulfed the valley, I felt the larger national
relevance of the Khwaja, who was also known as 'Hind-al-Wali', the Saint
of India. Banners to this effect fluttered from the colourful buses. The
journey was long and revealing, opening new vistas that belonged to Him,
that every tired and helpless soul felt they owned. It was in one of these
buses that I found myself, feeling the wind caress the tired eyes, of young
and old alike. '*Har dam ba libas-e-digar aan yaar bar amad, geh peer-o-
jawanshud* (Every time he appeared in a different garb, sometimes young
and at other times, old).'

The people in those buses were beautiful, vulnerable and tender,
shedding all trace of arrogance as they boarded the vehicle, which was to
be their home for the next fifteen days. They were themselves characters
from mystic verses: simple souls, love-crazy, living in these buses. Old
men wearing bangles as Khwaja-crazy faqirs—Khwaja *ki diwani*. They
danced like luxuriant trees in the wind, their glass bangles like leaves on
branches clinking on their crinkled wrists. These were moments of faith,
and droplets of *dua* shone on their foreheads. They were like *ayaats* from
the Quran '*Inallaha ma sabreen* (God is with the patient) . . .'

I was opening up to a new sense of beauty. I felt one with the simple
folk who were part of this journey, always at the receiving end, coming
back each time enriched. A journey from the self to the self.

To me it was a bigger experience than *Zooni*. For me, these people
in the buses visiting the Sultan-ul-Hind were beautiful and real. Their
journey was through Delhi, where rested Hazrat Qutubuddin Bakhitiar
Kaki, Hazrat Nizamuddin Aulia, Hazrat Nasiruddin Chiragh Dehalvi, and
then on to Ajmer Sharif. This was a journey people yearned to experience.
To cleanse themselves of the temporal world and enter the realm of the
heart. Seeing this grand yet touching spectacle of the travellers journeying
to Ajmer, I thought to myself that people of the Valley should experience
this phenomenon. The Sultan-ul-Hind was in India. Why would they
look beyond the borders?

The journey was elating, and I could hear answers blowing in the wind
to the questions that worried me no end when I had returned distraught
from the Valley. I talked to Mary, and she too was most elated with the
idea of bringing Abdul Ghani Namahali and his group of Kashmiri Sufiana
musicians, presenting them at the dargah in Ajmer and documenting them

through a film. It became a larger-than-life dream. I spoke to Shiv Shankar Sharma, the then director general of Doordarshan, of this thought. He jumped at the idea, and he sanctioned this on top priority as the Urs was about to commence. Urs is the celebration of the union of a saint with his Beloved, the Creator. Thousands of miles away, Jalaluddin Rumi's Urs is called Shab-e-Aroos, the night of union between Rumi and his Beloved, celebrated on 17 December in Konya. Always a magnificent day when the city is covered in snow and bare trees stand in rows with their branches raised to the sky. Something I would experience in time to come, when Rumi would become my new dream a decade later, to be made into a feature film.

The Urs of Hazrat Khwaja Moinuddin Chishti consists of a series of rituals ending in the *ghusl*, the bathing of the shrine. Whoever comes to experience this occasion is washed in his grace and beauty. They are immersed in purity.

My musicians from Srinagar arrived. We all met in Ajmer, where we stayed in a small hotel near the dargah. Shivshankar Sharma was indeed an outstanding officer of Prasar Bharati, during the long association I have had with the organization. He made things happen. He had visited Kashmir while I was shooting *Zooni*, and we'd talked about what should be documented in the valley after *Zooni* was over. But the valley never saw better days after 1989. Why? We will never be sure of the answer. Maybe they go all the way back to Partition and the unrest it led to. But those were the last of the better days.

Abdul Ghani Namtahali; his sons, Ghulam Nabi and Abdul Rashid, both of whom played the santoor; and the other musicians who played the rabab, saaz-e-Kashmir, the nut and the tabla, all arrived. We shot with them extensively in the dargah, taking the camera where the lens could never have tread before. Maybe because it was blessed by the tears of the *zaeereens* (pilgrims), cooking amid the smoke of their makeshift stoves, living in their makeshift homes under the shade of their busses.

Next morning, a musician who played the saaz-e-Kashmir came to me with tears running down his cheeks. He took me aside and told me of a dream he had last night. He wept as he said that I had received the greatest gift he could imagine from the Saint.

The Kashmiri *chhakri* (folk dance) took us into a trance. Its rhythm was in sync with the movement of hands cleaning the floors and walls of the dargah, as if perfectly designed for this activity. I still get goosebumps when I hear the line '*Ay gada karaṅ sada, salle ala Mohammada* (O faqirs, let's raise the call, bless Mohammad and his family).'

Music has an arresting sense of relationship, and this was the genesis of my newly found passion for the Sufi music of the Valley during the making of *Zooni*. Namtahali's group had a powerful sense of rhythm and melody, which has held me to the Valley. Bollywood was different. It was all about name, not passion, about not only talent but its commercial viability. Having been in Air India when embarking on *Gaman*, my approach to making that film was different. And my approach to Kashmir was different. I was far from its politics or its commerce, which was the one thing that Bollywood always saw.

In Ajmer Sharif, I saw a way of looking at the soul because of our intent and the company. Being there with Namtahali Sahab was a blessing I will always cherish.

Like the other pilgrims to the dargah, I had literally taken a full circuit. The film was a humble tribute of those afflicted by the pain of separation. '*Kushtagaan-e-Khanjar-e-Tasleem ra* (Those wounded by the dagger of submission).' The saint was fond of music, *sama*, and prayers, namaz. Thus, I called the film *Sama*.

This was to be the way things would proceed after the path of *Zooni* had closed for me. Poetry would come and receive me with open arms. Poetry of *Sama*. From that time on, I found new meaning in both poetry and music. My ustad, Ghulam Mustafa Khan, the great vocalist whom I had used in *Umrao Jaan* and *Aagaman*, showed me the way.

I am still on that quest and will always remain in search of greater and higher musical experience that would bring me to the threshold of the Divine. As long as my mind is open and my heart is free, new things will find me.

Meanwhile, people had lost the plot, and it was too late for *Zooni*. She was too bruised and battered to show the way. Bollywood was a cauldron of insecurity and ugliness. Small minds with narrow agendas subjugate giants and make them into pygmies. Money becomes the only criterion for art. Emancipation of the soul has vanished. After Partition, India did progress in leaps and bounds, but its qualitative and creative aspects never prospered. Films being one example. We lost our finer sense of culture, we lost Urdu, and we never dared to ask why. English became the way forward. We were falling into a colonial trap on the one hand and a communal one on the other. Today, we have lost a finesse that we had once prided ourselves on.

Zooni had been designed as a bilingual biopic, the first one at that. I wanted to share the history of our land with the world. Today, English is a necessary bridge. While we prided ourselves on being more English than the English, several English and American scholars were enriching themselves by discovering the scholarship of Persian and the spiritual wisdom of Rumi, Hafiz and Saadi. Unfortunately, India, at the grassroots level, was getting poorer and polarized.

Rumi has defined himself as placeless and traceless. He belongs to the soul of the Beloved. The everlasting concept of a faceless Beloved allows you to imagine beauty. You behold Beauty that is invisible. And when such an invisible beauty enters your being, you acquire an art that crosses all boundaries.

The mystics of the Valley had shown me the way. Their sense of formlessness had opened new vistas of interpreting craft.

In 1990 I met the famous Sufi scholar Seyyed Hossein Nasr. His book *Islamic Art and Spirituality* gave an intellectual insight into many things that were confused with orthodoxy—oneness and beauty and the concept of space.

For me, craft became the larger purpose of human behaviour and the ornament of nature in design. Design began to manifest itself with the geometry of knowledge as seen in the play of light and shade, thus creating a universal vocabulary of aesthetics attributed to the One Creator. Nasr opened up a philosophy of love and logic, which Rumi expressed in his *masnavi*. Having stepped into Delhi from a piece of paradise and a haven of craft, I thought everything he said made deep sense. He took me to Humayun's Tomb and the surrounding ruins, and to Arab Ki Sarai, which seemed to come alive with his presence. In Nasr's voice was a sacred resonance 500 years old. It spoke of a timeless truth.

Har naqsh ra ki deede jins-ash ze-la-makaanast
Gar naqsh raft gham neest aslash chu javedaanast . . .
(Every form you see has an archetype in this placeless world
If the form perished, no matter, since its original is everlasting . . .)
—Rumi

Nasr wrote of Hazrat Ali as being the head of every craft guild of his time. I was reminded of the Valley and the entire craft universe which kept reiterating the unity of Allah. This gave beauty to human effort. God has inscribed beauty in all things. I was preparing for a journey into craftsmanship, of which I had already had a stint in leather with Bharat, the craftsman from my Bombay days.

Delhi had become the centre of a design renaissance, with people like Pupul Jayakar, Kamaladevi Chattopadhya and others emerging as its doyens. Indira Gandhi was indeed the protagonist of the weaving world and with her inspiration, Pupul Jayakar could change the face of Weavers' Service Centres around the country. In fact, it was Pupul Jayakar who wrote to Rajiv Gandhi that *Zooni* should see the light of day, as Habba Khatoon was Indira Gandhi's favourite heroine in history. I had met Rajiv, and he was most positive about it. He assured me that even if his party had to stand guarantee alongside the Government of J&K, he would be willing to do so. One of his aides, now in the present regime, said that if Rajiv did so he would resign. It was then that I realized that such intelligent people were actually quite petty in the head! This was going to be my plight from then on.

It was then that Patwant Singh saw my short film *Sama*, which touched him deeply. He immediately wrote to Jagmohan, the then governor of J&K. He, too, refused to be of help, passing the buck to the popular government which was under Farooq Abdullah. The journey of putting *Zooni* back on rails introduced me to everyone who mattered. It showed me their pettiness and insincerity. I spent almost forty years in realizing my dream.

I lived in many strange places in Delhi while waiting for *Zooni*. I slept on the floor with no furniture in the flat. All I had was a thin mattress and a quilt. No one to look after me except Tahir, to cook two meals a day. I went from door to door in an effort to make the Government of J&K honour their guarantee for the completion of *Zooni*. Times were hard for me in Delhi and for people in the Valley.

Chapter 13

Call of the Soul

'*Khamosh kardam ai jaan-e-jaan-e-jaan-e-tu ba-go*
Zarra zarra ze-shauq-e-rukh-e-tu shud goya.'
('I am silent, speak thou,
O soul of soul of soul,
For in every bit of you I find meaning to my desires,
In each desire it is your face that speaks to me . . .')

—Rumi

I write this book as a dreamer's manual. For if you are a dreamer, you have
to be ready for many dreams to go unrealized, be broken, shattered. I had
to rise above my shattered dream called *Zooni*. I had to find my feet in this
world of utter helplessness. I had to see the good in this. Only minds like
the Sufi scholar Nasr could help you do this. I am glad I met him no earlier
and no later than 1990.

I had begun spending more time in Delhi in the hope of finding someone
who could bring *Zooni* to fruition. In between my trips to government
officials, politicians and potential financers, I met the architect Anil Laul
through S.K. Sharma of HUDCO. These were intelligent, forward-thinking
people of the time. They were looking at architecture as a new idiom of
public life. It was like starting life again, as I had done in Calcutta. I was
not looking at money as a sense of motivation. I was taught something else.

Sufism, *tasawwuf*, was teaching me that without a master there was no way to see the straight path, the truth. So when you are exposed to *mehfil-e-sama*, spiritual music, you realized the concept of a master, an ideal human. Sama almost always began with the 'Qual', a quote from Prophet Muhammad: 'Of whomsoever I am the Master, Ali is the Master.' This opened the doors of music like never before. It became a composition, an invocation to Allah. It taught the world the highest form of guru–shishya tradition. It gave new flight to creativity. For we were talking of beauty and love at the ultimate level—where the two became one.

Hazrat Ali was the greatest *ashiq*, lover, in the world, and this *ishq* for Allah was carried forward generation after generation. This ishq was coupled with knowledge—a knowledge which made the human soul universal and yet bow in humility. Hazrat Ali was taught to receive learning with grace, and he is known to have said, 'I am the slave of him who has taught me a single word.' And thus the Prophet deemed it fit to say for him, '*Ana Madinatul ilm wa Aliun babuha* (I am the city of learning and Ali is the gate).' The concept of the *pir-o-murshid* (master and disciple) therefore came to be exemplified through the Prophet and Ali's relationship—a relationship that will always illuminate the world through many *silsilas* (orders) and continuity of human lives.

I had begun to see things, feel people in a different manner, and the perception of pir-o-murshid became a modern creative experience through which I would see relationships differently. It was necessary to see the world through the eyes of love and beauty. One needed to be guided to understand the essence and the difference between the hidden and the revealed. Only through the eyes of the master could this be achieved. Soon enough I realized that this was a full-time engagement!

Kashmir was just one milestone. There were many more. There was too much beauty Allah had strewn around for his creations to see. But nothing was possible without the 'Qaul'. I feared that qawwali might become too commonplace if it moved out of the dargah, the shrine of a saint, from where true spirituality emanated and touched the soul. Touching souls was my main concern. I was neither a singer nor a writer nor a patron. How could I maintain the purity of this through my own artistic expressions? This is still my concern. There is a fine dividing line between sense and nonsense, and beauty is its silent measure.

Through the wisdom of Nasr, I began to see in Rumi the inner secrets of the Quran—mystifying, poetic, lyrical. I began to see the man behind the mischief, ego behind the power, cutting across all religions, Islam in particular. Misled Muslims and Hindus were their own biggest enemies, and colonial powers in India had taken full advantage of this. I was born in the midst of this experience, putting two and two together, measuring the past with the present, the present with the future.

The world was flowering on the one hand and being destroyed by subjugation on the other. Rumi was an element, like gold, that aways enhanced its value. He was the measure of each person's spiritual sensibility. He was a bridge between cultures, saving them from themselves, from self-destruction. The idea was to understand the beauty and purpose of His creations. He taught us to unlearn and learn. To learn from others, to acquire knowledge that would build bridges through which knowledge could be disbursed. Knowledge, as a means of enlightenment, not subjugation.

Religion was not designed to pit one against the other's faith but to celebrate each other: the commonality and the difference. India at its zenith, during the time of Mughal emperor Akbar, was this remarkable land that united people of varied castes and creeds. When all the craftspeople were treated as equal. When art and architecture were the result of a cerebral blend of philosophy and faith. The illiterate emperor would weep when he heard Rumi. He told his officials, 'Read Rumi. He will make you a better human. If you are human, this nation is human.'

The 1990s was emerging full of questions. What could one do? Maybe some of the answers to these questions would have led us to understanding the anguish of today. But politics drives one away from truth. Kashmir was full of politics. Every person was steeped in politics. Yet the alluring beauty of the Valley and its people was attractive and continues to be so today, and will remain so for all time to come. I was mauled by the happenings in the Valley, yet I am deeply touched by what people could do with their art and talent. I do not wish to make any claims, profess any promises, yet people have the power to change.

The nineties introduced me to Ajmer, where self-effacement was a prerequisite to receiving His grace. This empowered one to see beauty in everything. When you are witnessing His grace, you are witnessing His beauty. As a film-maker, my medium was about showing, not to be seen.

I wanted to make the world sensitive to beauty. *Zooni* was just a way, I realized, and if not that, then there would be other ways. I had chosen film, the most difficult of all the ways.

I returned to Bombay in early 1990 and tried to raise some money to take the journey of *Zooni* forward. I did not know where I belonged, what belonged to me, who belonged to me and to whom I belonged. These were days when Rumi began to dawn in the clouded horizon, calling out, come . . . come . . . That was my truth.

> *Biya biya ki niyabi chu ma digar yaari*
> *Chu ma ba jumla jahan khud kuja ast dildaari*
> *Biya biya wa ba har su-e rozgaar mabar*
> *Ki nēst naqd tu ra pesh-e ghair bazaari*
> (Come, come! For you will never find a friend like me.
> Where indeed is a Beloved like me in all the world?
> Come, come, and do not spend your life in wandering to and fro,
> Since there is no market elsewhere for your money.)
>
> —Rumi

I was opening my eyes to a place in the world I did not know. Kashmir was no more the paradise I knew it as. The world of Habba Khatoon was had no connect with the make-believe, ugly world of Bollywood. The world of *Zooni* was beyond the world of cinema. It was Habba's eternal search for her beloved. It was this search that gave her poetry and music. It gave a new meaning to nature, which has no questions and no answers. It was saga of the Sufis who said,

> *Tu ham chu vaadi-e-khushki va ma chu baarani*
> *Tu ham chu shahr-e kharabi va ma chu meemari . . .*
> (You are the arid valley
> I am the welcome rain
> You are the city in ruins
> I am its resurrection . . .)
>
> —Rumi

The mystics played hide and seek with beauty, and beauty with them. They drowned themselves in love, and love drowned within them. Through their words they pulled you to the shore and dragged you into an infinity of formlessness. Resonance was given a new meaning, and formlessness became the secret of the soul. I was in Delhi. I was waiting for someone to tell me where I was. But no one knew of my quest. The way was the way of Gharib Nawaz. Who was he, and why did he journey thousands of miles to where he was relevant, giving away all he had in the process? Ideas are shaped through quests and quests through ideas. Maybe I was wrong. *Zooni* was not to be made, and yet it was the need of the time. Whatever I did had to be done to reveal the quest and with it, the ugliness of the world that would not let me reveal the quest.

Each khanaqah was a world unto itself. Messages were presented as stories, that remained with you to light your path. The masnavi of Rumi had become a way of telling stories for centuries. It had taken centerstage of many a khanaqah and its bazaars, where cultures revolved. I was moved by the story of Hazrat Khwaja Moinuddin Chishti, his early life and travels. I wanted to tell his story in moving images. So as the next step to *Sama*, I decided to make *Seena-ba-Seena* (From the Heart to the Heart), a very humble tribute to someone larger than life. And it was this that changed my life. I woke up into a new way of understanding the world. Understanding successes and failures needed a creative and spiritual expression. It was the only way to realize the power of quest. A quest which had driven the Saint to India, made him settle in the desert, see the will of God. He was sent to make more saints, humanize emperors and equalize mankind. He was sent to liberate souls, create sama, mystical music. This was an uphill task. The unity of one creator, while acceptable in the higher Hindu philosophy, challenged the very basis of mythology, idolatry, culture and rituals. It was a conflict of ideas, and the arrival of a Sufi dervish on the horizon posed a threat to irrational thought, to an era of magic and miracles.

I had a desire to find my way into the world of the Saint who was thrown into the arid desert of Rajasthan to show light to the world. *Seena-ba-Seena* was my turning point, my epiphany. I got a poem written by Mohammad Ali Mauj, a producer at All India Radio introduced to me by Sardar Javed Khan, my talented friend from Rampur, truly a director's actor, but in many ways more learned than the director himself. His acting, knowledge of Urdu poetry, its elocution, music, singing always inspired me, and by using his knowledge and talent I thought of making a short, one-hour poetic film on the life and journey of Hazrat Khwaja Moinuddin Chishti. I got Khan Sahab to grow a beard and commit the poem by Mauj to memory, and travel with a group of Rajasthani bards in a camel cart through the expansive landscape, as if an invisible Khwaja was himself part of the journey. The story unfolded in layers, as the group traversed the desert towards the dargah. The concluding sequence was shot within the precincts of the shrine.

It was an elevating experience. Each portion was a slice of a mystical journey. Each milestone, a question. Why would this young man leave his soil and take this journey on foot to an alien land, through unfamiliar terrains associated with the amazing mythology of fertile imaginations? What had he come to seek? Had the Prophet of peace appeared to him and directed him to come to Hindustan as a torchbearer of love and justice?

It was Divine grace that brought the saint to Hindustan. He came with the message of Imam Husain, the Prophet's grandson. A solitary man's message of love, peace and equality, reminding the world what Husain stood for. In his words:

> *Shah ast Husain Baadshah ast Husain*
> *Deen ast Husain deenpanah ast Husain*
> *Sar daad na daad dast dar dast e yazeed*
> *Haqqa ke binaye la ilaha ast Husain.*
> (Husain is king, the king of kings,
> Husain is faith, the refuge of faith,
> Who gave his head but not his hand in the hand of Yazid,
> Husain was the foundation of there is no God but God.)
>   —Hazrat Khwaja Moinuddin Chishti

People have flocked to him for more than eight centuries to receive that clarity without which the soul is clouded. *Seena-ba-Seena* was a journey of the cleansing of the heart, the reflection of one soul in another that connects decades and centuries. Reflection is an important essence of this quest and journey. It removes the clutter of the mind and takes a novel, minimalistic view of creativity. It interprets unity in all its manifestations. Love and surrender in all its forms. It appears in people, places, poetry, sound, music and in the sacred dance, when the difference between the mind, body and soul is eliminated. This is sama in very abstract terms.

I got the *Seena-ba-Seena* project approved by Doordarshan. Somehow, Doordarshan has been my mainstay for simple thoughts like these. People in the organization held me in high esteem because of my non-commercial ideas about content. I worked on long-term thoughts. It was for this reason that, in 1983, Indira Gandhi nominated me to a high-powered committee for the development of software for television, which also included my colleague Shyam Benegal. In those days, S.S. Gill was the information and broadcasting secretary. Years later, I was nominated as member on the board of Prasar Bharati, for seven years, responsible for content development. This was the most barren period in my life. There was nothing that I could make happen.

In 1984, Mrs Gandhi was assassinated. I remember that morning distinctly. I was travelling by train from Lucknow—as usual, in an unreserved third-class compartment. There was a furore outside the grand Ghaziabad station. As the train chugged to a stop, smoke filled the early-morning sky and newspapers sold as intensely as tea. Amid the sounds of '*Chai . . . chai . . . chai garam chai*' came the announcement, '*Indira Gandhi ki hathya* (Indira Gandhi murdered)!'

I forgot the tea and snatched the paper just as the train pulled out. I was shell-shocked. I hurried out of the New Delhi station and took my familiar route to Sujan Singh Park, where I often stayed with Mala and Tejbir Singh. Mala is the daughter of the scholars Ramesh Thapar and Raj Thapar, and Tejbir, known to his friends as Jugnu, is the grandson of Sir Sobha Singh, the builder of Lutyens's Delhi. Together they edited a very relevant journal, *Seminar*. Both had inherited their parents' progressive outlook towards India, the exact opposite of that of Pakistan's. In fact, Indira lost her life to a misplaced sense of divisive politics that had begun to raise its ugly head. An anti-Sikh riot erupted, with Prithvi Raj Market, next to Khan Market, and Sujan Singh Park as its epicentres. The entire city was engulfed in mindless violence. The sky darkened with the smoke of ill-placed hatred. I took Jugnu and his brother's children along with their mothers, and checked into Ambassador Hotel under my name, while the men took turns guarding their home. Before this, I had no idea what violence meant. I knew Muslims were vulnerable, but at that moment I realized that Sikhs were no less vulnerable. A new sense of fear began to surface in India. I was to go on to Bombay by Rajdhani. When I went to board the train, blood was still being washed off in the compartments. I was shaken by this sight. I had no idea India could be so intolerant.

Displaced from Kashmir, I felt the same kind of helplessness then. *Seena-ba-Seena* opened a new world. It was a one hour film on the life Hazrat Khwaja Moinuddin Chishti. I had got Mohammad Ali Mauj to write a poem, which would be narrated by Sardar Jawed Khan to a group

of Rajasthani singers. I had seen Meera walking about in the Building
Centre in Delhi, run by architect Anil Laul, where they experimented
with alternative building technology in partnership with the Housing and
Urban Development Corporation. Meera was an architect working at the
Building Centre. I was taken up with her quiet grace and an aura of a
powerful sense of responsibility. I thought it would be a good idea if she
could be a part of the group of Rajasthani bards that were going to Ajmer
for the shoot. I asked Meera if she would be a part of the group. She smiled
and agreed. It was not much of a role, except being a part of a film on the
saint's journey from Chisht to Ajmer. I wanted a clean slate on which the
story of the Khwaja would unfold. That was my impression. I have always
lived on impressions.

I was growing out of the art of creating needs, into the art of reaching
out, but without any expectations. This was the Sufi way, as I was coming
to realize. And to carry big dreams on your shoulders without means
was no short of His *rahmat* (mercy) upon you. A heart-to-heart is an
unending source of gratification, both spiritual and aesthetic. The kind
that the Sufis lived with. People went to them for this endless satisfaction
and will continue to do so for all time to come. Their legacy is a miracle
for humanity. It makes the human being tender within and flexible in
behaviour. *Seena-ba-Seena* is about that miracle of the soul which will
forever flower, forever bloom. The poetry of the mystics was the fragrance
of this garden of the soul. From Delhi we drove to Ajmer, and for over a
week we shot *Seena-ba-Seena* at the dargah, and in the fabulous landscapes
and ruins in the vicinity.

From Ajmer I came to Delhi, following in the footsteps of the Chishtis.
Delhi came to be known as *Darul Auliya*, the city of saints. When we look
back, we see Delhi as a reflection of this spiritual mirror which had always
negated the power of politics and kingship.

It was in this cauldron of power and spirituality that Hazrat Khwaja
Moinuddin Chishti sent his disciple Hazrat Qutubuddin Bakhtiyar Kaki
in the thirteenth century, to spread the warmth of his divinity in this part
of the country that was always going to stand up as the torchbearer of truth
against the citadel of power.

Hazrat Bakhtiyar Kaki was a symbol of forbearance and patience. He
was so kind that he became the beloved of Delhi. This popularity became
a major problem, and he was asked to be taken back to Ajmer with the

Khwaja. But on the day he was to leave he was surrounded by the populace and not allowed to leave. He had to be left behind. He was always ecstatic in mehfils of sama, and one day, while a qawwal was reciting a poem by Jaam, he passed away in ecstasy.

Kushtagaan-e-khanjar-e-taslīm ra
Har zamaan az ghaib jaane dīgarast.
(He who is wounded by the dagger of submission
For him the Divine has created secret worlds.)

With the generosity of these saints, Delhi had become a centre of the Chishti order. Hazrat Nizamuddin Aulia, a disciple of Baba Fariduddin, succeeded Hazrat Bakhtiyar Kaki. Having lived and worked in Delhi for fifty years, he had seen a period of great political upheaval with the end of the Balban dynasty and the rise to power of Alauddin Khilji followed by the Tughlaqs. He survived through several dynasties with the Chishti philosophy of abstaining from politics. His relationship with Ghiyasudin Tughlaq was far from cordial. As the sultan was returning to Delhi from his campaign in Bengal, he sent a message to the Saint to leave the city before he entered. The Saint replied enigmatically, '*Hanooz Dilli door ast* (Delhi is still far away).' A grand reception had been organized for the sultan in a pavilion built by Muhammad bin Tughlaq outside the city. The pavilion collapsed and the sultan died—a miracle or sheer coincidence. Nizamuddin Auliya remains a living legend.

He was succeeded by Hazrat Khwaja Nasiruddin Mehmood. One day, a huge storm hit Delhi, blowing off every lamp in the city. Only Hazrat Nasiruddin's lamp survived. He was thereof called Chiragh-e-Dehavli. The fifth spiritual successor of Hazrat Moinuddin Chishti, he was the last of the Sufi saints of the golden age of the Chishti order.

When I arrived in the plains I began to see beyond the mountains. I began to see simple people like moments of truth. I felt like a lover, like Khusrau, the little that I knew of him, beyond the pages of history. He had been blessed by his *pir* since childhood, with a sense of sound in which the birds spoke to him. People flocked to hear that sound. As an eight-year-old, he watched a pigeon on the gate of Hazrat Nizamuddin Aulia's abode. As the pigeon strutted to and fro, Khusrau saw his might and majesty increase. He appeared like a regal bird of prey that adorns the hand of the sultan. He thought of the shaikh and a quatrain came to him:

> *Tu aan shah-e ke bar aiwan-e-kasrat*
> *Kabutar gar nasheenad baazgardad*
> *Ghareeb-e-mustamand-e-bar dar aamad*
> *Biyaadatandarun ya baaz gardad*
> (You are a king at whose gate of the palace
> Even a pigeon becomes a hawk. A poor traveller has come
> To the gate. Should he enter or should he return?)

There was no looking back. It is said that Nizamuddin Aulia at once asked one of his attendants to narrate the following lines to the boy sitting at the gate:

> *Biyaayat andarun mard-e-haqeeqat*
> *Ki bama yak nafas hamraaz gardad*
> *Agar ablah buvad aan mard-e-nadaan*
> *Azaan raahe ke aamad baaz gardad*
> (O man who knows the truth
> Come in so you may become my confidant for a while.
> But if the one who enters is foolish,
> Then he should return the way he came.)

Thus Khusrau was granted the company of the pir.

Since his childhood birds were his inspiration, the garden was his playfield. A space where different birds came and sang their songs, taught them to the others and flew away. They never said this was my land or your land. Till one day, when a gun fired in the Valley and the birds flew away forever. *Jahan-e-Khusrsau* is a land of birds under a piece of sky that joins many pieces of the skies. Khusrau spoke to me softly, gently, in meaningless and meaningful ways . . . *ta tum tarana nana* . . . He kept me amused through his childlike ways and rhythms, never once making me feel like that wounded bird from the Valley. He made me feel the beauty of being the target of the huntsman. The beauty of hope. Khusrau says:

> *Hama aahuvaan-e-sahra sar-e-khud nihaada bar-kaf*
> *Ba-ummeed-e-aan ki roze ba-shikaar khvaahi aamad . . .*

(The deer of the wilderness stand with their heads raised aloft
That some day the fair huntsman will make them his prey . . .)

Being wounded by the arrow of the Divine glance is the yearning of the Sufi.
Rumi whispers the same sentiment in another breath:

Ze-pagah mir-e-khubaañ ba-shikaar mi-kharaamad
Ki ba-teer-e-ghamza-e-u dil-e-ma shikaar baada.
(That fair prince goes out for his morning hunt
May our hearts fall prey to the arrow of his grace.)

I do not know what others felt about the Valley as it was then and the
Valley now. I see many wounded by this arrow and know not the cause
of this infliction. So the way to *Jahan-e-Khusrau* was through both
poetry and pain. Through beauty and hope. It was about perceiving the
limitlessness of the blue sky. I knew that Khusrau and Rumi would show
us the way of belonging to no place and every place. This evidence had to
pour out through art, through love and beauty hidden in the soul that we
are unaware of. Rumi unfolds it layer by layer, day by day.

Rumi had learnt the lesson of formlessness and placelessness at the feet
of his master, Shams Tabrez, who knew that the Islam he was seeking was
beyond that of his stick-wielding mother or an arrogant mullah's.

Tawhid, one formless Allah, is not easy. Each day you learn and forget.

Jahaan-dar-jahaan naqsh-e-surat giraft
Kudaam-ast aziin naqsh-ha aan-e-maa
(Images grip the world and the worlds within.
Which reflects us, have you asked of yourself?)

—Rumi

Rumi, in each ghazal, tells you of this wonderment and leaves you to
unlearn. I felt like the pigeon that Khusrau saw on Hazrat Nizamuddin's
rooftop. I could not see how anyone could turn this pigeon into a falcon.
Nasr could open doors to my inner falcon. A falcon that would scale great
heights and return to the arm of the sultan.

Ba shuneedam az hawa e tu awaaz-e-tabl-e-baaz
Baaz amadam ke sayad-e-sultanam aarzuust

(From love of thee I harkened to the sound of the falcon drum
I have returned, for the sultan's arm is my desire)

—Rumi

This transformation to the falcon who flies to the sultan's arm on the
sound of his drum is divine imagery. Because nothing is what is seems to
be. Like the worldly wine, there is no worldly sultan. In the world of the
Sufi, there is the hidden and the revealed. The master teaches you to reveal
the hidden and hide the revealed to the exact extent and degree he desires.

I was entering a different realm in Rumi's poetry . . .

Aañche na-burdast vaham aañche na-dïdast faham
Az tu ba-jaanam raseed qibla azaanï maraa
(You are what the mind cannot see, no wisdom comprehend
In that abstract form, you enter me, where I bow my head)

With the filming of *Seena-ba-Seena* I saw Meera revealed to me as a way
of the Divine. It is possible that she saw more than we saw. From smoking
a cigarette at sunrise sitting behind me in the Gypsy, she was transformed
into a true gypsy of the desert. This was the gift I was to receive from the
Saint. On 13 May 1990, we were married at the Kashmiri Gate Mosque
by Maulana Syed Ali. Sardar Javed Khan and my old-time production
manager, Ahraz, were witnesses.

I told my father, and off we went in the Shatabdi to Lucknow. Shaad
came to meet us in Kanpur. I think he was happy in my happiness. My
father was a little upset, as he was very fond of Subhashini's parents. He
said, 'You know what you are doing. Don't disappoint me in the twilight
of my life.' This hit me hard. What did he mean, and what was I doing?
I had dreams and responsibilities. He was concerned about both. Were
these ever going to converge with his? Parents often wonder about this
as they question their life. What will happen beyond them? What did
Kotwara mean to him, and was it ever possible for me to do anything for
its people?

This was the question I posed to Meera when we drove there in 1990.
I needed to introduce a muse in this place, which was in a state of ruin.
I loved ruins, but those in which the soul could find refuge. I look back
thirty years, and wonder at the now and the future. The soul is the essence

of the essence. It does not exist alone. It lives by gladdening other souls around it. The soul is a yearning, a sanctuary, it is many things that mystic poets use to reveal and conceal secrets.

I returned to Mumbai to see if there was a new dawn for *Zooni*. I got some money from a friend, Raj Chopra, to do a small schedule in Bombay. Would it make a difference?

Meera was an architect. I was always captivated by architecture, and I looked up to her talent to create spaces. Film spaces and real spaces. There was a lot to do with no means to do it! Each opportunity was exciting. The *Zooni* set in Bombay was one. I was fascinated by creating light and was enamoured by those who could. I had seen Bertolucci's *The Last Emperor* and was thoroughly impressed by Vittorio Storaro's work. I wanted to play with this light. A decade later I met Storaro, and he gave me his book *Writing with Light*. Each person had his share of writing with light, and this was another milestone for me. Meera had done her thesis on the play of light and shade in Islamic architecture, and the creation of the court of Kashmir was no different, except in its construction like a jigsaw puzzle. The jaali played a mystical role at different times of the day and the year. But people in Bollywood had lost their sense of wonder. They were terrified of anything to do with Kashmir. Still, I believed in what I was doing and was keen to find another part of India where I could complete *Zooni*.

I went all over the Kumaon region and Himachal Pradesh, but there was no location that could replace the Valley. I wondered how the displaced Kashmiri would feel in any other part of India. I asked myself what Jagmohan must have felt when he began the mass migration of the Pandits. Surely, they would prefer to die like thousands of their Muslim brethren in their own motherland. When I thought of this pain, I realized my pain paled before theirs. It was my destiny to live with this pain, and this is what poetry is all about. The poetry of *Gaman, Umrao Jaan, Anjuman* and *Zooni*. A sadness that adorned the voice of Asha Bhosle reflected in the anguished eyes of Dimple Kapadia. This was to be the fate of *Zooni*. The lockdown today reminds me of the curfews of Kashmir then. The country was ill-fated then, remains ill-fated now.

Meera and I were trying to come to grips with the new situation, torn between Delhi, Bombay and Lucknow, with Srinagar tugging at our heartstrings. Once again, painting came to my rescue. I had brought a lot of woodwork from Srinagar, with an equal amount of memories. Memories of nature, mountains in spring, autumn and the winter snow. I never realized that a place could have so much exterior with the interior. It reminded me of Joseph Allen Stein, an architect who breathed Kashmir in every breath. But people felt differently. They had no idea where their freedom was taking them. Freedom was at the top of everyone's mind. Was freedom living without fear, living without want? Or was it living with a sense of tradition, a tradition of beauty? Freedom seemed like a slogan to mobilize people into warfare.

Kashmir was like a sealed bank, under a bureaucratic stranglehold. I had seen this happening each day, making any prospect of a dream coming true more and more remote. I felt that a new energy, beyond the army and politics, was needed to reinvent the Valley. I could see Kashmir freezing into a static war-torn zone, like many regions where meddling had created a muddle with no solutions. My father's favourite phrase describing the USA, 'First meddle, then leave a muddle . . .'

Meera and I had been married only a few months, and she was trying to get to know my father, my Lucknow, Bombay and Naini Tal. Meera realized the gravity of these places and the way they would pan out for artists like us. Somehow, I believed that art would always pay off. Art applied to the larger human good. Wajid Ali Shah was deposed and sent to Matiaburj, and the one thumri he wrote, with the anguish of leaving Lucknow, lives on in human history: '*Babul mora nayhar chhoto jaye* (O my father, my home is being left behind).' It has been sung by every great singer in the subcontinent. Today, after 150 years, Matiaburj is said to be the tailoring hub of India, worth Rs 15,000 crore. This made me realize the *barkat* (blessings) of human skills, something that would resonate in my mind. The question was loud and clear. How were we going to make ends meet? My films had taught me the value of craft and couture, and they had, in turn, impacted the Indian haute-couture landscape. Seeing the temperamental nature of Indian cinema, craft was going to be our mainstay. Making people feel beautiful, making them sensitive to the handmade so that they develop a vocabulary of their own was most exciting.

Vapas nahiṅ phera koi farman junooṅ ka
Tanha nahiṅ lauti kabhi awaaz jaras ki.

(The orders of madness never went unheeded
the sound of caravan bells returned with resonance.)

—Faiz

I was different to my brothers and different to my friends. I wanted to see, to show and share what I saw. There was a tactile quality in this, which continues to live in me and is the reason for my being the kind of artist I am. I see people in their natural aura, of what they don and what it says about them and their milieu. These attributes constitute one's upbringing and legacy. My mother was always surrounded by bales of silks of different colours, chintz and laces of varying hues, and a battery of seamstresses working under her guidance as they made beautiful clothing for her and other members of the household, like all women of her time and age did. When you are brought up in such a world, in which creativity and human effort are part of your culture, you never grow out of it. You are always thinking of drapes and dyeing of various shades. It is a language which is as timeless as it is futuristic, layered with nostalgia as you traverse time and places and cover milestones of art. Art, to me, was therefore very human and sensitive.

The other layer was my father's wardrobe. In my childhood I had not seen such fabrics and styling in the streets of Lucknow. Having grown up in Scotland, he came back with the most elegant clothes and with the most charming photographs in them. By the time I gained my senses, he had switched to khadi, handwoven and handspun, a complete 180-degree turn. I was just an impressionable observer on a path of art. An art in which people were people and wore what they wore to be what they were. Each ensemble was a language, like Urdu, Awadhi and English.

Opening my mother's trunks and my father's wardrobe was a secret journey into my imaginative self each time. So, when I began to create characters for my films, they became real people of my dreams, more real than real could be, more truthful than they could ever imagine themselves to be. No one I knew had done it, because no one had integrated the element of time with the language of clothes. *Gaman, Umrao Jaan, Aagaman, Anjuman, Jaan-e-Alam, Zooni, Husne Jaana,* and so on.

Ameer Khusrau and Wajid Ali Shah, with a galaxy of thirteen other poets—Ghalib, Zauq, Nazeer Akbarabadi, Faiz, Firaq, Kaifi Azmi, Mir

Taqi Mir, Makhdoom, Mir Anis, Allama Iqbal, Quli Qutub Shah, Momin Khan Momin—all unfolded their poetry with their clothing to take you on the journey of time they had lived through. Their muse inspired romance and became legends. I found through this language a spiritual and cerebral dimension which continues to fascinate me. This is a world within a world. I made a series of eighteen short films on textiles and craft, and realized the beauty and excellence of human effort. It connected profoundly with nature and human habitat as a source of inspiration, as an endless discovery and interpretation of beauty.

This wonder taught me about art in which clothing continued to evolve as a metaphor, in the most delightful and endearing way. It is my desire to make a museum of this journey. Clothes are like poetry, no less, no more. Like music, they flow in the wind and speak in silence. I am often disappointed how characters in films are let down by the clothing. Clothing is beyond what meets the eye. In a moment it defines the trajectory of the character and the impact it creates. Imagine the cumulative impact of a persona on the mind of a viewer! An impact which no words can describe. A symphony, mysterious and unique.

The beginnings were simple. Taking small steps to create beauty that would ring true. Zainab Chauhan was our first muse, and it took some doing to make the clothes speak her language, our language. It was almost like an Urdu ghazal, in the voice of Begum Akhtar, taking one into the lost fragrance of Awadh. Zainab flowed with it, and it gave her the encouragement to be the muse like none other could have been. Her finesse and sense of detail made the craft flower, the colours bloom and helped us establish a reality from a dream.

Mary McFadden, who was the designer for *Zooni*, had stepped into Kotwara and exclaimed, 'This is a haven for craft!' And so it has been ever since. Our journey was to make people more beautiful than they could imagine themselves to be. We had to connect with the thoughts and ideas I had seen. We introduced the wide pajama worn a tad above the ankle. It took not just the city but the subcontinent by storm. We had explored every aesthetic manifestation in fabric and embroidery. Our chikankari, too, found a new idiom, which continues to be a benchmark. The detailing of the neck and the sleeve created by us was unique. Since then, it has been copied with eyes closed. 'Devil is in the detail' has been our philosophy, which made each garment intimate for each user. The story of our chikan is the story of thousands of lives, including that of the makers and the users. We have created legends from the soil, from which they'd emerged. We used live qawwali and kathak to present the beauty of embroidery, white on white, black and silver, and various pastel hues of spring. We were creating stories with the music from my milieu.

Chapter 14

End of an Era

'Che daani tu ki dar baatin che shahi hamnashin daram
Rukhe zarrin man mangar ki paye aahani daram.'
('How doest thou know what sort of king I have
within me as a companion?
Don't caste thy glance upon my golden face, for I have iron legs.')

—Rumi

With this ghazal, Rumi predicted his own death on 17 December 1273 in Konya.

My father came to Bombay to escape the harsh Lucknow winter of 1990. Shaad brought him home from the station, holding him, as he was far too weak to walk on his own. My brother Guddu's death three years back had been a huge blow to him. Guddu's children, too, were kept away from him. He wanted to get out of that gnawing loneliness in Lucknow and come to me. He loved children, and Murad and Shaad were a great solace. His chest had developed congestion, and his voice had become hoarse.

I wish I could spend more time with my father when he came to stay with us in Bombay, but I had to go to Himachal to find a lost Kashmir. My assistant, Alka Gupta, accompanied Meera and me. The hills of Himachal had similar wooden architecture, but I could not find the special features of the landscape and vegetation that was found in the Kashmir Valley, where I had shot so far. I could not figure out how to connect with the visual narrative of *Zooni*. My father's condition weighed on my mind too. We returned soon. Abba Jaan's health was failing. I rang up my Phuphi Jaan, his only sister, and asked her to come. Maybe it would revive him. Seeing her fostered a great sense of reassurance, and a slight smile lit up his sharp, aquiline face as soon as she arrived. I remember that day, in late January 1991, when I drove him to the hospital on Caddel Road, opposite Scottish Orphanage, and he took my permission to leave. I was alone in the car with him and could not bear this statement. He was very clear in his mind and had often said he didn't want to live beyond eighty. He was eighty-one. He felt that everybody had to live their own life. Why would anyone bother with an old man? He had too much self-esteem. If there was a true combination of a dervish and a king, it was him.

I spent my time in the hospital watching him, listening to the few words he would say. Other times I spent in the reception lounge reading Nasr's *Islamic Art and Spirituality* and poems by Rumi. I read and reread Rumi. It had a resonance with my predicament . . .

On the bed opposite Abba Jaan was Comrade S.A. Dange. I introduced them to each other. My father narrated a couplet of Ghalib's:

Ye masayil-e-tasavvuf ye tera bayaan 'Ghalib'
Tujhe ham vali samajhte jo na bada-khvaar hota.
(Your expression, O Ghalib, and your exposition of the Divine
You would have been a saint, were you not a slave to wine . . .)

For days after he passed away, Phuphi Jaan would recollect the times they had spent together. He was everything for her. That time expanded into a whole existence. Each day was a story in itself. Like when he had come to see her in Mussoorie as a child on his way to England, to study at Oxford. She spoke little about the times they had quarreled on petty issues. I could finally grasp how relationships were created, matured and peaked, to finally end up as stories. Stories were most important to Phuphi Jaan. She was here to live out the last chapter of her story with her brother. She came to experience how a soul left the body. I knew Abba Jaan's end was near and wish I had not left the hospital when that final moment came. When I came back I was told he had gone. The final moment was between brother and sister, which she describes till today with tear-filled eyes. Phuphi Jaan recalls how she experienced the soul leaving his physical body. She still recalls this moment at the age of 101, as I write this in 2021. (A few months later she passed away.)

My father's passing changed my life. 'Abba' was the first word I had uttered as a baby.

Then began Abba Jaan's return journey, embalmed in a coffin, in the hold of an aircraft . . . through the forest to Kotwara, where he had sped through in his grandfather's Phaeton as a child and later in his gleaming Isotta Fraschini as a young adult, ending in the old mosque next to his own father. All that he had left undone had to be done. Putting Kotwara right, where no one would be hungry and ill-clad. How could I, a mere struggler in life, realize a dream the size of that of an emperor, for his village, for his country, for humanity? I sat looking at his riding boots in awe. I still see them each day as I enter my home and climb up the stairs. I am glad he did not live to see the gory communalization of the country of his dreams. It was curtains down before the worst began to surface. Meera and I made the shift to Lucknow to slowly put things in order. I began to see life with his eyes. I wish he had seen the Internet and computer in his lifetime. His mind was made for that leap. A lot of my life after him is given to this thought: 'I wish he knew how easy access to information would become, how transparent things would be.' It seems he was preparing me for it. I am also glad that he did not live to see man become a slave to and an addict of technology.

The world after Abba Jaan was a different world.

The nineties saw a powerful upheaval. The demolition of the Babri Masjid in 1992 was a shattering episode. A curtain-raiser to a new brand of petty, ugly, intolerant politics. I understood what the other side of Awadh's *Ganga-Jamuni tehzeeb* was. I understood who created it, who cherished it and were enriched by it, and who now destroyed it.

The Sufis of Awadh were an important factor to look at the much-needed harmony for Awadh. They were the true propagators of the Ganga-Jamuni culture. The ethos of the khanaqahi culture was a world within a world. I met an *ahramposh faqir* (those clad in a single yellow garb) at the dargah of Aalam Panah Haji Waris Ali Shah in Deva, a short drive from Lucknow. Haji Waris Ali Shah was a Sufi saint who founded the Warsi Sufi order, which today has hundreds of thousands of followers the world over. He passed away in 1905. Not a single untoward incident had taken place in the dargah in the wake of the demolition of the Babri Masjid. The story of the faqir, too, was unique—how he came and found ishq, and stayed on. He was a village postmaster with the name Pandit Sahaj Ram Dikshit. Now he was called Khaki Shah. He believed that people acquired the attributes of their names. Deva was a window into hearts, a window into Awadh. What a faqir receives and returns is a secret known only to him and a chosen few, but the overflow is overwhelming, and it is this that purifies the ocean of humanity that surges towards it.

I was blessed to receive the grace of Sultan Syed Arif Ali Shah of Majhgavan Sharif in Bara Banki District around the same time. Arif Mian regaled us with mystic stories and poems. His followers were numerous, but he gave me pride of place in his company. His durbar was grand, with his huqqah constantly refreshed by his *huqqabardar* (one who tends to the huqqah). It was like a ceremony and the huqqah always travelled with him no matter where he went. Indeed, Arif Mian's presence and aura reflected in all those around him. He was a nocturnal bird and stayed awake all night praying. He often recited from the masnavi of Rumi to me. He left the physical world in 2009, on 17 December, the date of Rumi's death.

Arif Mian helped me buy a beautiful mare from the Dewa mela and kept her with him till I was ready to take her to Kotwara. What was it about horses that drew a non-sporty person like me to them? Maybe the art in them. The chivalry. The loyalty. Maybe it was the imagery conjured around Zuljhinah, the horse of Imam Husain, that drew me to it. Shams, my horse from *Zooni*, had been moved to Kotwara. The landscape in Anhalwara Palace, a mud fortress built by my ancestors in Kotwara, was adorned by a magnificent grazing horse who often broke into a gallop, reminding me of my great-grandfather's days, except with no means to support a world of horses. The green, moss-clad, crumbling walls of Kotwara were vying for attention. The echoes of Shams's hooves sought company. Once a year, during Muharram, he would be made into Zuljinah and electrify the countryside.

Dewa was a place near Lucknow where beautiful horses found their way every year around the end of October, on the occasion of the Urs of Haji Waris Ali Shah. As legend goes, one prosperous zamindar, Thakur Pancham Singh from Braj, a devotee of Lord Krishna, wanted to see the *raas leela*. So passionate was he about this that everyone who came to his door was presented with this request. He was left with no desire to meet with those who could not comply. He thus confined himself and this pious desire deep within him. One day, a faqir came to his door saying that the one who could make this happen had summoned him.

Thakur Pancham Singh got ready, as Radha would to meet her beloved, and set out on his long journey on horseback along with his retinue. He reached the banks of the Gomti River, which was in full spate. Haji Waris Ali Shah had a premonition that his visitor was about to reach the river and sent boats for them.

The thakur reached the banks and saw boats waiting to take them across the choppy, muddy waters. They reached the khanaqah of the saint. It was a saint the thakur had heard of but never seen. He was asked to close his eyes. As he obeyed the command of the saint, he saw the most enchanting and enthralling raas leela. The song rose to the sky as Lord Krishna danced with his gopis. What was this dance, and why did it unfold at the behest of this saint? Only those who seek beauty can know the real truth.

Pancham became a disciple of the saint. In him he saw his Krishna, the essence of purity. The saint said only three things: Worship one God; don't ask anything of anyone; and love everyone unconditionally. Pancham is said to have stayed on with Haji Waris Ali Shah all his life, and his mausoleum at Deva was built by him. This was the essence of Awadh—a composite culture, and people visited these shrines with reverence, not aggression. Each day in Awadh was soft, gentle, full of compassion and beauty. People who came from outside were welcomed with open arms, and they became part of it regardless of their caste or religion.

By the early nineties, it was not the same Awadh. It was a testing time. A time to show the mirror, polish the heart, reflect the soul. I thought of all I had done in Awadh and all that needed to be done. I was a man with no means but only intent. Jaan-e-Alam, as the last king of Awadh, Wajid Ali Shah, was referred to by his beloved populace, was secular to the core. He would speak to me as if I was him, in poetry and music. He would watch and dance through me. He wrote poetry with his feet, painted landscapes with his eyes. I saw my father in myself, and in him I saw Rumi. A sultan forever ready to enter receptive souls.

The Awadh of the nineties had come a long way. Yet the need for harmony was at an all-time high. People were polarized through divisive agendas, which were decimating the Ganga-Jamuni tehzeeb, slowly and surely. I could see this, as I was not a poet and was looking at the journey of life through poetry, not the journey of poetry through life. Allah has created humans to both learn from and to teach. Being a seeker is the biggest attribute of being human. And the most essential quality was humility. Colonial oppression had taken us into the dark ages. Into a world of hate, divisiveness and insecurity. The enlightenment and beauty of belonging to another faith was lost in the darkness of ignorance.

Vahshat ne hamse loot li dam bhar mein doston
Jo muddaton mein ayi thhi shaishtagi hamein . . .
(With the madness that took over us
The refinement that came with time, my friends,
Was in an instant gone . . .)

—Javed Kamal

I had always felt the togetherness of people of different faiths was an elevating concept, but not any more.

It was not the same Lucknow we had come to. Not the same city in which Umrao Jaan was born and died. In which Anjuman united her lot to fight for fair wages. This fight was of a different nature. An ugly one that had nothing to do with humanism and equality. I knew history was being written and history was being erased. The question was, which was faster?

Shankar Dayal Tiwari's son, Atul Tiwari, organized a seminar in memory of his father—Comrade Shankar Dayal Tiwari Memorial Seminar. The subject was most relevant to the times: '*6 December ko kya tuta* (What was demolished on 6 December)?' The Seminar was attended by intellectuals and progressive citizens of Lucknow. When my turn came to express my feelings, I said that 90 per cent of my relations and friends were Hindus, and that I did not want to live in a ten-percent mindset. This became the headline of a prominent national Hindi daily, '*Main das fisadi ho ke nahi jeena chaahta hun – Muzaffar Ali*'.

The following day, I met Atal Bihari Vajpayee at a wedding reception at the Taj Mahal hotel in Delhi. I was taken to a special VVIP enclosure, where he sat calmly, drink in hand. He repeated that headline and said, '*Bahot achha kaha . . . bahot achha* (Very well said . . . very good) . . .' He then took a sip from the napkin-wrapped glass and repeated himself. I so wished people understood what they said, meant what they did. Something had to be done. This was our historic 'Paigham-e-Mohabbat' march. With a group of friends, I decided to undertake a *paidal safar* (a march on foot) from Deva Sharif, via every dargah and temple en route to the Gola Gokarannath temple in the Kotwara region. Hundreds of people gathered and walked with us. I just wanted to feel reassured that the Awadh of my father's dream was intact, unscathed, untouched. With us was my mare, Saba, which Arif Mian had helped me buy.

Several decades later, as I drove into Lucknow on 23 February 2022, to cast my vote, I was asked by a journalist if I had a message for the voters of the city. I was reminded of that march. I said, 'Vote for those who will protect love and harmony.' Maybe my purpose is to make people understand the beauty and intoxication of harmony and integration. I can't change people radically but can certainly try to humanize them.

Lucknow after my father seemed more filled with him. I could see my present in the light of his past. One of his articles, entitled 'Cancer of Communalism', talked about the multidimensional emergence of an Indian mind before and after Partition. A well-defined graph that needs to be understood in the larger interest of the country. This was the Lucknow I was in. I was glad my father was not alive to see the new Lucknow. He would have seen his Indian Humanist Union wither away in the face of an emerging 'Bharat'. I felt a compassionate India had to be crafted and only composite culture could be the way forward.

I was torn between a legacy and a future. I wondered how different sects of the country felt. How individuals felt, at the subjugation of the idea of freedom. Art stood at a crossroads, maybe even sinking into an abyss.

During this period, I made a twenty-seven-part series, *Husn-e-Jaana*, for Living Media, India Today. It was a story based on the first revolutionary in Awadh at the time of the death of Nawab Asaf-ud-Daula. The year was 1800, and Wazir Ali Khan, the crown prince of Awadh, had shot Resident Cherry in Banaras. He was imprisoned in the spectacular fort of Chunargarh, on the Ganga, upstream from Mirzapur, a town known for its durries and carpets. The Ganga flowed saluting its weavers and craftspeople, hearing the silent wails of a king-to-be. The British had found as a successor, a Francophile cousin of the nawab, Saadat Ali Khan, and approached him with an offer he could not refuse. 'What will you give us if we place the crown of Awadh on your head?' Saadat Ali Khan giggled and said, 'We will give you half of Oudh.' He blushed coyly, as if he had won a fortune, which he had. But Awadh was halved. Wazir Ali was kept alive as a threat to the French nawab. A few years later, the Oudh nawabs were given the title of 'King' till, finally, the entire Oudh was annexed and its last king, Wajid Ali Shah, exiled to Matiaburj near Calcutta.

This was the essence of *Husn-e-Jaana*:

Hamein bhi jalva-gaah-e-naaz par lete chalo Musa,
Tumhein ghash aa gaya to Husn-e-Jaana kaun dekhe ga?
(O Musa, take me with you, so that if you faint
I will be a witness to the Beloved's beauty . . .)

—Jigar Moradabadi

The Quran and the scriptures preceding it talk of Moses going to the mountain of Tur, where Allah spoke to him—a blazing light, which was the beauty of the Beloved.

This was where the name for the series emerged from. The poetry that I used was written before 1800. I felt that metaphors and words had a fragrance of an era they were born in. And they could only be created if the poet and director were ready to dive into that era together, like Shahryar and I did in *Umrao Jaan* and *Zooni*, and were to do again later in *Daaman* and *Nur Jahan Jahangir*.

For *Husn-e-Jaana* I decided to go with the lyrics of the time. Maybe I wanted to feel and present an evolved and tolerant India just on the brink of a colonial takeover, still immersed in a culture of love and compassion. An India which was more advanced in thought than any other nation of the time. Mir Taqi Mir, Nazeer Akbarabadi and Hazrat Turab Ali Shah were poets who wrote with compassion, with the objective to unify man and spread the Sufi message of love. I was happy that I could embrace this sense of romance through *Husn-e-Jaana*. I studied these poets of love and found what I was seeking. The series, in today's context, is even more relevant, particularly with the far-reaching impact of OTT platforms.

Kotwara came alive with over sixty-odd locations. The tailors got busy, and the village folk opened their homes for shoots and readied themselves for bit roles here and there. We introduced many new faces and new talent, prominent among them were Nandita Das, Rubina Khan, Regina Bisaria, Rushdi Hasan, Murad Ali, Mazhar Kamran, Middhat Khan, Imran Khan and Manjari Chaturvedi. It was a mini industry of sorts. I composed the music, and Chhaya Ganguly gave her voice to the lyrics. The music was scented with a fragrance of a bygone era, which Bollywood clinically avoided. The purity of the sarangi that I had imbibed from Sultan Khan during the recording for *Umrao Jaan* could rip open the soul.

In Lucknow I discovered artistes who became part of my ensemble. Sadly, they are all gone now. The Lucknow of Wajid Ali Shah is bereft of its last sarangi player, Vinod Mishra. Indian culture exists in a vacuum today. It is here that composite culture begins to make sense, when music becomes a mingling of sounds, words and voices of Hindus and Muslims, learning from and creating with each other. It is all about putting their soul on the line to connect people with each other.

> *Tu aan qaatil ke az bahre tamasha khun-e-man rezi*
> *Mana bismil ke zere khanjar khuñkhaar mi raqsam.*
> (You are the slayer who relishes watching my bloodshed,
> I am that wounded who loves to dance under your bloodied dagger.)
> —Hazrat Khwaja Usman Harooni

Thus ended the series, strangely reflecting on the times.

It was an idea ahead of its time. India Today, being only a news company at that time, was not equipped to deal with fiction. They sold the rights to TV18, who packed up midstream. But nevertheless, I enjoyed making this series. The clap for the mahurat shot was given by Moti Lal Vora, the then governor of Uttar Pradesh, on location at the Gomti River flowing through the cantonment area near Bibiapur Kothi, where I had shot a song for *Anjuman* with Shabana and Farouque a decade back.

My father's absence fired my imagination. Though he'd led a very withdrawn life, and I was struggling with films elsewhere, I was privy to what went on his mind. He spoke to me in minimal ways, through memories, nostalgia and human values. He was a giant among intellectuals in Lucknow, a Lucknow he would leave behind to pygmies. He loved the taluqdars for their warmth and innocence, but was disgusted by their arrogance and stupidity. Little did I know that I was going to inherit this legacy. His endearing dinnertime stories would make anyone fall in love with them. They featured a host of unusual creatures so beautifully steeped in Awadhi dialect. There was a taluqdar who passed away leaving no one from his immediate family as heir. After much searching, a distant nephew in his early teens was discovered and nominated heir. The nephew had been brought up in an entirely Awadhi rural culture, and his grooming as a taluqdar had to start in earnest right away.

The first lesson was on the presentation of *nazar* (tribute) to the British Commissioner. He was taught to bow and present five silver sovereigns placed on a piece of velvet cloth to the commissioner. The nephew did so most perfectly, with the right respectful demeanour. But just as the commissioner stretched his hand over the coins, the boy screamed aloud, '*Are layin lihis rahe saar* (O, that rascal would have taken it away)!' While the boy had been taught how to present the tribute, he had not been told that the commissioner would place his hand over the coins and symbolically accept the nazar, which went into the treasury.

As a film-maker and painter, how could I enrich the world I was going to inherit? I painted this Awadh on celluloid through my films.

Qaiserbagh has always been Qaiserbagh. Always in the eye of the storm. I sat looking out of my father's window as he appeared to me again and again. There were times when I wondered if he was still here.

Chapter 15

To Be the Beyond

'Har kas ke be murad shud un chun mureed
Tu ast be surat-e-murad muradash mureedast.'
('To be a true disciple, don't have any desires.
You reach your goal without the longing for it.')

—Rumi

Having completed *Husn-e-Jaan*, I discovered that without wanting anything from it I had received a lot. Looking back, I see my efforts in the light of the aforementioned Rumi verse. The two are so inexplicably intertwined that it is nothing short of a miracle. It is a reassurance of faith. I was inching towards a mystical world, which I had begun to see in the beauty of nature and people. I was seeing, living Sufism on the soil of Awadh.

Kotwara itself was a melting pot of ideas, of the coming together of beauty and humanity. I wanted to do much for the people here and also live up to my father's last desire to see everybody prosper. Film was one way to do so. It had been the source of inspiration and was to become a means of emancipation. In fact, when Meera and I got married, the upliftment of Kotwara became our main mission.

Kotwara, through Meera and my work, acquired a new aura. The tradition of period clothing of Awadh for my films, and then as a couture statement, took several strides forward and added to a new vocabulary of

214

aesthetics and beauty. The costumery of Kathak became more sensuous and ethereal, setting new standards. Kotwara, named after a village, emerged as a brand to reckon with.

In the mid-1990s, we were invited to design a pageant of costumes for the launch of the Taj Hotel in Lucknow. This gave an interesting fillip to the Kotwara style, emerging from the court costumes of Awadh. From the elaborate *farshis* of *Umrao Jaan* to the fine *kamdani* embroidered dupattas, specially hand-dyed in a variety of colours, which my mother had worn, to the elegant *daglas* and *angarkhas*, donned by the male aristocracy, and their contemporary forms—our clothes were showcased to live music and dance, with models sashaying down the ramp. The event was replete with the splendour of the nawabs. The show was aptly titled 'Jashn-e-Awadh', and we were invited to stage several similar events all over the country. We emerged as trendsetters, inspiring many an Indian designer to use live music and dance, both contemporary and traditional, to add an element of eclectic dynamism to their own shows.

I also wrote three articles for the *Taj Magazine* then, on the costumes and Kotwara's refined culture to set a backdrop of Lucknow for visitors.

Ever since then and till this day Taj has been a part of the Kotwara story and Kotwara part of theirs, ' Kotwara is an invocation to many a nostalgic memories that moisten the eyes, heard in childhood, used in my films…all night I thought of you, all night my moist eyes smiled. For me as a painter Kotwara is my canvas. As a filmmaker, a screenplay. As an artist, an inspiration.' Taj magazine June 2022

Brand Kotwara was not just about clothing but a way of life and culture, inspired by a region and its arts. *Umrao Jaan* was certainly an inspiration, just as it had inspired many of our popular Indian couturiers. We were innovators in style, taking traditional Awadh and contemporary styling hand in hand. The costumes for my film *Jaanisaar*, set in 1875, showed the influence of the West on the East, particularly in menswear. The film, released in 2015, was an authentic and innovative documentation of the evolution of a lifestyle that began changing with the advent of the hybrid culture of the Raj.

Kotwara is a journey, a legacy of design passed on from Meera and me to our daughter, Sama. She has studied fashion design and development at the London School of Fashion. London continues to be a centre for fashion, with a cultural heritage that has influenced the world. Every modern global brand has a large presence in the city. London was the place to be for Sama. Today, we have a new atelier, established at our Delhi farmhouse during the initial years of the COVID pandemic; it has given us the opportunity to create an even better ambience for our clothing to come alive and for Sama to come into her own. The space is designed to speak the language of beauty, with my paintings in an architectural setting where everything comes alive.

While we dreamt of a future for Awadh that evolved out of its heritage of interdependence between craft and culture, the venom of communalism was spreading fast. This was in early 1993. The question of starting my own political party stared me in the face. My father had done so. Why not me? I happened to meet Moosa Raza, the then advisor to the governor of UP, and asked for his advice. He said I should join Mulayam Singh Yadav. I met him immediately, offering my unconditional support. I wanted to save those vulnerable elements that would continue to make us live in harmony.

Soon after the Babri Masjid demolition, Meera and I travelled in Mulayam Singh's Tata Estate to Allahabad, Faizabad, Akbarpur, Sidharthnagar and several other towns and cities, to feel at first hand the aftermath of the communal flare-up. He was a warm and surprisingly endearing leader, and I had some intimate, in-depth moments with him while travelling through the state together. He was truly a man of the soil. A true representative of the backward class, whose plight and pain he reflected. On my fiftieth birthday, in 1994, Mulayam Singh honoured me with Yash Bharati, an award for outstanding work done in art, culture and social work. It was indeed a very special moment, as he'd invited my actors and all other artistes to be present—Farouque Shaikh, Manjari Chaturvedi, Chhaya Ganguli, Ghulam Nabi Namtahali from Kashmir, Noorul Hasan, Madhusudhan from Bengal. The previous award was given to Harivansh Rai Bachchan. Meera and I flew in Mulayam Singh's official plane for this honour. It was here that I saw a nondescript, never-seen-before person inching towards Mulayam Singh, to be photographed in every picture at Amitabh's house and then later at my own house. This was Amar Singh, the maverick politician who was to become a game changer in UP politics.

Little did I realize that there was politics within politics. I was too simple, a perfect candidate to be taken for a ride. I fought four elections within a decade, came closer to people but became distant from my art.

Politics was still a game of numbers. Nothing had changed. But I made friendships that have lasted for decades.

I treated the elections like a film and advertising campaign. There was one Firoz Nizami, a Sufi poet who wrote poetry for my campaigns, which we recorded in Lucknow using local talent. The music remains part of my association with those memories. One Zaidi Sahib was my affiliate and adviser; he was also the editor of Chaudhri Charan Singh's *Kisan Bharat Patrika*. He was dedicated to me and upheld progressive values. The people I dealt with during my election campaigns, both my workers and the people of my constituency, were pure and simple. They did not see me as one who would win or lose. They saw me as a friend for all time to come, from the first election onwards. The outer trappings of politics had begun to wane. Election agents, polling agents, polling booths, the counting and declaration of results were alien to me. None of my elections were ordinary ones. The first election I fought was from Lakhimpur Kheri in 1993. I lost by 200 votes, when ten minutes back I had been leading by 2,000! The second I contested as an independent candidate, when I was briefly estranged from Mulayam Singh, in 1996. The third, again with Mulayam Singh's party, from Lucknow, against Atal Bihari Vajpayee, in 1998. I fought my last election in 1999, from Naini Tal, against the veteran politician Narain Dutt Tiwari, once the chief minister of UP and later of Uttarakhand.

I was motivated to fight for the sake of Lucknow, the city of my dreams, to save it from the ugliness of a culture that was fast taking over, with people losing their finesse and compassion. Having seen politics at close quarters, Abba Jaan believed that it was nothing short of a revolution. He had dreamt of this revolution through the window in his room, often talking to himself, gnashing his teeth. My father's son, I sat at the window overlooking the library. Was I real? Were those books still there? The library was in the hands of bureaucrats who had little idea what was in them. The world from the window was one of cacophony. People from nearby qasbas had migrated to eke out an existence—pulling rickshaws, selling bananas, mending punctures.

Our travels to Delhi grew more frequent. Often by train. I would see Atalji regularly at the New Delhi railway station, crossing the overbridge all by himself, dressed in his usual shalwar kurta, a dress which was abused as being 'Pakistani' in the aftermath of 6 December 1992.

I fought those who threw me out of a train from my reserved seat to Delhi. Just as the Lucknow Mail was pulling out of the station in Lucknow, a member of Parliament from Uttar Pradesh barged in and had me removed from my reserved berth while the TT looked on helplessly.

This gave me the reason to fight from Lucknow. This is what Amar Singh made Mulayam Singh see in me. I plunged into the fray. I discovered that an invisible layer of the RSS had taken over the cultural fabric of Lucknow and the entire Awadh region, a reaction to the Muslim League. The erstwhile Muslim taluqdars had shattered the Ganga-Jamuni myth by affiliating with the Muslim League around the time of Partition. They were secular to the core but stood by the communal forces of the League. Fighting against Vajpayee took me into every neglected corner of the city, most of which I had seen during the shooting of my films. I wanted to create a Lucknow of my dreams . . .

> *Saari duniya mere khvaaboñ ki tarah ho jaye, ab to le de ke yahi ek hai hasrat mujhko . . .*
> (May the whole world become like the world of my dreams, this is the only desire left in me . . .)
>
> —Shahryar for *Anjuman*

Lucknow was a VVIP constituency, and for me it was even more important personally. It had inspired oceans of art, gardens of poetry, rivers of music and mountains of craft which people created with their tender hands. Of course, everybody knew Vajpayee—some had seen him, but most he had not seen. The RSS was the interface between him and the people. His popular connect with the masses was that he was a poet with a powerful command of Hindi rhetoric. In one of his speeches, Vajpayee said, 'Don't think this is an easy fight.' Lucknow was indeed the most sophisticated electorate in the country and therefore held the key to power in Delhi. Mr Saptarishi, who was the director of NIFT Delhi and the election observer later, commented that this was the most refined Lucknow-like election. But Atalji was pitched as a prime ministerial candidate. There was no way he could lose. I was the sacrificial goat; there was no way I could win. I knew I was not taking on a full-blooded fight with full-blooded support.

There was a tacit understanding with Amar Singh that I had to lose. Having introduced the raw and simple Mulayam to a glamorous way of life, and with the likes of Amitabh Bachchan and Anil Ambani at his beck and call, Amar Singh had become indispensable. He was a master craftsman, gathering the party workers and supporters close to him, always ready to give them a hearing and in times of need, a shoulder to cry on, doling out money for elections, all the while estranging the unsuspecting Mulayam from his own cadres. Mulayam was no match for his maverick machinations, or maybe he was having too good a time to care. His priorities had changed. While as a politician he wanted to win every election, he was fast losing his sheen. His uncompromising nature as a man true to his socialist ideology began to wane. His popular title 'Dharti Putr' (Son of the Soil) did not ring true any longer. One day, he told Subhashini that he didn't understand what 'Muzaffar Sahab' kept talking about. 'Should I listen to him or save my seats?'

I went door to door with a smile and a firm handshake. This was politics. At my level, it was a mug's game. At a higher level of leadership, it was a game for mugs. There was no difference between the good, the bad and the ugly. My potential voters, too, were equally helpless. Scores of them told me on the train returning to Lucknow that they went to vote but their votes had already been cast. So you can imagine the overall impact of this *farzi* (fake/false) voting machinery!

Politics is all about the ego. People had to perceive you as a larger-than-life entity. Maybe that is why oversized statues are so popular in India. Statues which evince an aura worth worshipping. This was an art form that was perfected by the Greeks and Romans, and taken forward by the European church and colonialists. Scale and proportions achieved new heights and perfection.

Art is an unusual discovery of the world we live in and of ourselves. People are constantly in an active state of imagination, and it is this imagination that burns the other. The world is becoming crueller by the day. I was fortunate that as an artist I only went up to the shore and returned unscathed. I found Rumi, and he called me back. He, too, was a victim of politics and discovered a different ocean to immerse himself in. An ocean over which the sun rose and lit up the countless waves as symbols of ishq.

I could see the ugliness of politics, smell the stench of power, and after a few years I was able to purge it out of my system once I began to see people as a reflection of that enormous ocean of ishq which Shams had revealed to

Rumi. Today, as each day dawns, I see the essence of this dancing on the surface of each leaf, on the pages of each day gone by.

Painting to me is a peaceful way of whirling a brush on canvas, setting the imagination on fire. The people of the past could become a beacon for the future. My films were a gateway into the bazaar of beauty. How each moment spoke a hundred truths.

Rumi talks about this truth, this ishq, which empowers the world. I was seeking it and met many people who could celebrate this joy of faith. I noticed that amid the Sikh community I found faith in surrendering to ishq. They were immersed in *tawhid* (oneness of the Creator) and could tell the fragrance from a distance. They were poisoned during 1947 with ideas that were alien to them. When I fought my fourth election for the Samajwadi Party from Naini Tal, I found Sardars and Muslims coexisting in the entire constituency. I also felt the undercurrent of an anti-Sikh sentiment among the majority community, which had flared up in 1984.

Simplicity was lost in the politics of caste and communalism. Something which resurfaced in the time of Manmohan Singh, a man of the people, beyond the politics of manipulation. This was my last stint in politics, fully supported by the Sikhs who were fearful of their land becoming part of Uttarakhand and the policies of the new state, which posed the risk of alienating them from their large holdings.

My brief foray into politics was an unawarded Phd in human behaviour, which is best exemplified when you retreat from it, explained in Rumi's story of the bearskin.

A dervish was traversing through the bitter snow of Anatolia. The sun was sharp, and the wind was biting-cold. He saw a bearskin floating down the stream. He thought to himself, 'What a gift from God on this cold winter morn!' He jumped in to grab the bearskin but instead got carried down the river by it. The horrified onlookers urged, 'Leave the skin and save yourself.' To which the poor dervish replied, 'But the skin is not leaving me!' It was not bearskin, but the bear itself.

One day, while staying with my in-laws in R Block, New Rajendra Nagar, Delhi, I was surprised to see dozens of SUVs, Scorpios, Boleros and Safaris pull up outside the house. One after another, Sardars in kurta-pajamas draped with shawls, accompanied by a couple of gunners each, marched up the staircase into their flat. They waited respectfully for me, and as I came out they pleaded with me to fight from the Naini Tal seat, where the Sikh community was large in numbers. These Sardars had set up an Udham Singh Nagar Raksha Samiti, to prevent Udham Singh district from becoming part of Uttarakhand in order to protect their landholdings. There was one Mr Shukla who had set up this committee, with himself as its secretary. Huge funds were poured into this movement, which appeared to be a grassroots people's movement. Shukla had convinced Mulayam to give him this seat, which he had so intelligently crafted out for himself. But the Sardars thought otherwise. A quick calculation convinced them that it would be difficult for Shukla to wrench his seat from the political stalwart and several times CM, N. D. Tiwari. They needed a person with a powerful image, preferably a Muslim, since nearly 40 per cent of the constituency comprised Muslims. Muzaffar Ali, with a home in Naini Tal and an acceptability cutting across the hills and plains, would be the best choice. After much hesitation, I realized that they had done their homework and I had to agree. The bug of politics was still alive, and it needed this particular vaccination to purge it out of my system.

Meera and I plunged into the warzone. First was the nomination that took place at Rudrapur. It was something unprecedented—an endless sea of colourful turbans and the shining metal of cars, with Firoz Nizami's lyrics '*Sardar hai Muzaffar aur karwań hamara* (Muzaffar is the leader, and this is my caravan)' blaring in the air. Rallies were followed by meetings followed by a door-to-door campaign. Shukla followed me, a step behind, praising me to high heavens and then, just before leaving, cutting me to size by saying that I did not have a grip on the situation or that I was an outsider. And then there was the master of politics, Narayan Dutt Tewari. He would pop up from his custom-made SUV's roof with the plea that this was his last election, all the while praising me, saying that Muzaffar Ali still had a long innings to realize his dreams. What had to happen happened. I lost the game to Tiwari.

Politics had soiled me, with demented leadership misleading simple minds. I strongly believed the human soul was meant to transcend great heights, but there was no leader tall enough to take the lead. Amar Singh finally struck the last nail in the coffin when he told me, 'You are not a contraceptive that we use and throw away.' I was thoroughly disgusted. His crass remark explained this brand of Indian politics perfectly. The country had lost its grace and values, and I had to find an exit. It took me a few months to heal and change my tracks.

Rumi came to my rescue once again. Even today, in the days of lockdown, I look forward to receiving more precise direction from him. It was a creative way of perceiving the essence of a culture of unity. I am painting today, and as I do so I am being shown the path that leads, connects and becomes a bridge over deep ravines and wide rivers.

I was learning from what I had done in the past and was using my own experience to teach myself. Lessons in which strange characters show up, holding our future to ransom. Arif Mian had a good sense of humour. He had named his goats after some of these characters. And maybe in the course of time had them for dinner . . .

The nineties marked a transition between a generation, between cities where I lived and where I belonged. Between people who were petty and looked at only those film subjects that would suit a big star. Advertising, too, had become star-struck. No USP, no market research, everything was a star's testimony. Imagination and ingenuity were all coming to naught. Film-making was not going to be easy any more. I always invented subjects out of my own journeys and tried to imagine a world within a world. *Daman* was one such film. I had thought of a *Daman* earlier, which was about a love story of a young architect girl and a feudal prince in Rajasthan. This was before *Zooni*. Having abandoned the subject, the title remained glued to my head, as most of my films ended with 'an'. Now a new *Daman* began to form in my mind. A love story set in the time of Partition, with the lovers separated. The boy, having strong roots, stays on in India. The girl, forced to leave for Pakistan with her parents, is married against her wish. I can't imagine the emotional trauma in the minds of people of different generations following this holocaust.

Today, an imaginary wall has been created, which keeps growing higher. An unnatural wall between people of the same DNA. As she breathes her last, she does not see that formidable wall. After her death, her granddaughter comes to bury her in the family graveyard near Lucknow, to fulfil her dying wish, and relives her grandmother's past. The journey, as has always been, was through people, poetry, painting and places. I invited Shahryar to Bombay. By then it had become 'Mumbai'. Khaiyaam Sahab was doing the music, and Asha Bhosle gave the songs her voice. Besides the fact that each song was so overwhelmingly soulful, they all had the word 'daman' in them. *Daman* had many shades of meaning.

Manzar tarah tarah ke Daman meiñ bhar raheiñ haiñ
Ham ik naye safar ka saamaan kar raheiñ haiñ.
(Memories of many sorts I pack into my minds fold
As I prepare to embark on an unknown journey.)
—Shahryar for *Daman*

The music was to me no less than that of *Zooni*, full of nostalgia and the irony of history. The film was being produced by Gramco Films, a newly formed tentacle of the Gramophone Company of India. The executive producer was one Mr Dasgupta, an odd combination of a corporate sycophant, an egoist and a control freak. I had signed Manisha Koirala as the main protagonist. Opposite her we had to cast a young boy, her lover at the time of Partition, a role for which I was planning to take my son Murad Ali. For some reason, Dasgupta was opposed to this. He had other new faces whom he felt Gramco wanted to promote. This was a dead end. I did not want to be challenged on this score. I walked out of the film. Murad had shown potential, and I was sure that under my direction he would grow well. His first film was with Mani Kaul, and he then worked with Shyam Benegal, Sudhir Mishra, Yash Chopra and, much later, Tigmanshu Dhulia.

This was entirely unfair and impacted Murad's career as well as mine. My younger son, Shaad, realized that he had to find his own way in the egoistic quagmire that was 'Mumbai'.

The shattering of *Daman* revealed the ugliness of film politics to me once again. Camps and groups, rumours and espionage. When the film was abandoned, I found people closest to me in the opposite camp. So much for those who control the money and call the shots. Dreams were after all just dreams, cobwebs lurking in the dark corners of the silver screen. *Daman* was a film that would have defined the cinema I was searching for. A cinema of a film-maker's milieu and predicament. When I look back now, I feel Rumi was making a place for himself as a light that illumines the soul. He was removing the cobwebs that were settling in the mindscape. So whatever I was to do would be a guiding light. I was not going to be dictated by money. Today, in this time of confinement, I watch two to three hours of moving images. What are these images? Even with the best of choices, are they mirrors of the soul? The art of plotting stories is based on structured time and attention span, and the hook that holds you to a spot. It is an enjoyable ordeal which has emerged from the West. Unfortunately, we have lost the keys to the universe of that art form. We have sold our souls with our faces.

> *Ba numaye rukh ke bagh-o-gulistam aarzuust*
> *Ba gusha-e-lab ke qand faravanam aarzuust.*
> (Reveal thy face for a garden in full bloom I seek,
> Part open thy lips, for sweetness in plenty I seek.)
>
> —Rumi

Each day, as I walk reciting a poem of Rumi in Persian, I am transported to a land where characters from my films stay. Where I left them as frozen images on the screen of my imagination. Poets like Rumi unfold before you like an open sky, speaking of divine secrets and wonders. They are invisible yet tightly held to the strings of your soul. These strings are miracles of the divine partnership in one's journey of sunrise to sunset, of seasons that breed art through the magnificence of the dance of the soul.

> *Aye aftaab-e-rukh ba numaye naqab-e-abr*
> *Kaan chehra-e-mashashe tabaanam aarzuust . . .*
> (O Sun of the face, appear from beneath the clouds,
> aflame and aglow, a presence I seek . . .)
>
> —Rumi

Jahan-e-Khusrau was yet to be born. Places and people were playing their games, yet taking one to the source. Rumi began to dawn slowly on the horizon like the triumphal sun with the radiance of Shams of Tabrez. He was taking over the world. The era of Rumi had arrived with the Internet. It was the greatest idea in the history of communication. I wondered how a repartee on Rumi would sound between Ayatollah Khomeini and Raza Shah Pahalvi. Arch-rivals yet bound by Rumi. Rumi was here to bridge the gulf—a gulf that would keep expanding as it was being bridged. Rumi was not an end in himself, more like the unfolding of his own verse, exciting you with the diversity of his sense of unity. He was the reflection of the Quran and the beauty of him to whom it was revealed as the essence of truth preceding him.

I began to see beauty as an expression of talent, and talent as an expression of beauty. In both situations the artist was reporting to the soul. The marketplace was an ambience of culture, and the wares were small transactions of the heart. I was travelling constantly between Lucknow and Mumbai, comparing the two cities qualitatively. How could art survive and a renewed renaissance be ushered in?

You needed people who believed in beauty as an expression of talent, and talent as an expression of beauty. Meera was part of this conviction which made the comparison enjoyable. I had started to see such people as building blocks of an Awadh ecosystem which could continue to remain pure and endearing in the dynamics of socio-political change. In Delhi, I often met Syeda Naseem Chishti, who, in spite of her ill health, was full of spirit and zeal. Her passion for Urdu and storytelling was insatiable. Each day, she would phone me and recite new poetry and plead with me to make a film. She had recently translated Emily Brontë's *Wuthering Heights* into Urdu. There was a breed of Urdu scholars and lovers who were impassioned by English. My maternal uncle Dr Mohammad Ahsan Farooqi was one, and so were Firaq Gorakhpuri and Faiz Ahmad Faiz. They took to English because more students gravitated to it, and they saw a new sense of romance and creativity in it. In fact, my uncle infused this sense of romance and drama into my mother, who was brought up in a much-protected atmosphere. I remember being told that my uncle once turned out all the students who had never been in love from a class about Shelley the love poet. Mrs Chishti was an advanced version of this romance, someone for whom films were a new chapter in their lives. She got an assignment for making some patriotic songs for Doordarshan and requested me to direct them. One was 'Zara Thahar Jao'.

I saw Manjari Chaturvedi on stage in Ravindralaya, Lucknow. In her simplicity I saw the unaffected beauty and rhythm of a ghazal. She could say things with the gentility of her body language that masters would fail to do. To this day, she carries the same vulnerability on her face, writing verse with her feet and painting landscapes with her eyes. It was purity then, it is faith now. May Allah bless her.

I told Mrs Chishti of this find and said that I would like to work with Ustad Amjad Ali Khan as the composer. Khan Sahab did a tender job of this song, which was choreographed by Manjari's guru, Pandit Arjun Mishra.

The second in the series of patriotic songs for Mrs Chishti was on the army, using the 61st Cavalry. It was a journey into horsemanship, a world unto itself. Understanding fear and fearlessness. That is why a child is introduced to the horse from an early age. The horse is the quotient of power harnessed by man; he is the measure of courage, the yardstick of loyalty. These are attributes that inspire man to scale great heights which are otherwise not possible without the chivalry and valour of the steed. Thus began my journey into the world of horses, in a spiritual and artistic way. We joined the Riding Club in the Ridge opposite the President's Estate. It was here that the riding fraternity of Delhi converged, and one got the feel of the culture of the horse. Aroon Purie, who had produced *Husn-e-Jana* and, later, my music album *Raqs-e-Bismil*, also joined the Riding Club with his wife, Rekha.

I was drawn to the Indian horse, which inspired my art, emotion and spirituality. In the entire lot of thoroughbreds, there was one unpredictable and spirited horse called Sikandar. He was a Kathiawari stallion who would immediately command attention as he came from the stable. I would go to horse fairs and enjoy looking at these Indian breeds which varied slightly from region to region. You could see Arab blood, as horses in tens of thousands must have come to India with the Turks at the turn of the first millennium. They came with their steeds and dogs to hunt and explore, thus introducing new strains in the culture of the animal world and its imagery in painting and poetry, in myth and legend.

One of the many things I always regretted was not being able to ride with abandon. Another was not being proficient in Urdu. Both had enormous visual beauty—the form of the horse and calligraphy, the beauty of the soul. I struggled all my life to reach the threshold of these two arts. My horse Barak reminds me of magnificence. I feel like a king stroking his unridden back. He often enters my work as a sign of beauty. It takes years of concentration to achieve this.

I had bought him from Deva Sharif as a skinny five-month-old colt and decided that I would name him Barak if Obama won. Acquiring each horse has been a long-drawn story. Seeing the animal, falling in love with it and finally getting it.

One day, Meera and I were driving from Delhi to Naini Tal, and we saw the most beautiful creature move swiftly on the highway near a village called Joya. I had not seen a sight like that. I stopped, mesmerized by the nodding head and the flying mane of the beautifully proportioned creature heading towards us. I asked the rider, a young boy in his teens, if he would part with it. He said no and sped on. The vision stayed in my head. The horse was called Sher Ali. For the young owner, it was a triumphant moment to have said no. It was a balance of passion, pride and the means to be able to afford the two. But passion and pride are difficult to hold on to for the poor folk of this land.

> *Hai chor nagar yaañ muflis ki*
> *Gar jaan bachi to aan gayi.*
> (In a city of thieves, the poverty-stricken,
> If they do survive, lose their respect.)
> —Faiz Ahmad Faiz

Each time we crossed Joya, we stopped to meet the magnificent Sher Ali, as though we were stopping to see the Statue of Liberty. The desire to see him was unabated. The yearning to possess him increased. I had established many landmarks as Joya approached. A beautiful dargah on a mound on the left and another on the right. This time, the owner was in need. He himself asked if I would give Sher Ali a new home. He asked for Rs 25,000. Unfortunately, we were at a low point in our lives. We left crestfallen, on the pretext that we were in haste.

Finally, Sher Ali did set foot in Kotwara and performed in *Husn-e-Jaana*. He added to the glory of the Kotwara landscape.

Each route we took had a dargah, a tree, a person, a place, an animal that one would look forward to meeting or seeing on the journey. The journey also brought us face to face with craft and with what people did with their hands in the rural countryside.

With every animal was attached a legend, a happening, a journey. I was awarded the 'Yash Bharti' in 1994 on my fiftieth birthday. It came with a small cash component. I immediately set off for the magical animal fair in Soron near Badayun. We arrived at sunrise and witnessed the most glorious sight of horses emerging out of the mist. By the time the sunlight had begun to dance on their gleaming bodies, I had bought two gorgeous horses, Barkat and Mushtari, the former a black stallion and the latter a dappled grey mare. All these magnificent horses worked in *Husn-e-Jaana*, and added to the liveliness of the Kotwara stable and the beauty of the frame.

The protagonist of the series was a gypsy girl fleeing from the wrath of the British. Being a nomad, she had to have a hound. I found a beautiful Rampur hound in Hasanpur and called her Badli. She was white with grey, cloud-like patches. Dogs and horses became part of my life. Once I thought of giving away some dogs, so I asked my friend Colonel Sarpratap Singh if he was interested in them. I was taken aback by what he said: '*Ye wafa ke nishan haiñ, inhe alag nahiñ kiya jaata* (These are symbols of loyalty and are not to be parted from).' This has stayed with me. My daughter inherited this love for dogs from me, and we have moved, generation to generation, from breed to breed. From Rampur hounds to Rough Collies and now Salukis. There was a lot to learn from the dog itself.

> Happy is the one who lives the life of a dog. There are ten dog-like characteristics every believer should possess. First, a dog has no status among creatures; second, a dog is a pauper having no worldly goods; third, the entire earth is his resting place; fourth, a dog goes hungry most of the time; fifth, a dog will not leave his master's door even if he receives a hundred lashes; sixth, he protects his master and his friend, when someone approaches he will attack the foe and allow the friend to pass; seventh, he guards his master by night, never sleeping; eighth, he performs most of his duties silently; ninth, he is content with what his master gives him; and tenth, when he dies he leaves no inheritance. Elsewhere Hazrat Ali has said, 'Among dogs, good is found only in hunting and sheep dogs. Therefore, training and knowledge are so important that even a trained dog is considered a respected model being of some value to society.'
>
> —Dr Javad Nur Baksh in *Dogs from a Sufi Point of View*

The drift towards love, *tassawuf*, came in strange ways. Layer by layer, opening one up like a rose. And finally scattering its petals as a fragrance of love. I saw music and poetry in this, and images that moved in audio-visual narratives to be called films. The energy purified, distilled, poured itself into dance. For me, this metamorphosis of the human form became a language I began to understand without its vocabulary. *Wafa* (loyalty).

As I read Rumi, I see the hidden beauty of the narrative. The gradual revelation of the Beloved in various poetic shades in its ninety-nine attributes. Allah has blessed each of His creations to coexist in the silence of peace. He has given us the power of silence to hear harmony. To drink the wine of love, to dance with abandon.

Yak dast jaam-e-baada-o-yak dast zulfe yaar
Raqs-e-chuneen miyan-e-maidaanam aarzuust . . .
(A goblet in one hand to hold, the other free for my beloved's curl
And a wide-open field to dance, I seek . . .)

—Rumi

Words are written with the pen of silence and kept bottled up for higher purposes. In the wilderness of wonder, in the dance of the billowing sands. The mystics take you into the wonderland of mysteries with meanings within meanings, and essence within the essence. This is the ecstasy that the Divine has blessed all of us with to receive and scatter. That is why such stories are formless, ageless, placeless and timeless. Such stories don't die. They live to become stronger. They become icons without a face, lest they are worshipped and lose their intoxication like wine.

It's a presence that does everything good and bad, and yet remains true to its essence. So much so that He begins to resonate in every thought. Every simile and adjective is exhausted in praise of the one and only creator. At the end, he tells you to be silent; to listen to the soul, like the reed. To rise above the power of speech and use the power of hearing is to see the Unseen. As I read Rumi, I begin to believe in my 'self'. The self which dived into my own art to discover a Rumi for the world to see. Was I truly ready for it? I knew for sure that ever since 17 December 1207, the day Rumi left the world, the world has been ready for him. He was the essence of Islam, and yet belonged to every possible faith from every part of the world. He reiterated the oneness of an invisible creator just to prove that all mankind came from the same essence. I felt making a definitive feature film on Rumi was my calling. In 2003, I answered that call.

The intent of making a film on Rumi took me through several creative milestones. Unlike with *Umrao Jaan*, I had many more dimensions prescribed by Rumi himself to explore. The way to Rumi was a way into the world. A world he lived in, seen in a time we live in. Eight hundred years flying side by side. Looking at the evidence and inspirations. It was the coming together of mankind, which had been divided by rituals invented with each passing year. It was only poetry that could explain this journey. It was only silence that could penetrate this philosophy. Rumi wrote often of this silence because of the human need to hear the divine sound. The resonance of divine thought came from a presence that inspired beauty—*husn*, a countenance that defined ishq.

Zeen Hamrahan-e-sust anasir dilam giraft
Sher-e-Khuda-o-Rustam-e-dastanam aarzuust.
(My heart is weary of these weak-spirited companions,
The company of the Lion of God and the hand of Rustam in mine, I seek.)
                                                              —Rumi

Rumi gave one the desire to go beyond the being. He seamlessly joined the past with the present and the future, beyond the life of the ordinary. He illumined one with the rays of the sun, beyond which no light could penetrate. He described *tawhid* with an abstract yet creative logic illumined by the light of the sun, falling on every invisible facet of His attribute. Rumi made you think like him, because he thought like you, or at least made you believe so. Because he was ready to admit that his own mind was limited and His Beauty was enormous. He made it evident that his learning was as gentle as his teaching. And his teaching was nothing but wrapping and rewrapping His Beauty.

I started on a simple journey through others. The journey was designed to take others with me. Imaginative and energetic, creative and talented, those who had at least taken the path, leaving their egos behind. I had to understand Rumi from the context of my own soil. The Indian way. The way of the Chishtis.

Some friends had faith in what I was trying to do. They saw the larger picture of India as a country with a wide vision. Through these people I realized that bureaucracy had come of age. They could see the beauty of the confluence of tourism and culture. I had found this in S.K. Misra, who understood my work while making *Zooni* and what it meant for the country.

The nineties introduced me to the Ministry of External Affairs. I met K.C. Singh, who was a visionary of his time. He asked me to make a film on Muslims in India. It was an enormous subject. It was very easy to show the beauty and grandeur they imparted to the Indian landscape. But to show the present reality with a purpose was what KC expected from this. The film was called *Fragrance of Love*. This title was derived from a saying of Prophet Muhammad, that it was from the direction of Hind that I got the fragrance of love. I took the premise that the character of a Muslim in India is to extend service to his fellow countrymen, regardless of religion, caste or creed. The film went further to show how education was being designed for them to extend this devotion.

Narmada is the river dividing the country into two parts. On the northern side, the economic state of the Muslims was different from that in the southern region. All this emerged post 1857. The Muslims felt the British had decimated their heritage, and therefore learning English was to be avoided at all costs. India was emerging with English as a medium of education, and it took people like Sir Syed Ahmad Khan to make the Muslim a part of the mainstream and partner in nation-building. This film project took me to different parts of India to confirm this thesis, which became an antithesis and from which emerged the synthesis.

The Muslim issue is still relevant, and in the face of global Islamophobia, India needs to reposition itself with renewed logic. Surrounded by friendly Islamic nations and a hostile yet culturally alike Pakistan, India had to play a balancing act. Faiz, Nusrat and Abida will forever remain binding influences. In recent times, the anti-Pakistan rhetoric has blunted this great opportunity for a socio-political synthesis. But the cultural ecosystem is too strong for this lost opportunity to have a long-term effect. Through the Ministry of External Affairs, I found a way of being philosophically and artistically relevant to my country in more ways than one. Essentially, the relevance of my work had to do with films and culture, with a strong tourism spin-off, and Delhi accepted me for this.

Delhi was also emerging as a fashion capital. We were pioneers in this field, having reinvented chikankari and evolved a contemporary idiom for traditional Awadhi couture. In the early 1990s, we started a multi-designer store, Carma, in Delhi, with Rohit Bal, Suneet Varma, Geetanjali Kashyap, Rina Dhaka and Karuna Goenka. With our foray into fashion, Meera and I were being relevant to Kotwara and Awadh. A new genre of dressing emerged, born out of the poetic realism of *Umrao Jaan*, as well as a logical way to help the chikankari artisans I had introduced to the world through my film *Anjuman*.

Chapter 16

Follow Your Heart

'Khamosh aye baradar, fazl-o-adab raha kun
Ta tu adab nakhwandi juz tu adab nadeedam.'
('Silence, O brother! Put aside learning and culture.
Till Thou namest culture, I knew no culture but Thee.')

—Rumi

The silence that the great Rumi keeps taking you back to each time is the same silence echoing in a different time and space. A silence that is imperative to perceive the difference and the similarity. In silence you hear music, which becomes inaudible to your outer senses as it enters the soul. The body moves in complete surrender. You feel deeply at peace with yourself in the journey. In the art of all ages, we seek silence in sound. The beginning and the end of a note, the chirping of a bird, the blowing of the wind. The poetry of silence is the truth of art. When I watch leaves, they leave me bewildered. Is it because of the sheer impact of silence that one has taken into one's soul?

It dawned on me that bewilderment is the essence of Rumi. He had danced with the ecstasy of surrender in this bewilderment, breaking open all doors. An art passed on to him by Shams Tabrez. The light of the Holy Prophet allows this bewilderment to reach His lovers, His seekers, finding beauty in the majesty of His grace, each moment revealing a new dimension not revealed till yesterday. In Rumi's verse, lost in bewilderment, you find new forms. He has understood words as the music of a mystical ecstasy never missing a beat of the prescribed structure. A language born out of bewilderment is different from that which takes you through too many doors. It is the language of tawhid, where everything returns to the same source, like the falcon on the sultan's wrist. This image is indeed a divine philosophy, beyond what meets the eye.

Through Rumi, I am equally bewildered by what I know and what I can do with him.

> *Che goyam che danam ke ein dastaan*
> *Fuzoonast az hadd-o-imkaan-e-ma?*
> (What shall I say? What do I know?
> Of a tale so infinite and me so finite?)
>
> —Rumi

The moment I read Rumi, I was sure he was our man to lead us into the twenty-first century, where the heart would rule the head. I was going through a period where things needed to find their equilibrium. This was a time when I needed to meet minds with a heart. I met Shaykh Fadhlalla Haeri in London, a man of infinite wisdom and limitless peace writ over his face. He said the most obvious thing to me, but the way and how he said it was the turning point.

'Follow your heart.'

This was the turn of the millennium, and much was expected of the year 2000. It was more than just another year. It was the revolution of time. I made a one-hour film, *Raqs-e-Dil*, to be shown on this momentous occasion on Doordarshan. It was replete with mystical dance, poetry and music, and featured my favourite dancer, Manjari, with Navtej Johar performing in the sand in the first rays of the sun rising above the Yamuna at Divan-e-Khas, Red Fort, their shadows dancing on the beautiful inlays of marble and painted ceilings reminiscent of paradise. Simar Dugal, one of Kotwara's earliest muses, and Manveen Handa donned Mughal attires and moved through its exquisite arched interiors, riding into the future at the green turf of the Riding Club at the Ridge, in classic and vintage sports coupes—Richard Holkar's Bentley, R.N. Seth's Lagonda and Mansur Ali Khan Pataudi's 3.5-litre 1951 Jaguar. And finally, the old and the new came together in the midst of nature at the Bharatpur Bird Sanctuary. The film was shot by Amarjeet, an ace cameraman of Delhi, who literally danced with the handheld camera, like an ecstatic dervish, very much in the style of the film.

New ideas dawned with the coming of the millennium. Tajjali, a festival of this sacred thought, was presented on stage with musicians and dancers from Awadh, Punjab, Kashmir and Iran. Tajjali eventually shaped into a short film, *Rumi in the Land of Khusrau*, beautifully scripted by Anees Jung. Khusrau emerged in my mind as a true lover of India. Like a Sufi, he saw in India its limitless beauty that none had seen: in nature, geography, poetry, music, the wisdom and beauty of its people. He saw people as people, regardless of caste and colour. He saw the land of his birth beyond any land that surrounded it or from where people came to inhabit it. He was like his master and his master's master and his master, Khawaja Gharib Nawaz himself, a simple soul who changed the world. Music became a gateway to the heart and a connect to the soul. Thus, sama became the Sufi way. And to invoke this connect, every Sufi sama begins with the Qaul of the Prophet. *'Man kunto Maula fa haza Ali un Maula.'* I began to see a world within a world, beyond politics, beyond temporal power, beyond all forms of majoritarianism. Today, when we look back, the kingdom of the heart is all-encompassing and beyond all games of power.

So obvious and easy and yet the most difficult thing to do. Rumi followed Shams, and that was the most turbulent period of his life. He was opposed by his own son, many of his students and followers. But he followed his heart. And today, it is the greatest message for mankind. The liberation of yourself from your own self. From the shackles that are so dear to you. How could this journey become a film, particularly when you are the transformer and the one being transformed?

But the turn of the millennium came with a terrible setback. I had a major car accident on 15 August 2000. I got away with just a smashed right thumb. It did mean a lot for someone who had leant heavily on his hands for his art. It took a whole year for my crush injury to heal. I had just returned from Naini Tal, having prepped for *Raqs-e-Bismil*, which I was going to record in Abida Parveen's voice. I had convinced Aroon Purie, after much effort, of the idea. What he wanted and what I had in mind were two very different things. This has always been the case with those who control finance. Yet *Raqs-e-Bismil* has been one of the biggest and longest-lasting products of all time. These efforts find a place in the heart.

This, I have come to believe, happens from the Sufi dictum 'follow your heart'. I saw this in the mountains around me, in the magnificent trees that embraced these mountains, emitting a fragrance as the rains lashed to loosen their embrace. But the roots held them tightly, so that they didn't slip into the unknown depths of the green lake. The mythology became poetry, and poetry became rhythm and the rhythm, a melody. I waded through books and books to find moments that would touch the chords that drove my horse. And slowly I began to see light.

> *Zahid ne mera haasil-e-imaan nahiñ dekha*
> *Rukh par teri zulfoñ ko pareshañ nahiñ dekha . . .*
> (The preacher has not yet seen the essence of my faith
> He has not witnessed the tresses that hide the beauty of your face . . . .)
> —Asghar Gondvi

Each ghazal I chose and composed gripped the soul. They came alive in the monsoon mist rising from the Naini Lake.

In this, I saw the hills and the clouds covering them through the calligraphy of the *Panjatan*, in the glazed veranda of my home overlooking the bottomless lake.

Poetry is a bridge that helps you cross oceans and mountains. I was doing that in *Raqs-e-Bismil*. Sardar Javed Khan has often been my Naini Tal companion in poetry and found me nuggets of spiritual gold, which remain safe and secure in people's hearts to this day. Each dargah came alive with fragrance of ishq.

I had returned from Naini Tal, down mountains of illusions, into the heat of the plains, straight into this tragic night of the accident. My close friend Kanwaldeep Sawhney, sister of Simar Dugal's father, had given me her 1986 Mercedes 280S. A one-time beauty but still a head-turner. It was a metallic olive, with green leather upholstery that was reminiscent of my Isotta Fraschini. Inside, it was one of the most spacious cars I had driven in. It was Naresh Trehan's birthday, and I remember spending many hours that night talking to Madhav Rao Scindia about Congress in Uttar Pradesh. Signs had begun to show about the bleakness of its future, about which none of us could do much. I had flown with him to Lucknow sometime back and observed resentment amongst the party stalwarts of UP.

On my way back, I was already feeling sleepy, having driven into Delhi that very morning. I was in another world, listening to a ghazal by Farida Khanum. I didn't know when I fell asleep at the wheel. When I came around, I was sitting on the roof of the 280S, with its bottom up on the Ridge Road. Meera and I were upside down. There was no apparent pain or wound, but the car was covered in blood. Fortunately, some young boys from New Rajinder Nagar, who knew my father-in-law, found us and took us straight to the Ganga Ram Hospital, from where I was shifted to the Holy Family Hospital in Okhla. My right thumb, which had a crush injury, was patched up by Dr Pradip Sharma, an orthopaedic surgeon. It was a tough job to patch up a crushed thumb into some sort of functional form. They took skin from my thigh to graft on to my reconstructed thumb, and I needed daily dressing and painful rounds of physiotherapy in hot wax for a whole year. The reason for this narrative about the injury is to communicate that this was how pain entered the ghazals of *Raqs-e-Bismil*.

Each day I meet people and see the unseen connections that exist. The connection of diverse faiths with each other and the outer world. One learns to connect and yet keep alive one's own sense of that one Creator who is responsible for the unique oneness of the human being and all living creatures. In these human relationships, He reveals His grace and blessings. In my friend Ashok Kapur, I see the blessings and graciousness of Lord Hanuman, who is at the centre of Awadh's Ganga-Jamuni culture, where the slogan 'Ya Ali Bajrang Bali' resonated in the wrestling arenas of rural countryside. In the same transcending geography, Ashok's unconditional love for Hanumanji has extended like waves of blessings to friends like me through the decades.

Rumi helped me to understand the shades of beauty that man has been blessed with and is often unable to comprehend, despite all the worldly resources at his doorstep. More important for me is to perceive and inhale these layers of blessings that come to you all the time.

> *Har nafas awaaz-e-ishq mirasad az chap-o-raast*
> *Ma ba falak miravaem azm-e-tamasha karast . . .*
> (From the left and the right as I ascend
> I hear the voice of love . . .)

I began to see two ways of looking at the world. One was the way of moving images. D.W. Griffith, the father of American cinema, said in 1924 that a hundred years from that time, the language of moving images would truly unite mankind and end all armed conflict on the face of this earth. This impacted my mind, which was being torn between story and purpose, beauty and entertainment. I could see these bridges being formed in my mind. This was both a problem and a solution, when it came to mysticism. I said to myself that the physical Rumi was as important as the metaphysical one. The physical Rumi was like beautiful libraries and books leading to metaphysical journeys. But since the libraries had been razed to the ground by invaders like the Mongols, it was important to go beyond the books to the kingdom of the soul. The libraries were man-made, but the journey beyond was the journey of the soul. That kingdom had no boundaries, and thus none could invade it. Making a physical, tangible Rumi needed people who were measured in wealth and resources! And that was no easy a task to seek and find in the realm of the soul!

So to create art out of Rumi, around Rumi, was not as easy as it seemed. The journey of Rumi is beyond the physical form. Beyond the worshiping of idols, beyond form, beyond place.

Soorat gare naqqasham har lahza but-e-sazam
Vaa anke hama buthara ba pesh-e-tu bugdazam . . .
(I am a creator of images each moment I cast a new idol
Yet when I am confronted with thee, I smash them to pieces . . .)

So the quest for Rumi was for one who denied his physical existence.

Na az khākam, na az ābam
Na az arsham, na az farsham.
(I am neither of the earth nor water,
Neither of the skies or the earth below.)

Since he belonged to the soul of the soul, it would be too commonplace to give him a physical identity. His form is the remembrance of the formless.

Finding Rumi was losing Rumi. He would be found in tangible forms and lost in the formlessness of Allah. It was only in silence that he could be heard. This enigmatic soul could only be found in his verse, where he is either addressing or being addressed by Shams Tabriz, or is in discourse with the silversmith Salahuddin Zarkob. In the process of finding Rumi, one will find Shams in everyone and oneself in Shams.

In those inward moments I thought of an outward journey of Rumi. The journey of bewilderment and wonder. I began to connect with this enigma within myself through the wonder of his verse, in which I was lost. In 2000, I created a ballet, *Jaam-e-Ishq*, for the World President's Organization in the Taj Palace hotel, with Manjari and Navtej as dancers along with Simar and other models. From the music to the staging, the whole experience was an exploration of a verse of Rumi's, that would define the shape of things to come. It was meditation in movement. A journey that we had embarked upon, determining a new identity of aesthetics that was both hidden and revealed. This was going to open new doors.

One of my oldest friends in Delhi, Francis Wasciarg invited me to direct *Le Fakir de Bénarès*, a French opera with Fredric Leger as the conductor. The score had been written by a Jewish composer in the early twentieth century and was lost in the time of the Holocaust. One day, walking along the Left Bank pavement bookstores, Francis saw the score with a heading that intrigued him: *Le Fakir de Bénarès*. He picked it up instantly. It was a miracle of sorts. Something that was meant for Francis's eyes alone. A unique East–West bridge. So immersed was Francis in Indian culture that he had taken up Indian nationality. Meera and I were close to him, and he had great faith in us together. We spent a lot of time with him, and he requested me to become a trustee of the Neemrana Music Foundation. He also asked Meera to design the costumes.

Getting into a new zone not knowing French or how to read music seemed strange in the beginning, but I discovered two things. Acknowledging the trust someone puts in you and your commitment to art, and patiently allowing it to find its way to you. Francis was a man who could achieve this. He was a man of belief and commitment. He gave tourism and culture in the India of his time a new meaning. He believed in the story of the fakir, and through him I did too. In the opera *Sundra*, a homeless girl with a beautiful voice but a scarred face sings and dances with abandon on the colourful ghats of the Ganga in Banaras. One day, a handsome blind man, groping his way through the forest, hears her lilting voice, and a sharp spell of energy pierces through his body. 'How I wish I could see this miracle on earth . . .' Sundra, too, falls in love with him.

She realizes the effect her voice can have on the soul of this beautiful blind man. She gives him support, and together they go around asking for alms. This opens a new world for him. One day, Sundra meets a fakir, who is drawn to this couple. One beautiful and blind, the other scarred but with a sonorous voice that could stir souls. Hearing the blind man lament that his only desire was to see the face of his lover, the fakir gives Sundra a potion to apply to the blind man's eyes on the full-moon night and says that, God willing, he would see again. She is overjoyed but is in two minds. To apply or not to apply the potion? If she does, he will see her ugly face and instantly shun her. If she doesn't, it will be unfair.

Her love for him overwhelms her, and so, while he is asleep, she opens the bottle and takes the potion in her palms and rubs it all over his eyes. She then covers her scarred face and runs away. The blind man wakes up to a miracle. He is granted his sight. It was Sundra's love and belief that could make this miracle happen. Being able to see, he throws away his staff, but his joy is overshadowed by the disappearance of that source of tender love and support he had got used to. He searches for her everywhere and finally finds her hiding, face covered, in knee-deep water. He pulls her out and tenderly removes her hands from her face. He sees a face more beautiful than the moon shining upon it. The miraculous potion had transformed her into a matchless beauty!

I felt this miracle working through me, and the opera turned out as beautiful as Sundra at the end. Sundara was played by Francis's daughter Aude Priya. The opera was staged at the Siri Fort Auditorium in Delhi; the orchestra pit there was used for the first time for musicians as part of a spectacular opera. And we also performed at the Bhabha Auditorium in Mumbai. This was the power of trust and faith. India was slowly losing faith and confidence in art. In art that could perform miracles.

Delhi was a new place for me. Meera and I were finding our way into it. We had lived here earlier, in a Nizamuddin *barsati* belonging to Francis. I painted some collages there, and showed my work at the Carma Gallery and then at Galeries Lafayette in Paris. My collages were mystical landscapes of Kashmir, which are still present in my mind—maybe as an image of Zooni disappearing in the snow, in search of her beloved.

The world of Francis was warm and unique. His friends who frequented Neemrana formed a circle that remains the core of Delhi that is beautiful but slowly fading away. We are fortunate to have been part of that experience. We had some unusual fashion shows in Neemrana, using my musicians from Kashmir and Awadh, with Manjari dancing in ethereal costumes designed by us. Kotwara couture was coming of age. This was followed by an iconic fashion show at the Craft Museum in Delhi, which was the model Meher Jessia's first foray into choreography. We had, by now, developed a discerning group of Kotwara lovers, with Zainab still the most committed. She made us grow with her discerning eye. Wherever she went in Kotwara, heads would turn. There was an invisible Rumi that shone through her placeless Afghan presence.

Rumi is a young person's mirror today. Rumi's life follows the trajectory of a child born in 1207 to one of the greatest scholars of the time in Balkh, in present-day, strife-torn Afghanistan. The family flees the dreaded Mongols, who plunder and uproot all that falls in their path. One feels the plunder around and yet sees the divine hand rising to save it. The Beloved is as cruel as He is benevolent, appearing in different garbs all the time.

I felt like the child Rumi moving from city to city, wandering, experiencing the wonders of nature, living under the open sky with nothing but a tent sheltering me from the expanse of nature. Like Rumi, I heard nature speaking. Through birds and through people who understood the language of birds.

Rumi grew up with awe and wonder, each day writing on his mind's tablet the words that would take the form of poetry, which the world would reel under one day, like an ocean breaking the barriers of language and form. A timeless metaphor. Poetry spoke through Rumi, often like Solomon speaking the language of birds. With Attar, whom he met in Nishapur, he traversed the world of wonder and amazement. When his father died in Konya in 1230, he donned his mantle, yet felt ill at ease trying to fit into someone else's shoes. The more people expected of him, the more ill-adjusted he felt to take his place. He was born for a different journey, till one day, in October 1244, he met his mentor Shamsuddin of Tabriz. Shams was the dawn of a new light that changed the colour of Rumi's world.

I sit in my father's chair, looking out of the window, at the fading promise of the future. Yet the promise is empowered by the wonder of Rumi's pen, which had been dipped deep into the darkness of the ink of the night, and had risen with the triumphal sun, on the blank page of a white morning.

The story of Rumi is like the story of any one of us, just more intense and more focused. His union with Shams was powerful and short-lived. Shams was a man of the other world. He had severed ties from this world. He was seeking someone to share the light that illumined the inner world through the highly polished surface of the heart. When pressure of the outside world built up on Rumi beyond measure, Shams disappeared! This disappearance drove Rumi to a realization which could not have happened while Shams was there with him. And Shams knew this. Rumi went visibly crazy, as there was no one around him to blame. He broke out from his shell. He danced and celebrated in the streets, and wrote about his new-found freedom and ecstasy in the poems that the world will remember for all time to come. He had found that Shams was writing from within him!

Kotwara is where I am now. Timeless and static. Like Konya. Except more vulnerable. All I see is insensitivity and the devastation of the environment. Rampant cutting of at least 20,000 trees, which my grandfather Raja Raza Husain had planted over 150 years back. Nearly 60 feet of a kilometre-long forest has been denuded. The same trees and the same forest that I mentioned in the opening pages of this book. The same forest where no automobile had entered till 1924. The same forest where, at the railway crossing, my father and great-grandfather could have been lost to this world on their Phaeton. I am not against progress, but one can clearly perceive the insensitivity which is passed down from a corrupt, disconnected politician to a mindless administrator, both a cat's paw in the hands of the business world. This has rendered the rural countryside ugly and faceless. Cities are an even uglier manifestation of this phenomenon, where helpless rural folk migrate to and live in ghettos and encroached shanties, while the rich get richer and live in simulated sections of paradise.

Kotwara is always an inspiration as well as a rude shock. Bordering it is the holy town of Gola Gokarannath, with its Shiv temple built by my ancestors; the town is famous for having once had the largest sugar mill in Asia. We sit in the midst of all this and everything that makes this pristine beauty vulnerable. Just a hundred miles away is Lucknow, another dimension of this vulnerability. I look out of my father's window and wonder what Wajid Ali Shah must have dreamt when he created

Qaiserbagh, the garden of the king. I see the vulnerable city still conjuring up illusions of the past and a promise for the future. A city on the Gomti River, a tributary of the Ganges. Bathing in the Gomti on Ekadashi can wash away all sins. According to the Bhagavata Purana, the Gomti is one of India's transcendental rivers. It touches Jaunpur before joining the Ganges in Varanasi.

The fish from this sacred river became a symbol of good fortune both for its rulers and its populace. The two fish become the symbol of the rulers of Awadh, and remains so even with the present-day government. The piscine pair facing each other adorns every archway of the city, big or small. The tradition is so powerful that the entire Awadh region is full of doorways with this symbol. The city, with the fertile imagination of its Nishapur rulers, blending with the romance of Lord Krishna and the mythology associated with Awadh, opened the floodgates of ideas. Creativity began to surface in every form of craft.

The hammer and chisel, the needle and the thread gave form to the formless, and an everlasting identity to the region. They became sacred, like the Alam of Imam Husain, which adorns every Imambara of the city and for which it is known the world over. An elevating secular and sacred space that embraces each visitor. And the pair of piscine eyes lie frozen in wait.

> *Ba do chashme man ba chashmash che payamahast har dam*
> *Ke do chashm az payamash khush-o-pur khumaar bada*
> (With each breath
> Their two eyes
> Will receive messages from those eyes
> So breathtaking, so intoxicating.
> What will these messages be?)
>
> —Rumi

I tried to see this and make a connect with Rumi and his relationship with Shams Tabriz. This gave an abstract, invisible direction to my journey of making a film on Rumi. I had already made two episodes on Hazrat Ameer Khusrau, under a four-part series called *Paigham-e-Mohabbat*, the Message of Love. The other two were on Hazrat Khwaja Moinuddin Chishti and Alampanah Haji Waris Ali Shah. In my own way, I was already moving on the path that would enrich me with their poetry, which put into context the 'way', the Sufi way.

I had begun to see the 'way' and slowly share the 'way'. To be able to show the 'way' would be too big a claim for an ordinary person like me, but I can and should proudly claim being able to 'share the way'.

Jahan-e-Khusrau was this 'way'. I was getting lost in the verse of Khusrau and Rumi, in the poetry of Hazrat Shah Niaz and that of his descendants, all travellers of 'Qaul'. It was from this that the garden bloomed. The poetry of Hazrat Turab Ali Shah Qalandar of Kakori Sharif. Baba Fareed Ganjshaker, Baba Bulley Shah, Waris Shah, Hazrat Zaheen Shah Taaji. Their verse found a home in the ruins of *Jahan-e-Khusrau*, often in the voice of Abida Parveen.

I began to realize that Rumi and Khusrau were persons created to illuminate the inner world of man. Their creations were the most powerful tools in the hand of art. The journey into their lives was like entering a labyrinth of the soul, exploring tender feelings that made you swim in the ocean of delight and wonder, trials and tribulations, ecstasy and sobriety, surrender and intoxication. Whichever way you go, you are pushing the boundaries, for yourselves, for the others. Those whose soul is open, whose mind is free. This is the story of toys. Everything is a toy in the hands of the puppeteer. So make friends with him or become the puppet yourself.

It was all about pushing the boundaries. For me, then and now, the boundaries remain invisible. When I look here, he is there, when I look there, he is here. It is somewhere midway, in nowhere, that you encounter him. It is in the orbit that you understand a moving planet.

What is this Rumi that dwells everywhere and yet nowhere? Is he an intent or a purpose or just an index to a formless Allah and the soul in all of us? But a film is a film, an art, a technology designed for the soul. And today it stands amid millions in the bazaar.

So how does one find someone who is neither a buyer nor a seller?

I thought of looking for co-travellers. The Internet had come into being. I wrote to people either on the path or those who were artistic enough to liberate their art. The way for each was a path not travelled. From the outside the paths seemed like vast super-smooth orbits, all leading to that venerable world we term the soul. Otherwise it was a tough path, with challenging milestones and formidable barriers never taken before. The Rumians wrote of the soul, of a way to ride above it. They were all explorers of the soul. As the path got easier, one did not have to find them. They found you. Yet I was restless. I was a man of this world. I wanted to make Rumi. But there were other things that I could do to make my wait easier. Read poetry. Write my thoughts. Sketch ideas, moments of Rumi, his moments of illumination with Shams. Finding the Shams within . . . painting to discover the language of light in which the two souls were illumined in each other. Like the beauty of a new bride. Rumi is a good friend. One could be with him alone and discover oneself in the silence of darkness. Then why make a film? The child was restless and is still restless. I often wonder whether a child can make a film. And then it struck me. Why not find people of the heart to hold my hand?

Rumi discovered the art of surrendering. Of not knowing. The grace of admitting his ignorance. The beauty of being bewildered. So Rumi takes you wandering into a world of wonder, where the One God is manifested as a design of a richly crafted tapestry. Where idolatry is a creative dimension of the human imagination, where formlessness is a part of its romance. Rumi had to be shared through the medium of moving images. A medium which involves collective talent.

I wanted a cinematographer to give form to my dream. So I made a list of the five most acclaimed cinematographers. I first wrote to Vittorio Storaro, a man who claimed to 'write with light'. He had been awarded several Oscars, the highest commercial honour in the film world. I sent him a moving invitation by email, asking him to be a part of this Rumi journey. I waited and waited, and finally decided to write to the next one on the list. As I logged in, up popped the reply: 'Equilibrium of elements has been the quest of my life. Rumi will help me to find this important moment!' Vittorio was committed to the Rumi journey!

My cerebral engagement with him began on day one. Rumi began to appear as a man written in light, in shadows and silhouettes. I regularly communicated with Vittorio via email, till I felt it was time to meet. Meera and I went to Italy to meet him. He was as childlike as Attar. Full of optimism and wonder. This was the first gift I received from Rumi.

We reached Rome. I saw in the majesty of a church the presence of a questioning, wonderstruck Rumi. Sounds and spaces, words and meanings, language and feeling, began to disappear. Yet, this is not to deny the emotional connect each person has with his mother tongue, a language which he tasted with the milk that first touched the lips. Today, one can live with and in between many languages. I feel in Urdu and Farsi, and express in English. This is the reality of the colonial wave that drowned us, and we have emerged as unusual global creatures. From one ear I hear English, from the other Urdu. Urdu is the left side of the brain and English the right. Many books can be written about this, particularly in the subcontinent. I vividly remember my father promoting Roman letters and a people's language. However, the mother tongue will and should always remain the tongue that touches the soul.

I was reading Rumi's *Fihi-ma-Fihi, The Signs of the Unseen* in English. I had just met Vittorio, and we had talked about the idea of making a definitive film on Rumi. He was extremely enthused, and I felt that if *Fihi-ma-Fihi* could be shared with him in Italian, it would be a wonderful bridge. I was not talking to him about just a film; I was talking about how Rumi brought two diverse peoples and cultures on the same plane.

With the words from *The Signs of the Unseen* spinning in my head, I parted with him, and we decided to meet up later. The great thing about Rome is that you can walk into a basilica between shopping or your meetings. We went into the Basilica of San Giovanni in Rome. The inlay floor and painted frescos, with Latin inscriptions, took one into a realm of craftsmanship and art inspired by a spiritual force.

Fihi-ma-Fihi in Italian was on my mind. Our hostess, Neeman Subhan from Bangladesh, had even promised to translate it into Italian for me. It would take a few months. We came out of the basilica and walked towards St Paul's Cathedral. As we walked down the street, someone signalled me enigmatically to take a different route. We did so and came upon a quaint little bookshop There was nothing more charming than a quaint little bookshop. A beautiful-looking man, with long white hair, smiled and asked, 'Rumi?' I smiled back amazed. He pointed to a shelf. Staring right in my face was the translation in Italian of *Fihi-ma-Fihi—L'Essenza del Reale*, published by Libreria Editrice Psiche.

I made a copy of this book and gave the original to Vittorio. How it worked into him I don't know. But how it impacted me was more than a coincidence and just less than a miracle. However, a year later, when we went to Rome again, there was no such shop. And no one knew of it. In its place was an undertaker who said he had been there forever!

Rumi was an enigma, which came with so much beauty of thought that needed to be expressed. A phenomenon that needed to be discovered in people, in spaces, architecture, nature, mountainscapes, oceanscapes, in earth and soil, in snow and in rain . . . he was a life that was found in the arrangement of words, in the ninety-nine attributes of Allah. He was in calligraphy that crawled like a tendril into surfaces and spaces, in the lyrical arrangement of letters, each becoming as different as another human being dancing from right to left, sharpening the visual comprehension of each word through the combination of letters.

Rumi was an accident or a miracle. It was in human form that he found Allah and yearned for him in his absence.

Chapter 17

Keeper of Secrets

'Chashme maste ajabe zulf daraze ajabe
mai paraste ajabe fitna taraze ajabe . . .'
('O wondrous eyes full of langour,
O wondrous tresses wavy and long,
O wondrous wine worshippers,
O wondrous mischievous one . . .')

—Ameer Khusrau

As I feel like an outsider in the realm of poetry, I continue to be pulled into the higher reaches of mystic verse. Is the world ready for Rumi? Maybe not and it may never be, but each one of us individually is. This is a slowly emerging truth as conventional ways jam the path to the heart. Rumi started emerging as a script, and *Jahan-e-Khusrau* emerged as a show on the ground. A cinema of the senses. A mystical experience of art that captivates the memory. Words of the mystics pouring out their poetry for the Beloved. Surrendering their soul to invisible ears, to invisible eyes, in the coming together of melody and verse in their diverse and similar origins. *Jahan-e-Khusrau* is technology wrapped in the blanket of the soul. It has as many mistakes as art can make and still be called art. The mistakes are the humans standing humbly with folded hands in surrender. An epitome of endearment. A sign of *adab* (etiquette) before the one true majesty. The realm of forgiveness, of error and its acceptance. In such a state, the poetry of the mystics finds its way to you, overwhelming you with humility and wonder. A humility which Khusrau and Rumi wanted to share. A wonder which bridges time and space to prove His oneness and His creations.

> *Haq mago kalma-e-kufr ast dar inja Khusrau*
> *Razdaane ajabe sahib-e-raaz-e-ajabe.*
> (Khusaru, keep the Truth within,
> For here disbelief prevails,
> Wondrous is the source of mystery
> And He who knows the secrets.)

It was on 24 March 2001, in the ruins of Arab Ki Sarai, in the precincts of Humayun's Tomb, that this poem unfolded, like wild grass that was wafting in the night wind with the moonlight writing the verse on the tablet of the heart. Much like Khusrau may have imagined it to be with his Pir Hazrat Nizamuddin Aulia listening in rapt surrender, which love invokes as a tribute to the keeper of secrets. Over three evenings the moon took its course through tall dry trees, wondrous cirrus and cumulus cloud formations while the stars shone through them upon the audience.

Jahan-e-Khusrau made one realize how universal Khusrau was. The entire subcontinent resonated with the throbbing of his heart as the Iranians sang his ghazal:

> *Dil raft ze tan birun, dildaar haman dar dil*
> *Oftaad sukhan dar jaan guftar haman dar dil*
> (The heart is out of the body, yet He who
> Possesses it resides within the heart,
> Words absorbed in the being,
> The Beloved resounds within the heart.)
> *Yak shahre por az khubaan dah bagh por az golha*
> *Sad jaye naham deede dildaar haman dar dil*
> (A city full of wonder, ten gardens full of flowers,
> In a hundred ways I look.
> He who owns it is within the heart.)

There was an urge to share the ecstasy of mystic verse in voices that were blessed. The rhetoric of cross-border tension had not spilled over to the art of the spiritual world as yet, and Abida Parveen from Pakistan was my benchmark for using mystic metaphors. It was a blessing every day, for everyone. As I sat and chose poetry, she sat with the blank mind of a patient, eager-to-learn child. It reminded me of our time together during the making of *Raqs-e-Bismil*. I was certain we had touched upon something sacred. Something that was truly blessed. Something that touched the soul. Something I never knew existed or could come remotely near. These combinations were truly heavenly and needed to be recognized. The poetry that came to me was of Rumi, Khusrau, Hazrat Shah Niaz, Zaheen Shah Taaji, and a host of other mystics that knocked at the door of my heart. I had found a new *maqaam*. There was no looking back. I had begun to find poetry in everything, and such poetry had begun to find its way to me, in spaces, in the play of light, in painting, sketching, weaving or crafting in wood. I was a tool in His hands, pounding on the keyboard of the iMac.

The journey of the Sufi is what he undertakes for others. For the eyes of others, the ears of others, for the mind of others. But through the medium of one's own soul. In the process, the soul becomes someone else's, and you see beauty in everyone else. This is a journey I wish to share and these the footprints I wish to leave behind.

Finding this philosophy in everything is the way of the Sufi. It is manifested in all his acts and his arts. Eloquence is the essence of beauty. And thought is the form of the formless soul. You find this state in the presence of the Sufi.

Rumi takes you through this mystical journey, through his verse which reflects the presence of his mentor Shams, which becomes more radiant and ecstatic in their separation. From this emerges the wail of the reed, whirling in separation from the original source of Creation. A realization that was Shams Tabrez. He becomes your baton. A conductor who is weaving music with each stroke, a hundred different sounds creating a harmony that has kept the world going. The opera of wonder.

This is the essence of a Sufi's journey. When I travel, I seek this wonder, this dance of the soul, this bewilderment. I find myself all the time looking for two hands working together to create wonder. If you can't sing, you can clap. It is the rhythm of the hands that supplements the symphony of the soul. Silence is the language of the soul. In his silence we hear our own self. He enriches humanity around him. He sees the potential of those around as they are connected to each other at the level of the attributes the

Divine has given. A Sufi sees this and responds to them, and in this process sharpens them. This language of the soul has taken centuries to evolve and a lifetime to become engaging. The eye of a fakir sees through the human being, as if he is seeing on behalf of the most benevolent and the most munificent. This vision creates cultures, it enriches societies.

> *Vo basti ujarh jaye jahañ hoye na darvesh,*
> *Abaad hai har shahr faqiroñ ki nazar se . . .*
> (A place is deserted without the presence of a dervish,
> For it is he who keeps it forever alive . . .)
> —Hazrat Turaab Ali Shah Qalandar

I saw this truth in everything I did, everywhere I went. In every form of human endeavour, I noticed this blessing. The connect with nature and beauty, human effort and blessing. Particularly in what people did with their two hands and craft. The interpretation and inspiration of these elements to create lasting joy in their celebration. In my passion for the handmade, I saw endless blessings. I saw an unabated river of grace flowing through deft fingers and delicate eyes. Be it the weaving of pashmina, carpets, papier-mâché, the inlays in marble, metal . . . everything reinforced the unity and beauty and the interdependence of human beings. Hazrat Ali, the mentor of the Sufis, was the head of every craft guild in his time. He saw the hand of the Divine in the hand of craftpersons creating beauty in utility. I saw the divinity in the Ganga and the Jamuna, in the Narmada and the Brahmaputra. A resonance of love and unity.

> *Khusrau daryaa prem ka ulti va ki dhaar*
> *Jo utra so doob gaya jo dooba so paar*
> (Khusrau the river of love flows against the tide,
> Who entered was drowned,
> Who drowned came out at the other end.)

Jahan-e-Khusrau was one such journey. It evolved from year to year, poem to poem, melody to melody, voice to voice, clap to clap. We were unknowingly connecting nations, joining cultures, expanding the horizon of being and nothingness. Each year there was a struggle. Putting people together who did not know what had happened or was going to happen. This was a part of recreating this story. But slowly, people saw its inner beauty in themselves.

In 2003, we had a chief guest, a child in himself. He came with wonder, sat in wonder and went back wonderstruck! He had to leave early, against his wish, but protocol demanded it. When we insisted, in a childlike way he said he would lose his job! The next day came his awesome and wonderful letter:

> To Amir Khusrau, the Sufi poet, I was introduced through his poems. 'O, Emperor the shine and beauty of the crown what you are wearing, O, Emperor, I Khusrau, what I see in the crown, the pain and labour of poor men, crystal of blood.' With this poem ringing in my mind I reached the environment of *Jahan-e-Khusrau* on 28th February 2003. I lit candle lights. I saw beautiful candle light all around with the rhythm divine environment. The music, which was so powerful, it moved me. I find suddenly all the barriers of religions, language, culture all vanished as dust. Only breeze of unity of mind blowing. Oh, Almighty bless the humanity with your song of peace. I greet Raja Syed Muzaffar Ali of Kotwara for arranging such an excellent performance.
>
> —A.P.J. Abdul Kalam

The poets of the khanaqahs wrote with their soul, for the soul. And through them you see beauty in everyone.

Having started my poetic journey in Aligarh, I found in it a bitter struggle of love, life and art. I found my art being dehydrated by life. Yet I found that everything had romance, including the process of the dehydration. And Faiz was a master of this. In the worst of times, his words conjured up unimaginable romance. In times when everything was nothing and nothing was everything, when one revealed no wounds, and no one had the desire to mend, when the beloved was indifferent and the enemy oblivious of his presence.

Na kisi pa zakhm ayaañ koi na kisi ko fikr rafu ki hai
Na karam hai hampe habib ka na niguh hampe udu ki hai.
(To none are these wounds revealed, and no one cares to sew,
Nor upon me is the beloved's grace nor the eye of the evil foe.)

Words became ornaments in the garb of writing. In the words of Hazrat Ali, handwriting is the tongue of the hand and the eloquence of thought. I walked into the Khusrau of the past holding the hand of Faiz.

Jahan-e-Khusrau was a world within a world. Everybody enters that world through the narrow window of one's own self, in which you drown before you emerge at the other end.

Symbolism is the milestone on this journey. It protects you from the ugly interpretation of life by the *khirad* (intellect). And there were ways and ways of expressing this. *Jahan-e-Khusrau* was my way in the journey. It was also the journey of Rumi, and in both the journeys what runs parallel is a sense of wonder. Wonder in everything, in mystery, secret and submission.

> *Bahr-e-qatlam chu kushad tegh neham sar besujood,*
> *ou ba naazeajabe, man ba niyaze ajabe . . .*
> (He draws the sword, I bow my head,
> I prepare to die,
> Wondrous is his beneficence,
> Wondrous my submission . . .)

The word *ajabe* conjures up a question which has no answer in words. Wondrous is the nearest you can get. It is a code between Sufi souls. It is a statement of a state which has no address. Either you are in it or you will never even end up looking for it. Every time a daf player came from Iran, I would keep their dafs and give them to musicians from India who could think beyond all forms of rhythm. The way Khusrau thought. His way to art was not from the mind but the soul. It was above those elements that divided the human race—caste, religion, region, language. He could therefore reinvent music. My advantage was my being illiterate, yet aware each moment of the revelations of wonder. It was this wonder I found in common with Khusrau. Understanding Khusrau is as easy as understanding a child and as difficult as understanding a sage.

I had to make this happen. Khusrau had to become a millennial concept. Beyond drama and fiction. He had to become a design, a modern way of life. I discussed this thought with Chetana Sharma, or Chinoo, as she is known. With this came a sense of dedication. It was a long journey we were to embark upon. *Jahan-e-Khusrau* had to look timeless and modern. And so it did. We had to give a newness to tassawuf, hitherto trapped in a conventional garb. It had to go into the essence of its essence, and each year we reinvented it with a powerful contemporariness.

I felt empowered by this new design vocabulary, and it continues to inspire even today. In fact, the future has just begun for a spiritual design journey the world would like to live with. The journey extended into *HU: The Sufi Way*, a publication on the Sufi essence of the commonalities of cultures. Khusrau and Rumi were showing us the path.

Graphic design emerged once again as an extension of my creative soul. Like in my films, I have always given design pride of place in my life, and it is sad to see it missing in situations where it is needed most. It is not a part of our lives as it used to be in pre-colonial days. In colonial times, we made a complete departure, and in post-Independence India we began to lose the plot. Though the NID came up in Ahmedabad, Corbusier came to Chandigarh, Pupul Jayakar and Kamaladevi emerged with an enlightened government patronage, Bombay somehow became a hub of commerce, slowly moving away from Calcutta. Delhi and Bombay almost became twin cities, where many artists found the ease of creating art. Delhi also became a centre of news and documentary work, as government patronage of the latter grew. Doordarshan, India's only public service broadcaster, grew in size and network. The Ministry of External Affairs found it relevant to use the documentary way of presenting India's image to the world and empowering diplomacy. I had the opportunity to be a part of this process, as I have expressed earlier. I consider myself fortunate to have been a part of a shifting canvas, yet unfortunate to have not taken cinema to the world of my dreams. My last few years with Air India had empowered me with idea of the convergence of air travel, tourism and culture. I realized the power of an idea to conceive and promote travel through my Congresses and Conventions division, finding people with ideas and promoting their passion in the larger interest of the country. I was introduced to Niranjan Jhaveri in 1978 and he was aflame with the fire of jazz music. We started the Jazz Yatra in 1978 and kept the flag flying till he passed in 1990. Without the might of Air India, organizing Jahan-e-Khusrau was an uphill task. While we took baby steps, I continued to dream. Dream big. I dreamt of Rumi.

In 2004, we set up the Rumi Foundation with a group of friends and scholars. Dr Karan Singh was the chairman. I have been an admirer of him

since my Air India days, when he was our minister for tourism and civil
aviation. He was someone who could dream big, yet dream cautiously. It
was during this time that I started dreaming of a feature-length film on
Rumi. The vision of India's business mind and marketing acumen could
never fathom the beauty and importance of either Rumi or Khusrau. They
could not see the connect between art and spirituality and commercial
viability. Though India was a country of gurus, with unlimited economic
power, the transfer of this power into a world-class art language was and
still is a far cry. So the convergence of both Khusrau and Rumi was and
remains a unique way for the ever-growing world of the soul. A world
which was without boundaries. The world has come to realize this, and
also sees this as a challenge and a threat.

To divide and dominate markets has become the new order of things.
Human needs and interests are being fanned, and time is being swallowed
into a virtual world that is not the making of the soul. While everything
seems within easy reach, it is equally difficult to grab and sustain human
interest. Internet communication is at an all-time high. This is the era of
an invasion into our bedrooms, into our private and personal space and
time, whether we like it or not.

But somehow, the journey of the soul continues. The world of ecstasy
and bliss seeks new frontiers, breaking new barriers.

If poetry was the way today, why did I not become a poet? Maybe
I would have been a worried person, like most of the poets I met in life
or through books. A poet is a world that you have never seen enough of.
And this is what devastated Shams when Rumi said about Allah and the
Prophet, 'I have never known Thee as Thou should have been known!'

We return to *Jahan-e-Khusrau* year after year with the same bliss and
troubles. And I give credit to a woman who was truly beholden to Delhi. I
was lucky to say what I wanted to say about her in an episode of *Dilli Dil
Se*. She was Sheila Dikshit, who loved Delhi like a mother. I feel orphaned
with her passing. Sadly, soon no one will remember her.

A language is about what happens in it, about the soul that reverberates
in its nouns, adjectives, verbs, adverbs and its pronouns. Today, the soul is
like an ocean beating at the shores of human comprehension, knowledge
and understanding of the Divine. The seen and the unseen playing hide
and seek with one's soul. *Jahan-e-Khusrau* is a place where an *ashiq* wanders
in ecstasy on the streets of the Beloved. In the joy of the Beloved's quest,

he spins in abandon, on the streets, in the marketplace, amid friends and strangers, he cares not.

Na man behooda girde kucha-o-bazaar mi gardam,
Mazaq-e-aashiqui daram paye deedar mi gardam . . .
(I am not an aimless wanderer in the streets and bylanes,
Impassioned with love I wander to get a glimpse of my beloved . . .)

Jahan-e-Khusrau was this endless spin in the ruins, where the crumbling walls spin, where the trees dance in abandon, where the leaves that turn yellow spin till they fall on the ground to the deafening echo of the daf. Where spring treads gently on the grass growing wild. Where centuries-old poetry has been up in the clouds, free for lovers who spin to download at will. Where you see sound before you hear beauty.

Jahan-e-Khusrau opened up the realm of design as a function of an idea. There was no design without an idea and no idea without a design. A madness with a method, and method with a madness. The ecstasy with a bliss which was the essence of all cultures that united man. A sense of beauty which was a secret driving force of nature. A designer was not the one with the idea but the one who could see ideas within an idea. The idea was the original Sufi, the one who received divine transmission. The Qaul.

I began to see calligraphy as an expression of an idea. The thick and thin of a stroke that defined a spiritual context. Or a chain of thoughts that emerged as a design narrative. These were the lessons of *Jahan-e-Khusrau* that one was getting through the skills of Chinoo. The skills were spread out through several shades of design. The design of body movements inspired by calligraphic strokes in dance. Manjari became another designer within the idea of the idea. With His grace, the mystic metaphors through the exploration of human talent and skills, were unfolding to me like never before. Ideas that would radically transform life and art.

Design through Ameer Khusrau was a river of love manifested in every shape and form. It was a carpenter shaping ideas in wood. A weaver weaving magic in textiles. A human who saw a human without the curtain of the ego in between. I felt like a Khusrau who saw beauty in the common and uncommon folk. And everyone as a function of a divine design coexisting in an ecosystem, which again is a celebration of design.

Each poem was a step, a destination, a universe. The poetry of Khusrau took me to the threshold of Rumi, and Rumi brought me back to the threshold of Khusrau, and *Jahan-e-Khusrau* was the terminal from where these flights took off and landed. They opened up a universe of poetry that took one through the dramatic clouds of ecstasy, over varying snowscapes and deserts, oceans and rivers, and landed at the same tarmac of surrender. Exploring different freedoms of the air and a world without boundaries, with an unpredictable future. My aviation exposure with Air India was becoming my way of discovering secrets. All that you have been through in life finds its significance in the present that stands at the threshold of the future. And through this I was being enriched while enriching others. Becoming tolerant, becoming open to let the commonalities emerge and coexist. Allowing intoxication to overwhelm me . . . seeing the Beloved as a singular source of creativity manifested in the uniformity of creations.

As Hazrat Ali said, help always comes from unknown quarters, thus reinforcing the faith in the divine. Finding and working with Abida was a miracle in itself. Bim Bissel, a very dear friend and a beautiful soul, had asked me to introduce Abida at the American ambassador's wife's dinner, hosted for the International Women's Association in the early 1990s. I was so mesmerized that I presented Abida with a Quranic inscription of 'Naad-e-Ali' on agate, which I always wore around my neck. That was the beginning of a relationship that became the foundation of many compositions we did together. That voice was pure and free of ego and affectation. Poetry would enter her heart and come out of her soul. She was what made *Jahan-e-Khusrau* glow.

> *Mohse bol na bol meri sun ya na sun*
> *Main tohe na chaadoñ gi aye saañvare . . .*
> (Speak to me or don't, listen or don't listen,
> I will not leave thee my dark Beloved . . .)

This was written by Nawab Maulana Mauj in the style of Khusrau that is often attributed to him. I made Abida Parveen sing this ghazal for the first time in the first *Jahan-e-Khusaru*, in 2001. At that time, I attributed it to Hazrat Ameer Khusrau, using Nizam Piya as a reference in the rendition. The Sufi sees Lord Krishna as an eternal visible beloved, and much of their poetry in the colloquial idiom uses him as an icon of love.

Krishna has been a way of the Sufi expression of love and surrender, and has found its way into the realm of the heart. The *saañvra* was the keeper of divine secrets. The Sufis made him magical and endearing through their verse. The *khayal* (thought) became a metaphor in music.

It was through *Jahan-e-Khusrau* that I realized how tassawuf used the spiritual building blocks of Indian culture and Hindu philosophy, the unity of a formless creator as propounded in Advaita Vedanta, to connect with the *astha* of the Indian populace. The Sufis used their art and creativity to connect. They found in India a culture based on mythology, which gave the mystic mind of the Sufi the real life exploration of An-al-Haq.

I had found an old notebook of my father, comparing Advaita Vedanta and tassawuf. I had begun to realize the commonality in the matters of the soul and how Sufis made the rulers more understanding and compassionate. They accorded so much reverence to the evolved Hindu philosophy of the Vedas that it became a necessary bridge for crossing into souls. Dara Shikoh, the heir to the Mughal Empire, translated Advaita Vedanta into Persian as Majmaul Baharain, the Mingling of Oceans. At a time when Persian had an enormous footprint in the subcontinent, Majmaul Baharain was the most seminal book of Indian philosophy, thus opening its frontiers to the world.

Meeting Abida at this station of my journey was a milestone. My very first meeting with her had been in the late eighties. I happened to be in Mumbai, at a nature cure hospital next to my home in Juhu. Those were not the days of the mobile. I had just walked into the house to pick up fresh towels when the phone rang. It was Abida Parveen. She said she was there for a SAARC concert and the one person she wanted to meet in India was me. I called her to the hospital but realized it was stupid of me to do so. So she came home instead. I also invited Khaiyyam Sahab and Dimple Kapadia to meet her. That evening unfolded magically, leaving us mesmerized.

She had come with her husband. I would say miracles are always happening at each step, with each breath. It is the soul in quest which recognizes and seizes the opportunity to experience them. This was so true about finding Abida. I was brimming with lyrics that were like waves against the rocks on the shores of the soul. The wide ocean had a bright blue canopy in which Abida was circumambulating like a *huma*, a phoenix, a bird of paradise. She was a Sufi in spirit who instantly connected you with the divine through her voice. An artist free of the ego, with whom any wonder was possible. For me, this was a godsend. She had the potential to make my dreams into a reality, and turn my reality into a dream. I did an album with her and a group of Indian singers, to define the sense of freedom and the pain of separation, and commemorate fifty years of Partition in 1997. Indian singers sang verses of poets who had become part of Pakistan and Abida sang verses of poets who had remained in India. It was a moving chemistry of thought and ideas. I had proposed this idea to my friend Jay Vishwadeva in London, and it was published under the label Navras Records. In fact, this was my first meeting with Chinoo, who designed the CD cover.

Those like me, who were infants at the time of Partition, and those who lost their near and dear ones in that holocaust, had to grow out of that anguish and see the beauty in reconstructing futures and not harp on the rhetoric of communalism, which was an ugly colonial design to keep the fire aflame for an active arms market in the region.

> *Aahat si koi aye to lagta hai ki tum ho . . .*
> (At every sound I feel you have arrived . . .)
>
> —Jan Nisar Akhtar

Nostalgia, remorse, hope, anguish, philosophy and romance. This was the essence of *Paigham-e-Mohabbat* (The Message of Love). Each poem, each composition was heart-rending, and this was my second attempt at creating music, after *Husn-e-Jaana*. I knew no music, but I had acquired a sense of addiction music could create. I remember buying Protools and Digidesign, for designing the sound in 1997, in London, from the money I had earned in this project. I set up a studio of sorts and recorded a few albums there. But a complete lack of a technical bent of mind meant I could not master the technology. Still, I am aware and keep abreast of it, using it year after year. I believe in division of work, which helps minds work faster in communication technology.

Jahan-e-Khusrau was going to be an extension of that process, except there was a lot more to play with, learn and give. I wouldn't say teach, because I knew nothing to teach. Yet I had a plethora of feelings to impart. Thus, the journey of *Jahan-e-Khusrau* was about learning and imparting. My built-in humility, which grew with exposure to Abida, helped me to learn from musicians, singers and dancers. Through the light of their art I could see what they often overlooked in their art of teaching. They all contributed hugely to *Jahan-e-Khusrau*. People no longer alive, like Ustad Iqbal Ahmad Khan, Ustad Ghulam Sabir Khan, Astad Deboo, give me, and gave *Jahan-e-Khusrau*, so much of themselves. Ghulam Sabir opened up the floodgate of talent that he had nurtured in his sons Murad, Fateh and Amaan, along with many of his nephews and cousins.

I learnt as I created an open, seamless stage for mystical thought, a *raagdaari* for the free soul. Through Khusrau and Rumi, I realized that there was a new scale to measure man. Exactly the opposite of the Mohs scale of hardness, which is a scientific geological scale defined some 200 years ago. A new scale of softness. A variable scale that varied from person to person, from culture to culture, from time to time. Intolerance was its outer symptom and compassion its inner sign. Rumi and Khusrau nursed this inner sign. Ameer Khusrau had created a bridge of compassion between people. And that was the art of the Sufi. India, with its rich traditions of art and culture, was the most absorbent and fertile ground. In each part of the world there are various sorts of differences which hold humanity to ransom, and the Sufi is sent to smoothen the contradictions. The hardness of intolerance and the softness of compassion.

Each Sufi order is created to build these intangible bridges which cannot be seen, and so cannot be demolished. The scale of softness was therefore invisible. It can be called the realm of the heart. This was the premise of *Jahan-e-Khusrau*. A promise of compassion. Khwaja Hasan Nizami Sani, in an interview for a film I made for the Ministry of External Affairs on Muslims in India, entitled *Fragrance of Love*, said that the greatest blessing of Hazrat Nizamuddin Aulia was *gudazi-e-qalb* (softness of the heart), and 'tears of the eyes'. He attributed the martyrdom of Imam Husain in Karbala as the perennial fountain of the source of this blessing. From the khanaqahs and dargahs emanate the blessings, so much so that people look sanctified in their precincts. And this was to me the most wonderful experience. This was the aura of *Jahan-e-Khusrau* that began to emerge in my heart. It is difficult to plan, describe, predict and comprehend. It had to organically come of its own or forever dodge me. Such was the nature of service to a saint or to a sacred verse attributed to him. This has been a learning experience at a sacred university, where no certificates were given, no degrees awarded.

Upholding the sanctity of culture is a subtle, invisible process, which seems to grow out of our existence. I asked my father why he encouraged people to call him 'Raja'. He said 'Raja', like Raja Ramchandraji, was a scion, a custodian of tradition. When I look back, I find that till my generation, the rajas were the epitome of language, manners and grace, and some of them could even outdo the most charming courtesan in repartee.

I am stunned and disappointed to see that the way of art has been lost to the world, as the way of peace. The way of art is a fire in the belly, a fire that made the Rumis and Khusraus.

There was a time when men deserved to be called men. They set their standards, pitched themselves high, created milestones to which humanity continues to bow.

Tawhid, or 'Atma Brahma Asmi', resonated in different melodies beyond the realm of comprehension and understanding. Today, the content of *Jahan-e-Khusrau* is a subject of research and exploration of the soul. How the restlessness takes you on a search, through layers of mindscapes, through hidden secrets that a Sufi traverses to realize art as a way to *Haq, Satya* (Truth). He is the same flower in different soils, or is present as a different flower in the same soil.

In some part of this wide world, a Sufi asked of his disciple, 'What is the most commonplace element on this earth?'

The disciple replied, 'Coal.'

'And what is the most valuable of all elements?'

'Diamond.'

'And what are they both made of?'

He answered, 'Carbon.'

'That is right. And do you know what is the only difference between the two?'

'Pressure,' answered the disciple.

Pressure creates the ultimate beauty, and when the Almighty tests you with all the stress and strain in this world, He is shaping you to become invincible, beautiful . . .

It is pressure that charts out your course, creates an intricate tapestry of human relationships and ultimately shapes your art.

Dar Kaaba-o-butkhana har ja ki ravad Khusrau,
Dil baad ze tu badkhu deedaar haman dar dil.

(Be it the Kaaba or a temple, wherever goes Khusrau
In the heart is seen the same cruel Beloved
who resides within the heart.)

Khusrau saw in his pir, Hazrat Nizamuddin Aulia, the way to the Divine. One early winter morning, the pir, donning his typical tilted cap, walked on the banks of the holy river Jamuna, with his disciple Khusrau. He saw, with reverence, people praying to the sun and bathing in the waters. Hazrat Nizamuddin said, 'Har qaum rāst rahe dēn e va qibla gahe (See, people of each faith have their own way to the Divine).' To which Khusrau replied, 'Man qibla rāst kardam bar simt e kaj kulahe (But my way to the Divine is through the direction of a tilted cap).'

Kaj Kulah, a collection of Ameer Khusrau's Persian poems composed by me, and rendered in the voice of the maestro Ustaad Shafqat Ali Khan, of the famed Shyam Chaurasi Gharana, with a voiceover in English by my son Murad Ali, will remain an everlasting tribute to the saint and his disciple. Rumi and Khusrau will forever continue to water my art, and make miracles happen to soften hearts and refresh human souls. We salute their invisible sawaar (rider) on the horse of ishq.